FORGOTTEN HEROES

POLICE OFFICERS KILLED IN GREENVILLE COUNTY

DR. WILLIAM WILBANKS

TURNER PUBLISHING COMPANY

Turner Publishing Company

Turner Publishing Company Staff:
Editor: Herbert C. Banks II
Designer: Ina F. Morse

Library of Congress
Catalog Card No.: 97-60577
ISBN 978-1-68162-593-5

Additional copies may be purchased
directly from the publisher.

Author: Dr. William Wilbanks
All photos courtesy of Dr. William Wilbanks

TABLE OF CONTENTS

BRIEF HISTORY OF LAW ENFORCEMENT IN GREENVILLE COUNTY, S.C.

The "Upper Country" of S.C. was sparsely populated in colonial days and, since the office of the Provost Marshal was far away in Charleston, the few residents of the area formed an organization called "Regulation." The "regulators" were involved in debt collection and even in "supervising morals." According to a history of the "Upper Country" of S.C. by Sheriff Johnny Mack Brown, "by the winter of 1768 the Regulators were complete masters of the Back Country." However, the state of law enforcement was described by Sheriff Brown as being characterized by "anarchy and lynch law."

In 1772 the Colonial Governor appointed sheriffs for each of the seven districts of S.C. (Charleston, Beaufort, Orangeburg, Georgetown, Camden, Cheraw, and Ninety Six (the Upper Country). Robert Stark was appointed as the first Sheriff of the Ninety Six District that included what is now Greenville County.

S.C. declared its independence from England in 1776 and the frontiersmen of the Upper Country had to fight the Tories and the Cherokees, who were "incited by British agents to attack the Loyalists." The area later known as Greenville County had little or no law enforcement from 1777-1784 and was a "favorite refuge of rogues and thieves."

After the War of Independence ended in 1783 the General Assembly divided the Ninety Six District into six counties and Greenville County was created in 1786. The area had been opened to settlement in 1784 and "within two years practically all of the desirable lands in the county had been taken up, largely by Revolutionary soldiers."

Greenville County remained a part of Ninety-Six District until 1791 when the Washington District (comprised of today's Greenville and Pendleton Counties) was created and existed until 1799. In 1800 Greenville County became a separate judicial district with its own sheriff and court.

Several men served as Sheriff over what is now Greenville County in the "pioneer years" with the best known being Gen. Robert Maxwell who served from 1795 until his line of duty death in 1797. (A complete list of sheriffs for Greenville County from 1773 to the present is given in Sheriff Brown's history.) Early sheriffs received their income from fees, mostly for civil matters. However, the sheriff was involved in criminal matters and supervised local hangings before the state took over executions in 1912. The first known hanging in Greenville was on April 2, 1882, when three men were hung for burning the old Academy of Music in Dec. of 1879. A listing of hangings from 1882-1906 was given in the *Greenville News* on Feb. 25, 1906.

The town of Pleasantburg (Greenville) was laid out in 1797 and a courthouse was erected by 1800. The City of Greenville "elected" its first policeman (a "marshal") in 1845. A second marshal was added in 1851. The police "force" was comprised of only two men until 1871. Night policemen were added in 1876 and the first detective in 1891. By 1900 the Greenville Police Dept. had 16 men. The first black officers were hired by the Greenville Police Dept. in 1964. In 1996, the Dept. had 175 sworn officers.

·Until 1914 the county area outside of the Greenville municipal limits was patrolled by a sheriff and one or two deputies. However, in 1914 a "rural police force" with a chief and 10 or 12 policemen was instituted but lasted only a few years. The Sheriff's Office had only 10 deputies as late as 1935. In 1996 the Sheriff's Office had 296 sworn officers.

The history of law enforcement in Greenville County, and especially the history of officers killed in the line of duty, cannot be told without explaining the role of federal law enforcement officers in the county. Federal troops were stationed in Greenville after the Civil War under "Reconstruction" and stayed until 1877. U.S. Marshals arrested (sometimes with the help of federal troops) more than 7,000 southerners for violations of the civil rights laws (i.e., terrorizing blacks) through 1877. That role ended when the U.S. Supreme Court (in the *Cruikshank* case) denied the federal government the power to protect individual rights and left such protection up to state governments.

After the Civil War the federal government enacted federal revenue laws (i.e., taxes) on whiskey. Since many of the residents of the Dark Corner (i.e., the mountainous areas) of Greenville County made and sold whiskey, a "war" of sorts began with federal authorities and the "moonshiners." The federal Internal Revenue agents and the U.S. Marshals were supported by the U.S. Army until 1877.

Many local sheriffs and law enforcement officers were in sympathy with the moonshiners and, at best, gave little support to federal revenue agents after 1878 when U.S. troops left the state. At worse, some local officers actually arrested some federal Internal Revenue Agents and U.S. marshals. Also, when federal agents were assaulted or killed by moonshiners, the killers often went unpunished by local state courts where sympathy was more likely to be with the local moonshiners than with the "meddling" federal authorities.

However, a different twist on the "War against Moonshiners" resulted when the state of S.C., in 1892, created the State Dispensary giving the State complete control

over the sale of alcoholic beverages. This law began a period when both federal and state authorities sought to confiscate untaxed liquor and destroy "stills."

The most hated part of the new law was the section authorizing the State Constables to obtain warrants and to search private homes if they suspected that illegal liquor was stored there for sale. Darlington County openly defined the law and, in March of 1894, its citizens fought a "pitched battle" with the State Constables. In Jan. of 1907 the State Dispensary was abandoned and S.C. returned to local county option for liquor control until federal prohibition was enacted in 1919.

The shift from federal domination to state and local domination of law enforcement efforts against the moonshiners is reflected in that while two federal agents were killed in Greenville County by moonshiners in the 1870's, the only law enforcement agents killed in the county from 1904 to 1924 were three state and local officers.

The most remarkable aspect of the history of law enforcement officers killed in Greenville County is the extremely high number of deaths for the 31 years from 1904-1934 (a total of 19) and the total absence of any such deaths for the 30 years from 1935-1964. There were only 11 officers killed during the 32 years from 1965-1996.

Given that the total number of local, state and federal law enforcement officers in Greenville County totalled no more than 100 men during the period of 1904-1934, the total of 19 killed over 31 years is a remarkably high total. The total of 11 officers killed in the past 32 years, though tragic, probably represents a *rate* of officers killed that is only a very small fraction of the rate of officer killings from 1904-1934. Also, the 11 killed in the past 32 years includes 3 officers killed in traffic accidents and it is likely that several such police traffic fatalities occurred in 1904-1934 but were not recorded as "line of duty" deaths.

The relatively high rate of killings of police in the early years of the 20th century is not unusual as Dr. Wilbanks found that the rate of murders against police (not including traffic "accidents") in Dade County (Miami), FL, was 50 times greater from 1910-19 as in 1980-89 and 6 times greater in 1920-1929 as in 1980-89.

Sources: "History of City and Department of Police, Greenville, South Carolina," by Chief of Detectives L.W. Hammond, 1957; "Law Enforcement..," *Greenville News,* June 28, 1962, p. 28; "History of Sheriff's Office," by Johnny Mack Brown in *Proceedings of Greenville Historical Society,* Vol. 8, 1990; *The Lawmen: United States Marshals and Their Deputies, 1789-1989,* by Frederick S. Calhoun, Penguin Books, 1989; *A History of the Upper Part of Greenville County, S.C.* by Mann Batson, 1993; *P.D. Gilreath: High Sheriff* by John H. Gilreath, 1968; "Cops Killed and Cop-Killers: An Historical Perspective, by Wm. Wilbanks in *American Journal of Police,* Vol. 13, No. 1, 1994, pp. 31-49.

ABOUT THE AUTHOR

Dr. William Wilbanks

Dr. Wm. Wilbanks, 56, is Professor of Criminal Justice at Florida International University in Miami, FL, where he has taught since 1973. He was reared in Belton, TX, and graduated from Belton H.S. in 1958. He has "roots" in S.C. as his great, great grandfather, Henry Wilbanks and his son, Gideon Wilbanks, lived around Pendleton, S.C. in 1800.

Wilbanks received a B.A. from Abilene Christian College in 1963; an M.A. in Criminal Justice from Sam Houston State University in 1972; an M.A. from the State U. of New York at Albany in 1972; and the Ph.D. in Criminal Justice from S.U.N.Y., Albany, in 1975.

He has published 14 books including *Murder in Miami: An Analysis of Homicide Patterns and Trends in Dade County, FL, 1917-1983; The Make My Day Law: Colorado's Experiment in Home Protection* and a series of books on police officers killed in the line of duty (i.e., *Forgotten Heroes: Police Officers Killed in Dade County, FL, 1895-1995; Forgotten Heroes: Police Officers Killed in Bell County, TX, 1850-1994;* and *Forgotten Heroes: Black Police Officers Killed in Dade County, 1944-1995).*

Wilbanks has also published over 70 journal articles and book chapters and has appeared on national television 30 times from 1981-1996 including four appearances on CNN's "Crossfire" and two appearances on CBS' "60 Minutes."

NOTE TO READERS

On May 7, 1997, a new police memorial was unveiled in front of the Law Enforcement Center in downtown Greenville. The 3ft. by 6 ft. granite monument lists the names of the 33 law enforcement officers killed in the line of duty in the history of Greenville County. The memorial includes the words: "These law enforcement officers died in the performance of their duties in the county of Greenville, South Carolina. Blessed are the peacemakers: for they shall be called the children of God. Matthew 5:9"

The dedication at the bottom of the monument acknowledges the work of Dr. William Wilbanks who "discovered " 8 of the 33 names included in the monument and brought the complete list to the attention of county authorities. This book contains narratives of the life and death of the 33 Greenville County officers listed on the memorial.

Readers will notice that several of the slain officers included in this book were not known to law enforcement authorities in 1995 when research for this book began but were "discovered" during the course of the research. It is quite possible that there are other "lost" officers who were killed in the line of duty in Greenville County who are not included in this book. Dr. Wilbanks requests that anyone with information on additional officers not included here (or with information on "lost" descendants of the officers included) contact him at:

Dr. Wm. Wilbanks
Dept. of Criminal Justice
Florida International University
University Park Campus, VH302
Miami, FL 33199
Phone: 305-595-6102

#1 ROBERT MAXWELL
Sheriff of Washington District
Shot & killed while on way to court on Nov. 10, 1797.

THE EVENT

General Robert Maxwell, 45, the appointed Sheriff of Washington District (which included Greenville, Anderson, Pickens and Oconee counties) was shot and killed from ambush on Nov. 10, 1797, while on his way to court. One man was arrested for the killing and was tried and acquitted. Gen. Maxwell became the first law enforcement officer killed in the history of Greenville County and in the state of South Carolina and one of the first killed in the history of the United States.

On Nov. 10, 1797, Sheriff Maxwell was riding his horse to the Washington District Court in Pickensville when he was ambushed as he attempted to cross the Saluda River (near where the Piedmont Mill Dam was later built). "It was well known that Captain Maxwell would have to pass the place on his way to court." Four or five assassins, "dressed as Indians," were concealed among the bushes "on either side of the road" and shot Maxwell, wounding him fatally. He died two days later (Nov. 12) at his home.

General Maxwell had "collected several dedicated enemies both among political opponents and among the criminal class" and there had been earlier attempts on his life. On April 12, 1797, Governor Charles Pinckney announced a reward for the apprehension of "persons unknown" who had attempted to assassinate Maxwell on the night of Feb. 1, 1797. Another reward was announced by the Governor on April 29, 1797, for the apprehension of persons who attempted "to burn and destroy Robert Maxwell's buildings and property." It was generally believed that the attempts against the life and property of Gen. Maxwell were by his political enemies, the "Tories."

THE PERPETRATORS

Dr. William E. Kennedy, "a neighbor and a political rival," was suspected of being the "instigator" of the murder.

> Captain Maxwell and Dr. Kennedy were both gentlemen of high social position, neighbors, and intimate friends for several years. They were men of education, talents and property, and had the confidence, esteem and affection of all who knew them. They had a difference about a small bill which Dr. Kennedy had tendered against the Captain. They were both gentlemen of high temper, and strong impulse, and a bitter feud grew up between them from this trifling circumstance. (*Greenville News, 11/22/1871*)

The friends of Maxwell were determined to have Dr. Kennedy arrested but feared that this could not be achieved by "any legal process" as Kennedy had powerful political allies. The friends employed Gen. Blair, "who was famous as a detective in those times," and Ben Starrett, "a huge man of gigantic strength," to arrest Kennedy.

Blair and Starrett went to the village where Kennedy lived and checked into a hotel. Starrett got into a bed, feigned illness, and called for a doctor (Kennedy) to attend him. When Kennedy arrived he was "pinioned" by Starrett and was taken to jail. On the way to jail it appears that Blair and Starrett "beat and abused him very much on the road to extort a confession and succeeded."

At trial Dr. Kennedy's attorney had his client take off his shirt to expose the "bruises and wounds" to prove that the confession was coerced. Also, the defense presented "several persons" who saw Kennedy at home the morning of the murder. Kennedy was acquitted.

Dr. Kennedy was advised by friends to leave the area due to the bitter feelings of friends of Maxwell. He "moved to Georgia where he married a lady of fortune and great respectability" and died in 1825.

THE OFFICER

Robert Maxwell was born in Londonderry, Ireland, around 1753, the oldest child of John and Jane Maxwell. His parents were Scotch-Irish and his ancestors had been part of the English program to settle Scottish protestants in Catholic Ireland. The Scotch-Irish were mistreated in Ireland and developed a strong hatred of the English leading to several waves of immigration to the U.S.

Robert Maxwell came to the U.S. with his parents and siblings in 1765 when he was 12 years old. They landed at Charleston and took advantage of generous state land grants to Protestants willing to immigrate to Upper South Carolina, an area plagued by hostile Indians. The Maxwells settled about 10 miles north of the present town of Abbeville on land that had previously been Cherokee territory.

Young Robert was "ardent in his hostility both to Indians...and to Tories, who represented everything he hated about the English." He was a "fiery supporter of the cause of American Independence, a radical whig." In 1774, at the age of 21, Robert Maxwell represented the upper portion of South Carolina in the First Continental Congress which led to the English authorities setting a "price on his head."

During the American Revolution, he was a Militia captain, 1779-1782, often serving under Colonel Robert Anderson as he did in the defense of Star Fort at Ninety-Six against the Indians in November 1775, and as Captain of a ranger company of horseman in 1781. Between 1779 and 1782, he lost four horses while in service. His brother, John, served with and under him the last two years, during which time they fought in the battle of Watauga and engaged in a number of skirmishes against the Tories. (*The Maxwells of Greenville*, 1989)

After the War the state of South Carolina paid its Revolutionary soldiers for their service with land grants. General Maxwell (he was made a general in the state militia after the War) was given 1,892 acres about a mile from Piedmont and 15 miles south of the present Greenville. "He acquired other lands by grant and purchase."

The Maxwell "plantation" on "Golden Grove on Grove Creek" included a "huge log house" and 12 slaves and was called "The Grove." Though he held several public offices, he "made his living as a planter." His library of 50-60 volumes was unusually large for his day and "reflected his concern with the law and religion."

After the War Gen. Maxwell married Mary Anderson (born in 1766), the daughter of Col. Robert Anderson. Robert and Mary Maxwell had four children, all born at the family plantation in Greenville County.

Public service for Robert Maxwell began with the creation of Greenville County in 1786. He was appointed Justice of the Peace for Greenville County, February 27, 1788 (also served in 1789); as election commissioner, 1789; and as a delegate to the State Constitutional Convention, 1790. The new State Constitution established Greenville as an election district, and Robert Maxwell represented his District in the Eighth (1789), Ninth (1791) and Tenth (1792-1794) General Assemblies.....

When the judicial District of Washington, comprised of Greenville and Pendleton counties, was formed in 1791, he served as a commissioner to superintend the building of a courthouse and jail, and on November 12, 1794, was appointed by the Legislature as Sheriff of Washington District for a four year term. The Commission was signed by the Governor on December 9, 1795. (*The Maxwells of Greenville*, 1989)

Sheriff Maxwell was buried on his plantation. In 1996 his gravesite "just off the Augusta Rd. near the Ware Place" is still visible in the Maxwell Cemetery. The grave is marked by a "massive concrete stone" erected by one of his sons with the inscription:

> In Memory
> of
> Robert Maxwell
> who died in 1797
> He was a Whig
> a Soldier and
> a Christian

The grave of Robert Maxwell was vandalized 170 years after his death. Four men were charged with the desecration of the grave after the skull from the grave was found hidden in the closet of one of the vandals. The skull was returned to the grave.

Robert Maxwell was survived by his widow, Mary Anderson Maxwell, and four children: Anne, 9, John 6, Elizabeth 3, and Robert, 2. The descendants of Robert Maxwell have been thoroughly traced by Albery Charles Cannon, Jr., a 7th generation descendant of Robert Maxwell, in *The Maxwells of Greenville*, written in 1989. In 1996, Rev. Albery Charles Cannon, 59, was an Episcopal priest in Greenville.

The name of Robert Maxwell is inscribed (East Wall, Panel 35, Line 8) on the National Law Enforcement Memorial in Washington, D.C., and a plaque bearing his name is displayed at the S.C. Criminal Justice Hall of Fame in Columbia.

SOURCES: Primary Source=*The Maxwells of Greenville* by A. Charles Cannon, Greenville: 1989; *Greenville News*, Nov. 22, 1871; *Greenville: The History of the City and County in the South Carolina Piedmont* by Archie Vernon Huff, Jr., Columbia: U. of S.C. Press, 1995, pp. 42,51-55,105,422; *S.C. History Magazine*, Vol. 24, p. 77; and interview with Rev. Albery Charles Cannon.

#2 VAN BUREN HENDRIX
Special Deputy for U.S. Marshal
Shot & killed during arrest attempt on Feb. 12, 1877

THE EVENT

Van Buren Hendrix, a "special deputy" for the U.S. Marshal, was shot and killed on Feb. 12, 1877, while attempting to arrest an escaped federal convict 15 miles north of Greenville on the Asheville road. His killer was tried but acquitted.

According to the *Charleston News and Courier*, Hub H. Garmany, had been incarcerated in the Greenville County Jail for the federal offense of "illicit distillery" but escaped. Sheriff Perry D. Gilreath, who was in the first year of his 23 years (1877-1900) as Greenville County Sheriff, offered a reward of $20 for Garmany's arrest. Special Deputy Hendrix, "who was not an officer of justice" (i.e., was not a full-time law enforcement officer), had evidently had been made a "special deputy" to pursue Garmany and "it was to secure this paltry sum of money that Hendrix was working."

Records maintained by the historian for the U.S. Marshal's office indicate Hendrix accompanied Deputy U.S. Marshal W.F. Gary to arrest Garmany at his home in the "Dark Corner" of Greenville County.

They arrived at Garmany's house, who stood in the doorway with a double barrelled shotgun and ordered them not to approach. They did advance and he fired and killed Hendrix on the spot. He then fired at Gary and missed him and Gary left. (Files at U.S. Marshal's headquarters in Washington, D.C.)

Reports indicated that Hendrix was killed instantly. Newspaper reports indicate that Garmany was later pursued by Revenue Agent Wagner's mounted patrol, "supplemented by a detachment of United States troops, under Lt. H.H. Adams of the Eighteenth Infantry" (federal troops were stationed in S.C. under "Reconstruction" until later in 1877).

The agents and army were also searching for a party of men who had stormed the Henderson County, N.C., Jail to in an attempt to rescue "Fisher, one of the distillers recently wounded in the attack on the United States Commissioners' Court in that county." Local citizens had driven off the raiders and wounded several.

THE PERPETRATOR:

The 1860 census of Greenville County, S.C., listed Hubbert H. Garmany as 13 years old and living in the "Panther Community." His father was listed as John Garmany, 54, and his mother as Cynthia Mariah Garmany, 44. Two brothers were also listed: William H., 16, and Barney, 6. Thus in 1877 Hubbert Garmany would have been 30 years old, William Garmany, 33, and Barney Garmany, 23.

John G. Garmany (Hubbert's father), 85, died in 1890 and was buried at the Ebenezer Baptist Church on White Horse Rod. north of Travelers Rest. His mother, Cynthia Garmany, 60, died in 1876.

Garmany surrendered to Sheriff Gilreath "some weeks afterward" and was tried for murder. He was acquitted in July, 1877, on the ground that Hendrix fired first though Deputy Marshal Gary "swore that neither of them attempted to fire on Garmany."

However, the *Charleston News and Courier* put a different twist on the killing of Hendrix by Garmany. The newspaper reported that

When Hendricks shot at Garmany, which he did twice, the latter had his child in his arms. The people think the killing justifiable under the circumstances.

On the same day Jackson Ward, living at Glassy Mountain Township, whilst walking in the highway, with one of his children in his arms, was shot at by a revenue officer named Johnson, and the child killed. Johnson is in jail. Although now a revenue officer, he was formerly engaged in illicit distilling. (*Charleston News & Courier*, 2/15/1877)

The Greenville *Enterprise and Mountaineer* on Feb. 21, 1877 (before the trial), reported that Hendrix shot at Garmany as the latter had a child in his arms and stated that "the people think the killing justifiable under the circumstances, severely condemning the reckless hazarding of an innocent life."

The Greenville and Charleston newspaper coverage may have been affected by an anti-federal marshal bias on the part of the local press. The Greenville *Enterprise and Mountaineer,* on July 4, 1877 (during the trial of Hubbert Garmany for killing Marshal Hendrix), made its views quite clear in an editorial.

The greatest abuse under which the people of the State are now laboring....is that of the Internal Revenue Service. The Deputy United States Marshals constitute the centre of this abuse. What we need now from President Hayes....is a reform in this service. That great and aggravated outrages have been committed upon our people there is no question. It is true that much illicit distilling has been carried on, which we condemn, and which all of our best citizens condemn; but the manner in which the Deputy Marshals discharge their duties in endeavoring to enforce the laws, is not now, and never has been, calculated to break it up. We think the very best plan to remedy this evil, is to dismiss the entire force of Deputy Marshals now in the service, and to fill their places by other persons, who are of a better class of men.

Since the war, few, if any, good men could be induced to serve the government in this department, and the consequence has been, bad men and men of indifferent characters were the only ones who could be induced to fill these positions. Greenville *Enterprise and Mountaineer,* 7/4/1877)

Local newspaper coverage indicated that the trial began on July 3 and ended on July 5, 1877. Only a brief mention was made of the end of the trial:

The case of the State vs. Hubbard Garmany, for the killing of Van Buren Hendricks, was continued to its final end, upon the re-assembling of the court on Thursday last. After able arguments from the attorneys engaged on both sides, the Judge charged the jury, who retired and brought in a verdict of not guilty. (Greenville *Enterprise and Mountaineer,* 7/11/1877)

Hub Garmany returned to his moonshining activity and, a little over a year later, killed a second U.S. marshal, Rufus Springs. (See the next narrative in this book on this case.) Garmany was also acquitted for that killing.

It is no surprise that Garmany was acquitted for both killings as the jurors who tried him may have been quite sympathetic to him in view of the hatred of federal government officials, including marshals. It should be noted that federal troops were still stationed in S.C. as part of "Reconstruction" and actually accompanied

Internal Revenue Agents and U.S. Marshals on "whiskey raids." On March 7, 1877 (four months before the Garmany trial) the Greenville *Enterprise and Mountaineer* reported that a raid supported by federal troops arrested 16 men in the Dark Corner and "seized seven illicit distilleries of whisky" and destroyed 7,000 gallons of liquor.

Van Buren Hendrix was also resented because he often worked "undercover" in what would today be called "stings." The Greenville *Enterprise and Mountaineer* published "a talk" with the "celebrated outlaw" Lewis R. Redmond (actually a moonshiner) on its front page on July 10, 1878, and he recounted his numerous "run-ins" with federal agents, including a prior undercover arrest by Deputy Marshal Van Buren Hendrix. It was clear that to the local newspaper, the outlaw Redmond was a folk hero while Hendrix was a villain.

In fact, not only was there considerable local feeling that moonshiners who shot marshals should be acquitted but there was also considerable feeling that the marshals themselves should be prosecuted for shooting moonshiners.

> It seems that the shooting of illicit distillers has got to be a common past time with the United States revenue officials. We hope some of these infamous scoundrels many be brought to justice for their murderous acts. We think it is a shame and a disgrace to a great nation like ours to send agents to shoot down, like beasts, the ignorant, half civilized men who make a few gallons of whiskey, while…dishonest revenue officers everywhere go scot free. (Greenville *Enterprise & Mountaineer,* 2/28/1877)

THE OFFICER

Little is known of Van Buren Hendrix (sometimes spelled "Hendricks" in news coverage). No death certificate was filed and he is not listed in the 1860 and 1870 S.C. census. It is possible that he was an "outsider" who was brought in as a deputy marshal from another state.

Hendrix' bravery was evident in that he was pursuing Garmany in spite of a previous experience that resulted in a serious wound. In Jan. of 1877 Hendrix, as a "special deputy," had accompanied Deputy U.S. Marshal E.H. Barton to arrest a "notorious desperado" (actually a "moonshiner"), Lewis R. Redmond, in Pickens County. After arresting Redmond and seizing his wagonload of contraband whiskey, the two men started for the town of Easley but Redmond escaped along the way.

A few minutes after the escape, the two officers were attacked by Redmond and others. Hendrix was "dangerously wounded in the abdomen" but recovered in two or three weeks and accompanied Deputy Marshal Gary on the raid that resulted in his death. Deputy Marshal Barton was shot in the leg. The wagonload of whiskey was recaptured.

A few days later, Redmond and a party of men surrounded Deputy Marshal's Barton's house in Pickens County and took him prisoner. They searched his house but found nothing of value except a check for $100 from U.S. Marshal R.M. Wallace. They forced Barton to endorse the check and forced his wife to go to Easley and get a merchant to cash the check. They then left with the $100 in cash and Barton's best horse. Redmond and his men boasted in town of their daring raid and Marshal Wallace complained that "not a man spoke of interfering to prevent the outrage."

Marshal Wallace further complained to Attorney General Devens:

The distillers exert a powerful influence in this way and officers are thrown entirely on their own resources. In the County of Pickens (which adjoins Greenville) Redmond and his gang are openly defiant of Revenue officers, deputy marshals and the Sheriff of the county and his deputies. Several shots have recently been exchanged between the officers and the outlaws but no captures effected. They have many spies everywhere and whenever a party of officers moves a report is once carried to their haunts and they are on the alert … . Several men have left their homes in consequences of threats against their lives and there is a general reign of terror in half the county. (Letter from R.M. Wallace, 4/22/1878)

The year 1877 seemed to have been a particularly dangerous year to be a special deputy to the U.S. Marshal. R.M. Wallace, U.S. Marshal for the District of S.C. reported to the attorney General that three special deputies were killed in S.C. during that year. The other two were apparently killed in retribution for helping federal revenue agents.

In June of 1877 Special Deputy Alfred McCreary of Pickens County accompanied the marshals on a raid which resulted in several arrests and the destruction of a still. A few days later he was shot while plowing in his field by someone hiding the adjoining woods. The assassin was never captured.

Also in June of 1877 Special Deputy James Letford of Spartanburg gave information to revenue officers and assisted deputy marshals to arrest some illicit distillers. Several days later he was dragged from a train near Landrum and shot and stabbed by four men while "others stood with drawn pistols and ordered the crowd not to interfere." Marshal Wallace complained that the Sheriff of the County (Spartanburg), several of his deputies, and "at least two hundred citizens saw the whole affair from beginning to end and made no effort to prevent the murder or to arrest the murderers after it was done." Marshal Wallace further complained that

firing on Deputy collection and Deputy Marshals in the mountain sections of this state while they are attempting to arrest illicit distillers and peddlers of contraband whiskey has become so common as to excite but little comment and the officers begin to regard that as an unpleasant performance incidental to the discharge of their duties and are prepared to return it. (Letter of Dec. 31, 1877, from U.S. Marshal R.M. Wallace)

The name of Van Buren Hendrix is inscribed (West Wall, Panel 61, Line 13) on the National Law Enforcement Memorial in Washington, D.C., and, on a memorial at the headquarters of the U.S. Marshal in Alexandria, VA. In 1996, a plaque bearing his name will be displayed at the S.C. Criminal Justice Hall of Fame at Columbia (this memorial had not been aware earlier that Hendrix was killed in S.C.).

SOURCES: *Charleston News and Courier,* Feb. 14,15, 1877; The Greenville *Enterprise and Mountaineer,* Feb. 21, March 21, July 4,11, 1877, July 10, 1878; Letter of Dec. 31, 1877, and April 22, 1878, from R.M. Wallace, U.S. Marshal for the District of S.C. to U.S. Attorney General Charles Devens; 1860 census of Greenville County; and Greenville County criminal court case #3388.

#3 RUFUS H. SPRINGS
Deputy U.S. Marshal
Shot & killed on moonshining raid on April 19, 1878

THE EVENT

Chief Deputy U.S. Marshal Rufus Springs was shot and killed "by parties in ambush" while on a raid on an illegal still near Glassy Mountain in the northern part of Greenville County on April 19, 1878. The killer, who had been acquitted for the killing of another U.S. marshal the year before, was again acquitted.

In 1878 the U.S. Government was making a great effort to stop the making of "moonshine" whiskey in the Dark Corner of Greenville County and thus assigned several "Revenue Agents" to Greenville County to enforce the "whiskey law" which added a 90 cents per gallon tax on whiskey. The law

was bitterly resented by the people in the mountains and resisted in every way possible. Quite often a Revenue Agent, or an informer, in the Dark Corner was killed and it then became the duty of the sheriff to arrest the person who did the killing. Generally speaking, the mountaineers hated all law men but they loved, respected, and trusted Sheriff Gilreath. (*P.D. Gilreath: High Sheriff*)

A lengthy account of the killing of Deputy Marshal Springs is given in a book by Frederick S. Calhoun, the historian of the U.S. Marshals Service. Calhoun said that Springs along with seven other "revenuers" left Greenville on April 18. The federal "revenuer" needed the deputy marshals because only marshals or deputies could arrest the illicit distillers. The authority of the "collectors" (i.e., Internal Revenue agents) extended only to seizing illegal stills and untaxed whiskey. The deputy marshals were also utilized because "they were men who were good with a gun and accustomed to the dangers of pursuing lawbreakers."

The raiding team had already destroyed four illegal stills before the incident on April 19 that resulted in Springs' death. The fatal incident occurred "in the vicinity of Hog Back Mountain."

Now, early in the afternoon of April 19, 1878, the raiding party was ready to move against its fifth illegal still. Deputy Collector H.H. Gillson, the Internal Revenue officer in charge of the raiders, ordered three of the men to remain on guard with the horses. Gillson took the other four men, including Deputy Marshal Rufus Springs, with him to charge the still house. ...

As they got closer to the shed, they broke into a dash, rushing across the last few dozen yards. Converging at the door, the revenuer kicked it open and burst into the stillhouse. They found no still. ...

Knowing that the moonshiners must still be in the area, Springs insisted on looking through the woods around the house. As the deputy marshal along on the raid, Springs knew he was there to make the arrests. ...

Springs stepped outside the house ... (Moss and Springs) stood a half dozen paces apart, their backs to the shed. Both men felt the tension. Neither man spoke.

A single rifle shot shattered the stillness.

"Lord of Mercy, I'm shot," Springs groaned. "Shot through." He slumped against the side of the stillhouse, dead. Panicked by the gunfire, Moss instinctively ran. He sprinted directly ahead into the woods, running wildly past three armed strangers. Startled by his dash, the bushwhackers had no time to fire at him. Moss kept going.

The remaining revenuer converged again on the stillhouse. Gillson galloped up with the horses. Without pause, they tied Spring's body across his saddle and fled. For several miles some men followed them, but a sudden mountain squall discouraged the chase. Gillson and his men made it back safely to Greenville. They found Moss waiting for them there. (*The Lawmen: United States Marshals and Their Deputies, 1789-1989*, by Frederick S. Calhoun)

The *Greenville Enterprise and Mountaineer* reported that the shot "entered back of the right shoulder and lodged against the ribs of his left side, cutting the main artery." Coroner Rayne held an inquest "on the body but no information was elicited as to who were the guilty ones."

THE PERPETRATOR:

U.S. Marshal R.M. Wallace of the District of S.C. wrote to Attorney General Devens requesting approval for the offering of a $200 reward for the arrest of Springs' killer but added that if the reward were not approved, he would pay it himself. The reward was approved by the Attorney General.

John H. Gilreath reported in a book about his grandfather, P.D. Gilreath, Sheriff of Greenville County from 1876-1900, that the man who killed Agent Rufus Springs was a "mountaineer" by the name of Hub Garmany.

A warrant was issued for his arrest, and early one morning Sheriff Gilreath left Greenville headed for the mountains and Hub Garmany's home on Gap Creek. Hub was not there but his father, John Garmany was, and the sheriff talked with him. After some persuasion, John Garmany told the sheriff where Hub was hiding and gave complete instructions on how to find the place. Following these instructions the sheriff walked along mountain paths, through ivy thickets and over log-bridged streams, until he came to a rail fence. About twenty feet from the fence Garmany stepped from behind a big oak tree, with a gun in his hand, and told the sheriff to stop where he was and not come any closer to the fence. The sheriff talked with Hub for a long time and as he talked he eased forward, a few inches at a time, until he reached the fence. Presently he told Hub he was tired and would sit on the fence while talking—and this is what he did. On this—as on most missions—the sheriff was unarmed. They continued to talk for a long time and then Hub stepped forward, gave the gun to the sheriff and said: "Alright Sheriff, I am going to trust you."

Late that night the sheriff, with his prisoner, arrived at Greenville and drove directly to his own home. They ate a good supper and the sheriff told Hub to sleep in one of the bedrooms upstairs. The next morning they ate breakfast together and walked to the jail. Hub was tried at the next term of Court and acquitted. (*P.D. Gilreath: High Sheriff*, pp. 29-30)

Hub Garmany was apparently the same man who had killed Special Deputy Marshal Van Buren Hendrix on Feb. 12, 1877. He was acquitted of that killing and had returned to his moonshining activity. According to Gilreath, Garmany was also acquitted of the killing of Marshal Springs though no confirmation of that could be found in the court log book or in the local newspaper.

Since killing a federal officer was not a federal offense in 1878, the marshals had to rely on the state and local governments to prosecute those who assaulted or killed marshals or other federal agents.

But the local southern courts frequently showed little sympathy for them, being much more concerned for the accused than for the attacked. The moonshiners and others who were charged with attacking deputies and revenuers often went unpunished, and the state and local governments frequently used their own power and authority to hinder the revenuers and deputy marshals and to protect the distillers. In one absurd case, Deputy Marshal Will W. Deavers was indicted by the North Carolina courts for destroying personal property after he took his ax to an illegal still. (*The Lawmen: United States Marshals and Their Deputies, 1789-1989*, p. 133)

Two months after Deputy Marshal Springs was killed, four deputy marshals (Hugh P. Kane, William Durham, Robert P. Scruggs and G.W. Moose) were indicted for murder by a state court for the killing of Amos Ladd, an "illicit distiller" in Pickens County. Ladd had evidently been hiding Lewis R. Redmond, the notorious Pickens County "outlaw" (i.e., moonshiner). The front pages of the Greenville *Enterprise and Mountaineer* were filled with this case for several months as the U.S. Marshal's office, fearing that the four men would be convicted in state court, tried to get the case transferred to federal court. The case became a test case for the jurisdiction of state vs. federal courts. The log book for Greenville criminal (state) court does not list the names of any of the four and thus it would appear that the four were eventually transferred to federal court and probably acquitted.

THE OFFICER:

Little is known of Rufus H. Springs. The U.S. Marshal's headquarters gives no information as to his age, family, etc. He is not recorded in the 1870 census for S.C., N.C. or GA and there is no record of he or his family in Greenville. He may have been an "outsider" brought into Greenville by the chief U.S. Marshal.

However, there were apparently three men named Springs serving as deputy marshals during this time. No indication is given in the newspaper as to whether they were related. In May of 1878, only a month after Rufus Springs was killed, the Greenville *Enterprise and Mountaineer* reported that Deputy Marshals William Springs, John Springs, and T.H. Blackwell were involved in an altercation that ended with William Springs hitting a citizen over the head with a gun. Springs was charged with assault for what the newspaper called "an outrage." (No record could be found of the disposition of this case.)

Also, in March of 1877, "two young men with the Revenue service named Springs" who were "under the influence of spirits" were arrested and taken to "the calaboose." The two Springs men were each fined $20. The June 26, 1878, *Enterprise and Mountaineer* reported that William L. Springs "now confined in jail under the charge of grand larceny,, has been relieved of his commission." This report included the following words which clearly indicate the "local" attitude toward the "federal" marshals: "If the rest of the Revenue officials were relieved of their commissions also, no great wrong would be sustained."

U.S. Marshal R.M. Wallace of the District of S.C. reported to Attorney General Charles Devens by letter on April 22, 1878, that Rufus Springs was his "chief deputy in that section of the state" and was a "very intelligent, energetic and efficient officer." He described Springs in another letter as a "brave man and a faithful officer."

Marshal Wallace also told the Attorney General that Springs discharged his duty faithfully to the Govt—but at the same time he was careful to secure to the citizens every right to which he was entitled under the law. He arrested and brought to trial a large number of offenders against the revenue laws in that section but no man can complain of any unkind or unfair treatment at his hands. (Letter from R.M. Wallace, 4/22/1878)

Marshal Wallace also told the Attorney General that he was satisfied that Springs was not killed due to any "personal malice but because he was an officer attempting to enforce the law." He complained that during the prior two years the officers in three or four counties in "that section" had not dared to go out "without combining together for mutual protection." He noted that "many" officers had been shot "repeatedly but without serious results previous to this time."

Marshal Wallace also noted that "so many officers have been threatened and injured and killed in that country that men of the best standing in the county" would not face "the dangers of holding office under the Govt. for the consideration offered." He added that "another great drawback in securing the service of good men is the fact that no provision is made for the benefit of their families in case of their death in discharge of duty." He urged the Attorney General to seek a law providing for death benefits for those officers willing to work in the "mountainous sections of the South" who were in "constant danger" of losing their lives. He added that "I know that such a provision of law would give more dignity to the Service and secure a better class of men in the Service."

The illicit distillers and their abettors and the men who sell for them are made up almost exclusively of the more reckless and improvident classes of the community—they receive some sympathy from some men who still cherish a bitter hostility to any act of the general govt— and are encouraged by political demagogues. The more intelligent classes and men of property would prefer to see law enforced but they live in constant dread of the distillers and their friends and do not dare to give any information or even to furnish food and forage to the officers who may be attempting to capture offenders against the law. (Letter from Marshal R.M. Wallace, 4/22/1878)

The name of Rufus Springs is inscribed (East Wall, Panel 10, Line 14) on the National Law Enforcement Memorial in Washington, D.C., and on a memorial at the headquarters of the U.S. Marshals in Alexandria, VA. In 1996 a plaque bearing his name was added to the S.C. Criminal Justice Hall of Fame in Columbia (that memorial had been previously unaware that he was killed in S.C.)

SOURCES: *Enterprise and Mountaineer,* March 14, 1877, April 17,24, May 29, June 5,12, July 3,10,24,26, Sept. 11, 1878; *The Lawmen: United States Marshals and Their Deputies, 1789-1989,* by Frederick S. Calhoun, Penguin Books, 1989, pp. 130-132; *A History of the Upper Part of Greenville County, S.C.,* by Mann Batson, 1993, pp. 476-7; *P.D. Gilreath: High Sheriff* by John H. Gilreath, 1968, pp. 29-30; and files of Historian for U.S. Marshals Service in Alexandria, VA.

#4 JAMES PATRICK TUCKER

Greenville Police Dept.

Shot by a man at railway station on April 12, 1904 (died April 13)

THE EVENT

Officer James Patrick Tucker, 48, a 16-year veteran of the Greenville Police Dept. was fatally shot on April 12, 1904, by a drunken night watchman who was angry that the officer had arrested his negro cook. The killer was in turn fatally wounded by a second officer at the scene and died of his wounds four days later.

At 9:00PM on Tuesday, April 12, 1904, Greenville Officers J. Patrick Tucker and Z.J. Brown were on routine patrol when they met Ellis Sanders, a watchman of the Southern Railway, on King Street at the rear of the beer house near the railroad station. Sanders began to curse the two officers because, earlier that day, they had arrested Pearl Lollis, his negro cook, after she and another woman "got into a difficulty."

Sanders had earlier gone to the "guard house" and bailed out the cook and cursed her for getting arrested. Officer Tucker saw Sanders shortly after he bailed her out and the watchman seemed friendly and even thanked Tucker for arresting Lollis.

However, Sanders began drinking after supper and his mood changed for the worse. As Officers Tucker and Brown approached Sanders (at 9:00PM), he began to curse them saying, "God damn your souls, you knocked me out of my supper. You arrested my negro cook." Officer Brown rebuked Sanders and said, "that will not do." At that point Officer Tucker later testified that he

> put his left hand on Sanders' shoulder in a friendly way, and said, "that has got to be stopped." He jerked out his pistol and shot me. I said: "Brown, I am shot through and through by Sanders," and then I walked

The family of James P. Tucker knows he is in this photo although, they do not know which one he is.

off and he then shot Brown and Brown shot him. (dying statement from Officer Tucker, *Greenville News,* 4/14/1904)

The later investigation indicated that Sanders used two pistols (.38 calibre Colts) to fire at the two officers and fired three shots from each pistol. Officer Brown emptied his revolver at Sanders and fatally wounded him. Officer Tucker never unholstered his weapon and fired no shots. Officer Brown later testified that he was ten or twelve feet from Sanders when the "duel" occurred.

After Sanders fell, Brown, though wounded in the leg, went to the aid of his fallen partner and took him to his home on Highland Ave. (only a few blocks from the scene) and called for a doctor. Officer Tucker was comforted at his home by his family and friends and by the mayor and Chief of Police as he awaited the doctor. Tucker tried to tell the the Chief of Police what happened but he weakened and was told to be quiet and rest. The mortally wounded officer told some of his friends that he did not expect to recover. When the patrol wagon and the physician arrived to take him to the hospital, "he bade farewell to each one of his family as he was being lifted on a stretcher to the wagon."

At the hospital, just before being placed on the operating table late Tuesday night, Tucker made a statement (quoted earlier) that was signed and recorded in case he did not survive. The officer died at 3:00AM the next day (Wednesday), six hours after he was shot. The "immediate cause of his death was hemorrhage, shock and incipient peritonitis." The autopsy revealed that he had fifteen punctures in the intestines and two in the bladder. "The ball entered the left side of the abdomen and ranged downward lodging in the opposite hip near the skin."

After Officer Brown had carried away Officer Tucker, Sanders got up and "staggered" to a small restaurant near his room and said, "Boys, I'm shot." He was taken to his room and a doctor was called. After examining him, the doctor had little hope he would recover. Sanders was later taken to the hospital where he died four days later (on April 16). He had been shot in the chest "in the region of the heart." In an interesting sidenote, the *Greenville News* reported on May 8, 1921, in summarizing the seven Greenville officers killed in the line of duty that Sanders died "in the hospital, later, after he had been operated upon he tore open the wound to his stomach and died."

Officer Brown was well enough to report for duty the next day. He was charged with the killing of Sanders and was tried in the court of general sessions and acquitted on May 30, 1904. Sheriff Gilreath testified to "Brown's character as a worthy officer and told of Sanders' reputation for lawlessness and disorder." The "ante mortem statement made by Officer Tucker just before he was placed on the operating table in Dr. Black's sanitarium, was "proved" by Mayor Mahon.

It appears, however, that the "trial" was more of a public airing of the circumstances of the "pistol duel" as after Solicitor (prosecutor) Boggs presented the evidence to the jury he announced "that he did not think the facts produced could warrant the State in asking for conviction, and he therefore consented to a verdict of 'not guilty.'" The jury then returned the verdict of not guilty and Brown was released by Judge Townsend. Officer Z.J. Brown was still on the force seventeen years later in 1921 when Officer Burroughs was killed.

THE PERPETRATOR:

Little is known of Ellis Sanders other than that he was the night watchman for the Southern Railway. This incident was not the first time that Sanders had tried to take the life of an officer.

Several years ago while under the influence of liquor he attempted to shoot Chief Kennedy and would have done so had it not been for Sergeant Gunnels, who shoved the weapon up before it was discharged. *(Greenville News, 4/13/1904)*

It does not appear that Sanders was prosecuted for the intended murder of Chief Kennedy as no mention was made by the newspaper of a conviction and he surely would not have been able to work as a night watchman with a record of attempted murder. Sgt. Gunnels, the officer who saved Chief Kennedy's life, was killed in the line of duty in 1911.

The newspaper also reported that Sanders died "with sealed lips" and made no effort to contradict the statements of Tucker and Brown that he had shot them in a drunken rage. No relatives came to claim the body of Sanders though he was thought to have a brother in Gaffney.

A coroner's jury ruled on April 15 that Tucker was killed by Sanders and that Officer Brown killed Sanders in self-defense. The jury also ruled that Pearl Lollis was an accessory *before* the fact as witnesses testified that she bragged to acquaintances that the police would not arrest her because they were afraid of Sanders and "if anyone ever bothered her she would make Sanders fix them." Another witness testified that while Sanders was drinking shortly before the murder he "pulled his revolver and remarked, 'Tucker and Brown don't like me, and I am going to get even with every one that had anything to do with it.'"

It is interesting to speculate as to what would have happened to Sanders if he had lived. An editorial in the *Greenville News* on April 14 (after Sanders' death) spoke approvingly of lynching and suggested that "while our people want the law to take its course, they will demand vengeance and punishment" if they perceive that justice was not done in a case like the murder of Officer Tucker by Sanders.

Also, it appears that Pearl Lollis was charged with murder as she was "implicated with Sanders" in the killing of Tucker. She was scheduled to be tried in the Court of General Sessions beginning on May 30, 1904.

THE OFFICER

James Patrick Tucker was born on June 16, 1855, in Gowansville in Greenville County to J.P. and Elizabeth A. Peace Tucker. His brother-in-law, Bony Hampton Peace, bought the *Greenville News* in the 1920's and the Peace family owned the newspaper through the 1980's.

"Pat" Tucker moved to Greenville in 1877 at the age of 22 and operated a store on Washington St. near Main. Tucker, 33, was "elected" to the Greenville Police Dept. in 1889 during the administration of Mayor Rowley and served as a Greenville officer, "with the exception of two years," until his death. He was a 13-year veteran of the Dept. upon his death. Officer Tucker and Officer Z.J. Brown were longtime partners and friends and even resembled each other in appearance. Tucker had an excellent reputation as a police officer as evidenced by the newspaper headline:

Tucker was Fearless
Dead Officer One of the
Bravest Men in Greenville

There never was a braver member of the police force in Greenville than James Patrick Tucker. He was not afraid of anything. While he was often in the midst of danger he never flinched, never showed the white feather, and always got his criminal regardless of all risk and difficulties. The records at the station house for a number of years will prove that he made more arrests than any other officer, and he took none but real offenders. ...

It was often said at police headquarters that when a man was needed for a dangerous assignment it was best to send Tucker. He was cool, he was not easily ruffled, and being familiar with all manner of crooks he understood how to handle them. The fact was illustrated Tuesday night. When Sanders became violent. Tucker walked quietly to him, placed a hand on his shoulder and mildly suggested that there was no occasion for any row. And he was killed for his pains. He might have shot when he saw that Sanders was mad, but not having any blood in his own eye he suspected none in his slayer's. Officer Tucker was known by nearly every citizen of Greenville. He was admired for his fearlessness and he made friends because he had the right sort of heart. (*Greenville News,* 4/14/1904)

The newspaper editorialized on April 14 that Officer Tucker "did not court trouble, but on the other hand he endeavored to pacify one whose character and deed proved his unworthiness." Tucker also told a friend before his death that he realized that he had been mortally wounded but "did not wish to kill Sanders, although, he could have done so easily."

One story about Officer Tucker that was passed down in oral family history involved his ability as a hypnotist. After a robbery at a railroad station Tucker hypnotized a man to help him remember the robber. The subject not only remembered the robber under hypnosis but also told the police where he could be found and the robber was arrested.

The funeral was held on April 14 at the First Baptist Church and was conducted by Dr. Z.T. Cody. The city bell tolled for 30 minutes to announce the service. Immediately after the funeral the "cortege" walked to Springwood Cemetery for the burial service conducted by the Improved Order of Heptasophs, Conclave No. 739. The City Council, a detachment of firemen, "and the entire police force accompanied the remains to the cemetery."

James Patrick Tucker was survived by three children, Charles Earl Tucker, 19 (born in 1885), Patrick Riley Tucker, 18 (born in 1887), and Elizabeth Adeline Tucker, 13 (born in 1891). In 1996 Officer Tucker's grave is easily found at Springwood Cemetery in downtown Greenville. A 10 ft. tall stone monument in Section D at Springwood marks the grave of Tucker. It reads:

JAMES PATRICK TUCKER
Born June 16, 1855
Died April 13, 1904

It appears that the 10 ft. tall stone monument marking the Tucker family plot was erected as a public tribute to the fallen officer. On May 23, 1904, several hundred people attended a mass meeting at the Grand Opera House "for the purpose of making arrangements to raise a monument to Policeman J. Patrick Tucker" as a "mark of appreciation from the people whom he served so faithfully for more than fifteen years." It was proposed at the meeting "that a monument should mark his grave" and that "a tablet inscribed to his memory" should be displayed at City Hall.

Col. James A. Hoyt spoke of the dead officer's long service as a member of the police force and also

> spoke of the continual and almost universal violation of the laws prohibiting the carrying of pistols and the sale of alcoholic beverages. These two things he said, were the cause of nearly all the homicides in South Carolina which were tarnishing the State's fair name. The intoxi-cated man and the ever ready pistol were the most fruitful causes of the frightful, useless sacrifice of human life. In contributing to the fund for the monument to Officer Tucker, Col. Hoyt said, the people would not only be doing honor to a man who deserved the gratitude and loving remembrance of the people, but they would be doing more. They would place the stamp of their disapproval upon the pistol habit and illegal traffic in whiskey. Hoyt's address was strong and forceful and left a deep impression upon his hearers." (*Greenville News*, 5/24/1904)

Senator A.H. Dean also spoke at the "mass meeting" and "paid a beautiful tribute to the memory of the veteran policeman:

> his bravery and fearlessness in the discharge of duty, his courage and fairness were universally known....and if ever a man deserved a tribute at the hands of his fellow citizens, that man was "Pat" Tucker. For more than fifteen years this gallant officer had watched and guarded the people of his native city. In the cold, dark nights of winter Policeman Tucker was at his post watching, ever on the alert that no harm should befall the sleeping women and children of Greenville. And the end of the man! He had given his life, a sacrifice for the cause of law and order. (*Greenville News*, 5/24/1904)

At the conclusion of the meeting, Mayor Mahon appointed six members of the police force to "receive subscriptions" to the monument fund from the six wards of the city.

Officer Tucker was buried beside his wife, Judith Belle Peace Tucker, who died at the age of 26 on April 8, 1891. Patrick R. Tucker, the son of James Patrick Tucker, who was a jeweler on Washington St. for many years, died on April 26, 1957, at the age of 70 and was buried by his father and mother and wife, Annie E. Long Tucker, who died on June 29, 1924, at the age of 32. Patrick R. and Annie Long Tucker had three children: Louise, Estelle and Patrick R. Tucker, III.

Officer Tucker's daughter, Elizabeth Adeline ("Addie") Tucker Watson, lived in Greenville until her death on Dec. 5, 1983, at the age of 92. She was buried in Christ Church Cemetery. Addie Tucker married Frank Leland Watson and the couple had three children: Frank R. Watson (born Oct. 30, 1920); Annie Lillian Watson (Jan. 10-1917-July 12, 1982); and Robert Patrick Watson (March 30, 1927-May 27, 1971). She was survived at death by nine grandchildren and ten great-grandchildren.

Officer Tucker's grandson, Frank R. ("Buddy") Watson, 75, remained in Greenville in 1996. He was a Sgt. in the U.S. Marines and fought in the Pacific theatre during World War II. He worked for the *Greenville News* for 45 years and played the bass fiddle for the Rhythmaires, a local band that played in Greenville for over 40 years.

Another son of Officer Tucker, Charles Earl Tucker, worked as a jeweler in Rock Hill, NC, until his death at the age of 50 on Jan. 26, 1936. He had three sons, James Riley Tucker (1907-1970), Charles Clement Tucker (1908-1996), and John Peyton Tucker (1913-1974). James Riley and Charles Clement (who was a well-known "portrait painter" in Charlotte, NC) had no children but Dr. John Peyton Tucker (an optometrist) and Lillian Tucker had two sons and six grandchildren. One son, Dr. Tom Tucker lived in St. Simon, GA, while the other, John Tucker, a broker, lived in Coral Springs, FL.

In 1996 many descendants of Officer Tucker lived in S.C. Dr. Patricia S. Watson, the wife of one of his grandsons, was on the faculty of the College of Criminal Justice at the U. of S. Carolina in Columbia. She established the James Patrick Tucker Scholarship at the University for the senior Criminal Justice student with the highest grade point average each year. One source of the scholarship fund was royalties from her book *(Guide to South Carolina Criminal Law and Procedure)* published by the USC Press.

The name of J.P. Tucker is inscribed (East Wall, Panel 35, Line 3) on the National Law Enforcement Memorial in Washington, D.C., and a plaque bearing his name is displayed at the S.C. Criminal Justice Hall of Fame in Columbia. Tucker's badge (#19) is displayed at the Law Enforcement Center in Greenville along with the badges of several other slain City of Greenville officers.

SOURCES: *Greenville News,* April 13,14,15,17,19, May 24,28,31, 1904, May 8, 1921, Dec. 7, 1983; Grave markers at Springwood Cemetery; interviews with Dr. Patricia S. Watson, Frank Watson, Louise Helton, and Lillian Tucker McNabb.

#5 WILLIAM J. COX
Magistrate
Shot and killed during attempted arrest on May 14, 1904.

THE EVENT

Magistrate William Jerry Cox, 35, of Austin Township in Mauldin was shot and killed by "bootleggers" on May 14, 1904. Both bootleggers were sentenced to death and one was hanged.

Magistrate Cox received a report by telephone on Saturday, May 14, 1904, that two negro men had been seen "transporting contraband liquor" on the road between Mauldin and Simpsonville. Cox left his house accompanied by his constable, T.M. Austin, in pursuit of the bootleggers. Around 6:00PM, Cox and Austin overtook the buggy driven by the bootleggers about a mile and a half from Simpsonville and called on them to "halt and surrender."

The team was stopped immediately and both men jumped from the vehicle to the ground. One negro threw up his hands in token of submission, but the other broke and ran about thirty feet. He then turned and opened fire on the officers.

Seeing his companion resisting, the negro who had surrendered also drew a pistol and began to shoot. Judge Cox drew his pistol and fired four times, but before he could discharge the last chamber he fell unconscious and mortally wounded. (*Greenville News,* 5/15/1904)

Constable Austin, who had been armed with a double barrel shotgun, "struck out for Simpsonville for help" when he "saw his chief fall." He "collected" a "posse of citizens" at once and returned to the scene where the wounded magistrate was "found lying in the road in a pool of blood."

Sheriff Jefferson D. Gilreath, who served as Sheriff from 1900-1908 following the 24 year tenure of his father, Sheriff Perry D. Gilreath, was called to the scene and, with a small posse of four men, pursued the bootleggers to Laurens County. Upon reaching the vicinity of the Jeff Hughes Plantation (12 miles from Simpsonville), the posse learned the identity of the two negroes and the location of their homes.

THE PERPETRATORS

At sunrise on Sunday, only 12 hours after the murder, the Sheriff and his posse surrounded the home of Fletcher Byrd.

Just then Fletcher came out and seeing the officers, he broke and ran, making a wild dash for liberty. Chief Hall, who was more than two hundred yards from the fleeing negro, at the suggestion of Sheriff Gilreath attempted to shoot the fugitive with a Winchester rifle, at the same time calling to him to halt and surrender. Fletcher discovered the other members of the party in front and he doubled back like a rabbit and ran into the house. The entire party then closed in. Trouble was expected, for the negro was known to be a desperate character, but instead, to the surprise of every one, he emerged from the front door a few moments later and threw up his hands, begging the officers not to shoot. (*Greenville News,* 5/17/1904)

Fletcher Byrd told the Sheriff of the "whereabouts" of his brother, Palmer Creswell (also known as Bulger Byrd), who had been with him at the murder scene. Creswell was quickly arrested and both brothers confessed to the shooting of Cox but claimed self-defense.

Little is known of both men but the *Greenville News* did report that both had families living between Fountain Inn and Simpsonville and were concerned for the fate of "their wives and children."

The two captives were taken by train to the state prison at Columbia for safekeeping as the Sheriff feared that the two might be lynched if returned to Greenville through Simpsonville and Mauldin. They arrived at the penitentiary only 24 hours after the murder. An editorial in the May 17 *Greenville News* lauded the Sheriff for avoiding a lynching and recognized the likelihood of such an event.

> The citizens of this county are not of the lynching sort, but there are times when men believe that prompt vengeance is necessary. We are glad that the negroes were not swung to a tree and riddled with bullets. That would have been deplorable and it would not have been a credit to the Piedmont section. They must answer to the court and their necks should pay the penalty.
>
> The coroner's jury has fastened the murder on one of the negroes. One was guilty of killing the magistrate, but both stood together, fighting to save a lot of contraband liquor, and in the eyes of the law both must stand convicted. Greenville county cannot afford to dismiss them with a short term in the penitentiary, and if the court cannot determine who fired the fatal shot, then both should be sent to the gallows. Certainly, one must hang, but if there is the least question of doubt, hang the guilty pair. (*Greenville News*, 5/17/1904)

As mentioned above, the coroner's jury under Coroner Black held an inquest "over the body of Magistrate Cox" at Simpsonville on Sunday, May 15, only hours after the arrest of the two brothers. Dr. W.P. League testified that the fatal bullet "entered the neck at the base of the skull and ranged upward and into the brain." Cox was killed "instantly." T.D. Wood, a member of the posse which arrested the two Byrds told of the confessions made by both men.

The "principal witness" at the inquest was Constable Austin who was present at the murder. He testified that:

> We drove around them and stopped, and by the time we got out of the buggy the two negroes got behind their buggy. Each one had a pistol in his hand. I threw my gun on them and ordered them to hold up their hands and they held them up and had their pistols in their hands. One of them backed back some distance. I still stood in the same place and kept my gun on both of them and Mr. Cox walked up to the one that stood behind the buggy. I did not know their names. When Mr. Cox got to the one that was at the side of the buggy, I turned my attention to the one that was back behind holding up his pistol. I leveled my gun on him and he fired at me and I fired back at him. By that time there was several shots and the buggies ran together. I backed back and grabbed the lines. When I grabbed the lines I looked back and saw Mr. Cox lying on the ground. I grabbed the lines and left. (*Greenville News*, 5/17/1904)

Byrd and Creswell were kept in Columbia until the May, 1904, term of the court in Greenville when they were brought to Greenville and "hurried to the jail." Their one-day trial was held on June 2, 1904, in the Court of General Sessions before Judge D.A. Townsend before a court room "filled with people."

Solicitor Boggs prosecuted the case for the state and presented D.M. Austin, the constable at the murder scene, as his star witness. Austin repeated the testimony he had given at the inquest that both negroes fired at he and Cox. The prosecution claimed that Creswell fired the first shot but that Byrd's shot killed Cox. The state conceded that Creswell "did not hit anyone" but that he was equally guilty under the law.

O.K. Mauldin of Mauldin and Townes defended Byrd and Creswell though the speedy one-day trial and the fact that he "offered no testimony whatever" for the two defendants raise questions as to the quality of the defense. Also, the *Greenville News* quoted Mauldin as telling the jury that he "neither sought nor desired to represent" the two brothers but that Judge Townsend had directed him to do so. He added that "the duty was not at all pleasant" and "had been thrust upon him."

The defense attorney did argue that the attempted arrest by the two officers was illegal since they had no warrant as required by law in cases of suspected transport of illegal liquor. Thus the two officers "acted without authority of the law and were the aggressors in bringing on the difficulty." The fatal shooting of Magistrate Cox was thus, Mauldin argued, a case of self-defense and not murder.

The jury took only two hours of deliberation before returning a verdict of guilty without recommendation of mercy thus mandating a death sentence. Byrd was silent at the sentencing but Creswell "cried out and begged the judge to be merciful." Judge Townsend told the two men that he had no choice under the law and then sentenced both to be hanged on July 1.

An editorial in the *Greenville News* urged "state authorities and the courts" not to "interfere" with the sentence of death.

> In the eye of the law their hands are stained with a terrible crime and they richly deserve their fate. Except for the good work of Sheriff Gilreath these black fiends might have been lynched, yet how much better does the record appear, now that they have been tried by a court of law. It would not be right to hang them, unless the jury was absolutely sure of their guilt, simply to counteract the spirit of mob law, but to be merciful with them would encourage mobs to take the law into their own hands. A verdict of this sort will cause the public to have more confidence in the justice of the court, and all respect for it will be lost if the sentence should be commuted or a new trial granted. ... Let us hope, then, that Byrd and Creswell will die on July 1, and let no wave of consideration or sympathy save them from the trap of death. (*Greenville News*, 6/3/1904)

Contrary to the "demands" of the editorial, there was a new trial and a commutation. Attorney Mauldin filed an appeal for the two condemned men as they were returned to the state prison at Columbia pending the decision of the court. The appeal was denied and the two men were returned to Greenville and were sentenced to hang on Nov. 10, 1905. Attorney Mauldin asked that the two death sentences be commuted to life imprisonment but the Governor refused.

However, the day before the scheduled hanging, at the urging of defense attorneys Mauldin and Lewis Dorroh, the Governor "wired a respite for Creswell" granting him a 30-day reprieve while he sought a new trial. Fletcher Byrd was hung as scheduled on Nov. 10, 1905, in the county jail yard on Broad St.

In 1905 each county conducted its own hangings as the state did not take over this function until 1912. The *Greenville News* mentioned on Nov. 10 that Fletcher Byrd was the ninth man to die on the scaffold in Greenville. According to an article in the *Greenville News* on Feb. 25, 1906, the gallows was first used in Greenville on April 2, 1882, for the hanging of three negroes convicted of arson in the burning of the Academy of Music in Dec. of 1879. This 1906 article described the eight prior hangings in Greenville County.

The *Greenville News* published a lengthy description of the hanging in its Nov. 11, 1905, issue. The hanging was conducted by Sheriff Gilreath who "slipped the black cap over his head" as both stood on the scaffold. The hanging was only semi-public as the only spectators allowed into the jail yard to witness the hanging had to have "passes" from the Sheriff. Chief of Police Becknell and his men "patrolled the walls seeing to it that no unauthorized persons entered" the jail yard to witness the hanging. The authorities heard a rumor that a mob, angry at the reprieve granted to Creswell, might try to lynch him on the same scaffold used to hang Byrd. One interested witness was Palmer Creswell who apparently saw the execution from his jail cell.

Byrd was allowed to make a final statement to the witnesses and said that he was ready to die and that he "realized what he had done and that it was right that he should give life for life." He expressed the hope that "others of his race would take warning from his example and let gambling and whiskey alone." Then he "looked slowly about him, and calling each of a group of his friends and relatives by name, told them a lingering good-bye."

The S.C. Supreme Court granted a new trial to Creswell which was held on September, 12, 1906. Solicitor Boggs again prosecuted the case while Creswell was defended by Lewis Dorroh. Creswell was not found guilty of murder but of "manslaughter with a recommendation to mercy." Neither the court file nor the newspaper coverage reported the sentence imposed by the judge for the manslaughter conviction. Since the S.C. Dept. of Corrections has no records of release dates until the 1950's, no information is available as to how long Creswell was incarcerated.

THE OFFICER

William Jeremiah Cox was born on May 6, 1869, in S.C. to Lewis Robert Cox (Aug. 19, 1845 - May 3, 1909) and Susannah Elizabeth Hyde Cox (Aug. 20, 1844 - July 2, 1903). His great, great, great grandfather, William Cox, Sr. (1730-1814), was a resident of Greenville County upon his death in 1814.

Wm. J. Cox married Mary Myrtle Watson (born on Oct. 20, 1871), the daughter of James Franklin and Mary Frances Walker Watson. Wm. J. and Mary Myrtle Watson Cox had an infant daughter who died on Oct. 10, 1895. Myrtle died at the age of 25 on May 27, 1895.

Wm. J. then married Elizabeth Vaughan (born on Dec. 18, 1882) and the couple had two daughters, Myrtle and Willie Cox (the grandchildren of Wm. J. Cox). Myrtle Cox married Cecil Dewitt Boney and had three children, William Jerry Boney, Carolyn Ann Boney and Eugene Dewitt Boney (the great grandchildren of Wm. J. Cox).

Willie Cox married Frankie E. Kitchen and the couple had one child, Don Kitchen (the grandson of Wm. J. Cox). Don Kitchen was a veterinarian in Greenville for many years.

William J. Cox was buried in the Bethel United Methodist Church cemetery in Mauldin. In 1996 his grave marker can be easily found at the Bethel cemetery on Holland Road just east of Mauldin near the Bridges Rd. exit to Interstate 385. The family plot is marked by a seven ft. tall Woodman of the World grave monument for Wm. J. Cox at the back of the cemetery. The grave marker reads:

William J. Cox
May 6, 1869
May 14, 1904
One loss at home
One more in heaven

Also buried in the Cox family plot are Wm. Cox's first wife, Myrtie Watson Cox, 25, who died on May 27, 1897; the infant daughter of Wm. J. and Myrtie Cox who died on Oct. 10, 1895; Wm. Cox's second wife, Elizabeth Vaughan, 76, who died on Sept. 25, 1959; and William Jerry Boney, 50, the grandson of Magistrate Cox and the son of Myrtie Cox Boney and C. Dewitt Boney, who died on Oct. 28, 1981. Wm. Jerry Boney's grave marker includes the words, "National Council of Churches, New York."

Dr. Wilbanks could not locate any living descendants of William Jerry Cox in 1996. Several descendants (e.g., Carolyn Ann Boney and Eugene Dewitt Boney) were though to have moved to New Jersey. Historians in Mauldin and "old-timers" present at the annual reunion of the Bethel United Methodist Church had no knowledge of the whereabouts of any of Cox's descendants.

The name of William J. Cox will be added to the National Law Enforcement Memorial in Washington, D.C., in 1997 as his line of duty death was unknown to the memorial before research for this book. A plaque bearing his name will also be added to the S.C. Criminal Justice Hall of Fame in Columbia in 1996.

SOURCES: *Greenville News*, May 15,17,28,31, June 3, 1904, Nov. 10,11,12, 1905, Sept. 12,13, Nov. 13, 1906, Sept. 27, 1959; Greenville County Criminal Court case #6305 at State Archives in Columbia; *Mauldin's Legacy and Its People* by Mae Walker, Mary Forrester, Martha Clyde and Karen and Adam Fisher; Cemetery index of Greenville County; grave markers at Bethel United Methodist Church in Mauldin; Genealogical information on the Cox family provided by Dallas W. Griffin of Mauldin, S.C.; and interview with Lillian Henderson Eaton.

#6 WILLIS FOSTER
Greer Police Dept.
Shot & killed by bootleggers in Greer on July 2, 1904.

THE EVENT

Night policeman Willis Foster, 36, of the Greer Police Dept. was shot and killed by bootleggers on July 2, 1904. Three bootleggers were charged with the murder but were acquitted at trial.

On Saturday night, July 2, 1904, Officer Foster, "a large, mustachioed man who took very seriously his duties as night patrolman" had "supper" with his wife and two children before going on night patrol duty. "He carried a pistol in a holster strapped to his left side and a 'billy' stick as he patrolled the dusty streets." One of his primary duties was to be on the lookout for bootleggers as Greers (as it was then called) was "on the fringes of the so-called Dark Corner of the state" and "served as a center of trade for many moonshiners and bootleggers."

Some twenty years before, the streets of Greers had been cluttered with saloons and many citizens had lived in fear of ruffians attracted to these establishments. In 1879, the state legislature finally acted and closed the bars. The problem was not completely solved by this action, however. The absence of competition stimulated business for those not deterred by the letter of the law. This was the situation in 1904. The police made very effort to uphold the liquor laws. Bud Littlefield, a veteran officer, and later a chief of police, was no-nonsense man who,

Greer, South Carolina Officer Willis Foster, 36, was shot and killed by bootleggers on July 2, 1904. Willis posed for this studio photo only hours before his death. His name is inscribed on the National Law Enforcement Memorial in Washington, DC.

as a day patrolman, earned quite a reputation for his firm but fair enforcement of the law. (*Greer Citizen*, centennial edition, 1976)

On that fatal Saturday night, Officer Foster relieved Officer Littlefield, the day patrolman, and started making his rounds. Around 10:00PM, Officer Foster was in the area "near the site of the old Wayside Inn when he spotted a man duck into nearby trees. Foster recognized the man as a known bootlegger and suspected that he had a cache of whiskey stored nearby. The officer followed the suspected bootlegger "into the trees." A few moments later, several people at a nearby cafe heard three shots and ran outside to investigate.

They found patrolman Foster lying at the edge of a grove of large oaks. His pistol was still in its place; Foster had been ambushed by the man he was following. The officer died before he could be moved. The lingering scent of gunpowder and the two small, round holes in Foster's new uniform poignantly summed up the events for the gathering crowd. (*Greer Citizen*, centennial edition, 1976)

The bullet wound that caused the officer's "instant death" entered his body through his chest and then went through his heart. One arm was also "terribly shattered in the region of the elbow" by another bullet. A quart bottle and flask of illegal liquor was found near the body providing one clue to the identity of the killer(s).

Sheriff Jefferson D. Gilreath, the son of legendary Greenville Sheriff Perry D. Gilreath (1876-1900), was called to investigate the case and arrived in Greer on Sunday morning, July 3. He spent five days in the city gathering "a mass of circumstantial evidence" with the help of Chief Becknell of Greenville, Chief Constable Hall, Constable Charles, Deputy Sheriff Holcombe and "several officers from Greer." By Sunday night several men were arrested as suspects and/or as witnesses.

THE PERPETRATORS

Magistrate Westmoreland, acting coroner, began an inquest on Monday, July 4. Nearly twenty witnesses ("most of whom were white men") were called during a two-day inquest before the coroner's jury directed by W.C. Cothran, a Greer attorney. After five hours of deliberation, the jury ruled that Officer Foster "had come to his death at the hands of Boyce Stone and that Watt Nobles was an accessory both before and after the fact." The names of Watt and Jim Nobles and the negro George Downes, who were also arrested for illegal distribution of liquor, "were more or less connected with the evidence brought out at the hearing, all of which, however, was circumstantial." All four men were "from the neighborhood of Greer."

It was alleged in the inquest testimony that Watt and Jim Nobles, accompanied by two negroes, both named Downes, went to Greer Saturday afternoon with nine gallons of whiskey, "which they concealed in the woods just beyond the limits of the town." The two negroes were sent into town "to drum up the trade for the evening." They returned later and reported that "the crowd" would be out that night to buy the liquor.

Also, according to the inquest testimony, Boyce Stone spent the night with a relative in Greer and aroused the relative later in the night and said he had dropped a quart bottle and a flask during the earlier part of the night and that he had to find them. The two men dressed and went in search of the missing bottle and flask (which had been found by the body of Officer Foster). While "passing along the street" they heard the blood hounds (brought by Sheriff Gilreath from Greenville) and "sat and listened." Stone suddenly announced that he would not look for the bottle and flask any longer and the two returned to the house.

Testimony also indicated that Stone had been seen earlier Saturday afternoon with a revolver and was heard to remark that "there was going to be trouble for any one that interfered with him." After the shooting he told another man that "if any one had seen him with that pistol and heard what he had said it might put him in a bad fix." Another witness testified that Jim Nobles remarked after the shooting that Foster "was a scoundrel and ought to have been shot." Another witness testified that Watt Nobles was at the scene of the shooting.

In addition to Stone being charged with murder and Watt Nobles being charged as an accessory before and after the fact, George Downes and Jim Nobles were arrested and charged with "violating the dispensary law."

The *Greenville News* editorialized that Foster was killed "because the outlaws feared him" and praised the law-abiding citizens of Greer for their efforts "to free themselves from the bandit liquor gang" which was responsible for the "assassination" of Policeman Foster. The gratitude of the citizens of Greer was shown by the erection of a 7 ft. tall monument at his gravesite commemorating his heroism while discharging his duty.

The first murder trial of Boyce Stone, Watt Nobles and George Downes began in the "winter term" of 1904 but ended in a mistrial—due to the illness of a juror—after nearly all the evidence had been presented. The second trial began on Tuesday, May 9, 1905, before Circuit Court Judge Prince of Anderson. A total of ten attorneys were involved in the murder trial. Solicitor Boggs prosecuted the case with the assistance of Alvin H. Dean and T.P. Cothran. Watt Nobles was defended by H.J. Haynsworth, B.M. Shuman and George Johnstone; Boyce Stone by O.K. Mauldin and H.K. Townes; and George Downes by T.K. Earle and B.A. Morgan.

Jury selection took eight hours on May 9 and required the calling of a second panel of prospective jurors. Defense attorneys were allowed a total of 20 "arbitrary objections" (i.e., challenges without specifying cause). Since the death penalty was a possible punishment for murder, those expressing objections to the death penalty were eliminated from the jury.

The *Greenville News* reported that the conviction depended "almost solely on circumstantial evidence." The large number of lawyers led to considerable bickering among the attorneys for the prosecution and defense as did the transcript of witnesses' testimony from the first trial which was introduced as evidence. The state depended upon witnesses saying that they saw the defendants near the scene of the murder and that Stone and Nobles had uttered threats that they would kill any police officer who interfered with their sale of illegal liquor. The prosecution took two days (May 10 & 11) to present its case followed by two days (May 12-13) of testimony from the defense. Watt Nobles took the stand in his own defense while Boyce Stone did not.

In a strange twist, the prosecution told the jury it did not seek the conviction of Townes, the negro, since "there was no evidence tending to show that he took any part in the killing." However, it appears that he remained as a defendant at the trial.

On Saturday, May 13, 1905, the jury deliberated only one hour and twenty minutes before returning a verdict of not guilty for all three defendants. The acquittal was not unexpected though some observers thought a conviction for murder with a recommendation for mercy was likely.

No one ever expected the two white men to be found guilty of murder, without the usual fringe, the recommendation to mercy, which saves the prisoner from the halter, but there were many who confidently expected a conviction with the life sentence. (*Greenville News,* 5/14/1905)

However, the jury, "laboring under the impression that there should be punishment of some sort at least" convicted Nobles and Stone of "carrying concealed weapons, or rather of carrying unlawful pistols." However, Judge Prince judge threw out these weapons convictions since such convictions were illegal without conviction on the murder charge.

Little is known about Watt Nobles, Boyce Stone, and George Downes. The newspapers did not even report their age and they were not listed in the 1900 SC census. Also, no record could be found of their (later) death in the index of SC deaths (which goes through 1934) or the cemetery indexes of Greenville County.

By the time of the second trial "day patrolman" Bud Littlefield had become Chief of Police in Greer. His problems with bootleggers continued and on Dec. 8, 1905, he engaged in a shootout with a "crazy drunk" negro bootlegger, Lewis Bruton. The bootlegger was killed and an inquest ruled the Chief shot in self-defense.

THE OFFICER

Willis Foster, 36, was born on Oct. 18, 1867, in S.C. According to the 1900 S.C. census (taken on June 4, 1900), his parents were also born in S.C. and Willis was a "farm laborer" who spoke English but could not read and write. Willis Foster lived on the farm of his mother-in-law, Mrs. Eliza Pennington, 58, in Chick Springs, a township of Greers. The 1900 census indicated that Willis Foster, 32, had been married for three years to Mattie Pennington Foster, 28. Mattie's two sisters, Mary Pennington, 31, and Annie L. Pennington, 22, also lived on the Pennington farm. The 1900 census listed the two children of Willis and Mattie P. Foster as "Cohen D." (born in Oct. of 1897) and "Laura L." (born in Jan. of 1900). Both names were listed incorrectly as the correct names were Coan and Lucille. A third child, Edith M. was born on Sept. 4, 1902. At the time of his death, Willis Foster was survived by his wife, Mattie, 31, and by three children, Coan, 7, and Lucille, 4, and Edith, 2.

Earlier on the day he was killed, Officer Foster had "posed for a portrait at C.W. Drace's photography studio. The portrait, to be a gift for his young family, showed the officer in his first uniform." Foster had waited for some time before he was able to afford his new uniform and "his pride was obvious to all who saw him that morning" before and after his photography session. That photograph is included with this narrative as it was obtained from Officer Foster's granddaughter, Maxine McNatt.

Only one paragraph was devoted to the funeral of Officer Foster in the Greenville News on July 4. The funeral was held on Sunday, July 3, "and the interment followed immediately." The newspaper reported that the Officer's wife and three young children were "left in a destitute condition because of the tragedy."

Willis Foster, 36, was buried in Edgewood Cemetery in downtown Greer. The citizens of Greer erected a 7 ft. tall stone monument to mark the grave of the slain officer. In 1996, the grave marker still stands in Edgewood Cemetery and reads:

W. FOSTER
Oct. 18, 1867
July 2, 1904
Erected by the citizens
of Greer in memory of
Officer Foster who was
assassinated in 1904
while discharging
his duty

Others buried in the family plot near Willis Foster are C. Pennington, his father-in-law (1897); Eliza Jane Pennington, his mother-in-law (1915); Mary E. Pennington, his sister-in-law (1907); and his widow, Mattie Jane Foster (1941), and child, Edith M. Foster (1904). Edith, 23 months, was born on Sept. 4, 1902, and died on Aug. 19, 1904 (six weeks after her father's death).

Mattie Pennington Foster, 68, the widow of Officer Foster died Jan. 30, 1941, and was buried in Edgewood Cemetery in downtown Greer. Her obituary in the *Greenville News* indicated that she was a "member of one of the oldest families of Greer, being the daughter of the late Cunningham Pennington and Eliza Jane Alexander Pennington." Her father, Cunningham Pennington, 62, died in 1897 in Greer and her mother, "Janie" Pennington, 74, died in 1915 in Greer. Mattie was born at Oneal "but had lived in Greer since she was eight years old." She was a "devoted member" of the First Baptist Church where her mother had been a "charter member." The 1915 Greer Directory listed the widow "Maggie" Foster as working as a clerk at the "Famous Dry Goods Store" in Greer.

Mattie Foster was survived (in 1941) by a daughter, Mrs. Gus (Lucille L.) Lewis, 40, of Henderson, TN, and one son, Coan D. Foster, 43, of Greensboro, N.C., and by "ten grandchildren."

Officer Foster's daughter, Lucille Foster Lewis, died at the age of 93 on Oct. 9, 1993, in Henderson, TN. Her only memory of her father (who died when she was 4) was of his lying on their porch after he had been "brought home from being shot." Lucille married Augustus Evans (Gus) Lewis in 1918 while he was in the Army at Camp Sevier, S.C. They moved to Henderson, TN, following World War I, and Mr. Lewis farmed and later operated a diary. He died in 1978. In 1993 Lucille was survived by five children, four grandchildren, and five great-grandchildren.

In 1996, the four living children of Lucille Foster Lewis were Maxine McNatt, 76, of Jackson, TN; Joe F. Lewis, 66, of Jackson, TN; Annie Laura Beckworth, 62, of New Albany, MI; and Martha Lee McMinn, 59, of Blanchard, OK. A fifth child, Mary Emma Rouse, 55, died in Memphis, TN, in 1996. These five children had a total of five children and eight grandchildren (the great, great grandchildren of Willis Foster).

Coan D. Foster, the oldest child of Officer Willis, married Emma Frances Dodson in 1918 and lived his adult life (working as an air-conditioning engineer) in Greensboro, NC, and died there in 1979 at the age of 82. In 1996 the survivors of Coan D. and Emma Frances Foster were Frances Boone, 76, of Greensboro; Clara Smith, 74, of N. Myrtle Beach, SC; Margaret Gottschalk, 72, of Greensboro, NC; and *Willis* Edmund Foster (named for Officer Willis, his grandfather), 70, of Chattanooga, TN.

The four children of Coan Foster had a total of 3 children (Clara's daughter, Judy Moore, 51, worked for the U.S. Foreign Service in Paris; Margaret's daughter, Donna Ford, 39, lived in Greensboro; and Edmund's daughter, Sandy Lee, 46, lived in Chattanooga, TN). Sandy Lee's two children (Michael Lee, 24, of the U.S. Army and Christopher Lee, 20, of Chattanooga) were the great, great, grandchildren of Officer Willis Foster. None of the descendants of Officer Foster lived in Greenville County in 1996.

The name of Willis Foster is (incorrectly) inscribed on the National Law Enforcement Memorial in Washington, D.C., as *"William Zonk Foster."* Descendants of Willis Foster in 1996 were surprised to hear the name "Zonk" as the only name they knew was "Willis Foster." "Zonk" may have been a nickname by which he was known by other police officers.

Foster's date of death is also incorrectly listed by the National Memorial as Jan. 1, 1904, rather than July 2, 1904. Descendants of Willis Foster, when "found" by Dr. Wilbanks in June of 1996, were not aware that their ancestor's name was on a national monument in Washington but several planned to visit the monument in the near future. Martha McMinn provided a print of the photo of Officer Foster taken on the day of his death for this book, for the national memorial data base, and for the Greer Police Dept.

The name of Willis Foster (actually "William Zonk Foster") is also displayed on a plaque at the S.C. Criminal Justice Hall of Fame in Columbia, S.C. The Greer Police Dept. displays a photo/plaque honoring Officer Willis at its headquarters building and he remains the only Greer officer ever killed in the line of duty. On Sept. 18, 1996, the *Greer Citizen* published an abridged version of this chapter to remind its citizens of Willis Foster, the only law enforcement officer killed in the history of Greer.

SOURCES: *Greenville News*, July 3,4,6,7,8,9, 1904, May 9,10,11,12,13,14, Dec. 9, 1905, Jan. 31, 1941; *Greenville Mountaineer*, April 10, 1897; *Chester County (TN) Independent*, Oct. 14, 1993; *Greer Citizen*, centennial edition, 1976, Sept. 18, 1996; 1900 S.C. census of Greers, S.C. (E.D. 21, Sheet 3, Line 85); 1910 S.C. census of Greers, S.C. (E.D. 8, Sheet 11); Greenville County criminal court case #6390; and interviews with Maxine McNatt, Martha Lee McMinn, Annie Laura Beckworth, and Frances Boone.

#7 OLIVER S. GUNNELS
Greenville Police Dept.
Shot & killed at railway station on Feb. 17, 1911.

THE EVENT

Sgt. Oliver Gunnels, 62, a 26-year veteran of the Greenville Police Dept., was shot and killed at a Greenville railway station "in a desperate pistol duel" by a man who was in the middle of a "crime spree" that began the day before and continued until his capture in GA on Feb. 22 after he shot and killed a railway conductor. The killer was lynched on Feb. 24 at Warrenton, GA.

The incident that led to the fatal shooting of Sgt. Gunnels began between the hours of 2:30AM and 3:00AM on Friday, Feb. 17, 1911. Sgt. Gunnels and Officer B.V. Johnson were walking down Augusta St. toward the downtown area when they noticed a man emerge from the "railroad cut" near the "Vardry St. crossing" with a bag or grip hung over his shoulder. The "lone stranger" was walking the 300 yards toward the railway passenger station. Since the freight train had just passed, the officers suspected that the stranger had just jumped off the train.

The officers followed the man to the station and saw him enter the "colored" waiting room. Gunnels and Johnson approached the door at the same time and Gunnels opened the door with his right hand as he shined his flashlight into the room with his left hand. Officer Johnson later said that simultaneously with the flash of the light

the man raised his revolver and fired. The first shot pierced Gunnel's abdomen, and he fell back against the door facing exclaiming, "Johnson, I'm shot: kill him." Before the stranger could fire a second time I had my pistol out and opened fire on him. The second shot he fired struck Gunnels in the right thigh and "Sergeant" receded toward the south end of the station. The third shot from the man's revolver pierced my right leg. All the while the man and I were exchanging shots with lightning-like rapidity. I had a Smith & Wesson, .38-calibre pistol and I think he was armed with a .32 calibre Colt's magazine revolver. I fired four times and pulled the trigger of my revolver again but the cartridge failed to explode. I receded then and the man sprung through the door, firing as he ran. When on the outside he wheeled about, ran backwards a short distance, and fired several more shots, the first one being fired at Gunnels, who was in the act of sinking to the ground, and the remaining ones being fired at me. He then fled and I turned to assist Gunnels. (*Greenville News*, 2/18/1911)

Officer Gunnels was rushed to the hospital and died a few hours later (at 7:00AM). Dr. W.C. Black, the coroner, later determined that Gunnels had been hit with two shots. One shot severed the femoral artery which caused the bleeding that led to his death. The other shot entered the abdomen and lodged in the spinal cord. The steel-jacketed bullet taken from the body was found to be the type used in magazine type pistols.

Neither officer approached the "tramp" with any thought that he might be armed and dangerous. What they did not know was that the stranger, later determined to be a "mulatto" named Arthur Young, was an escaped convict from a Greenville chain gang and was in the midst of a crime spree involving the burglary of several buildings. The bag Young carried contained burglar tools and he realized that, if caught, the possession of burglar tools was a "penitentiary offense" and that he faced additional time (up to 10 or 20 years) for other charges. Thus Young probably felt "hemmed in" at the station and "had no other thought than that of escape" and to accomplish the escape "he would murder everything that stood between him and liberty."

The police did not determine the identity of the killer for several weeks. After the police investigation failed to come up with immediate leads to the killer, local citizens hired a Pinkerton detective to track down the killer. The $275 fund to pay the Pinkerton man was raised from contributions of $1 to $25 from local citizens. The local citizenry was concerned that three of its police officers had been attacked in recent days. Officer Jim Noe had been attacked some weeks earlier and two days before the murder of Gunnels, Officer T.J. ("Uncle Tommy") Cureton had been shot by a deranged man.

In response to this "crime wave against police officers," the Board of Police Commissioners met on Feb. 24 and authorized an increase in the size of the police force and the purchase of automatic or magazine revolvers. Prior to this time police officers had to provide their own weapons and, given the low salary of officers, were being "outgunned" by the criminal element. The Commission noted that Officer Gunnels' revolver was "old and extremely rickety" and was no match for the weapon used by his assailant in the shootout.

THE PERPETRATOR

The killer of Gunnels was not positively identified as Arthur Young until after he was lynched by a mob in Warrenton GA. Young had boarded a train near Augusta, GA, on Feb. 23, and when questioned by Conductor W.W. Thompson and a railroad detective, he pulled his pistol from his pocket and fired, killing the conductor. Young was wounded, captured, and taken to the jail in Augusta where, two days later, he was taken by a mob and lynched.

The Pinkerton detective, W.B. Fitzgerald, and a team of officers from Greenville were tracking Young and "just missed him before the lynching." The body of the bullet-riddled and lynched Young was sold by the Warrenton, GA, sheriff to a medical college in Atlanta. Greenville Officer Hendrix Rector (later Sheriff of Greenville County from 1913 to 1919 when he was killed in the line of duty) obtained the body from the medical college and brought it back to Greenville so that it could be identified.

At a reconvened coroner's inquest on Feb. 27, several local citizens who knew Young identified his body and Officer Johnson identified the body of Young as that of the man who shot him and killed Officer Gunnels. Other witnesses identified Young as the man who burglarized several stores in Williamston several hours before he shot Gunnels and as the man who "cracked" safes several days earlier (from Jan. 11 to Jan. 30) in Easley, Owens and Laurens and in three towns in GA. The coroner's jury ruled that Officer Gunnels had been killed by Arthur Young.

One man who identified Arthur Young at the inquest was J.I. King, "a farmer residing several miles below Greenville." He testified that the dead negro was Arthur Young and that he was raised on his farm and "had lived there until a comparatively short while ago." Another man identified Young as a "familiar character in the police court and the chain gang" in Greenville.

The *Greenville News* left the impression that the case would never have been solved without the work of Fitzgerald, the Pinkerton Detective, who "connected" the various crimes to the same man and eventually tracked him to GA where he was lynched. There was also a report in the newspaper that several citizens questioned why bloodhounds were not owned by the local police as Young could have supposedly been tracked and captured immediately with the use of dogs.

THE OFFICER

Oliver S. Gunnels, 62, was born on Dec. 5, 1848, in Cooley's Bridge, S.C. His obituary in the *Greenville News* reported the story of his near death as an infant. His father, who lived on the "old Sullivan plantation in Dunklin township" was instantly killed by lightning in 1849 while he held his infant son, Oliver, in his arms. "The father was killed on the spot but the babe was not even bruised."

Oliver moved to Greenville as a young man and was employed at the Camperdown Cotton Mills for several years. In 1885, at the age of 37, Gunnels was elected a member of the Greenville Police Department. With the exception of one year, he served on the Greenville force from 1885 to his death in 1911, a period of 26 years. During his time on the police force, he served as acting chief, as first sergeant and as second sergeant. He was elected as acting chief by the Board of Police Commissioners on Sept. 12, 1906, when Chief T.L. Becknell was forced to resign. At the time of his death he occupied the position of patrolman but was still referred to by colleagues and citizens as "Sergeant."

Sgt. Gunnels was famous for one particular act of bravery. The *Greenville News* reported on April 14, 1904, that Sgt. Gunnels "several years before" saved the life of Chief of Police R.H. Kennedy (who was Chief from 1885-1890, 1893-1906, & 1908-1911) when Ellis Sanders attempted to shoot him. Gunnels "shoved the weapon up before it was discharged." This story was reported in the newspaper after Officer James Patrick Tucker was killed (and another officer wounded) by Ellis Sanders on April 12, 1904.

The funeral for Sgt. Gunnels was held on Saturday, Feb. 18, 1911, at the Pendleton Street Baptist Church. A funeral procession of city officials, police officers, and others followed the casket carried by six fellow officers from the Gunnels home on Greene Ave. to the church for the service. The church was filled with mourners for the brief and simple service conducted by the Rev. Dr. Henry Miller, pastor of the church.

From the church the funeral procession "wended its solemn way through the streets" to Springwood Cemetery. The gravesite was "heaped high" with numerous "floral offerings" with "one of the prettiest being from the wives of the policemen who, perhaps better than anyone else, can sympathize with the policeman's widow." The Masonic Lodge No. 31 was in charge of the graveside services.

The City Commission agreed to pay all medical and funeral expenses for Officer Gunnels and to give his widow her husband's salary for the "entire month of February." Evidently little thought was given in those days to pensions for the families of officers killed in the line of duty.

Oliver Gunnels, 24, married Sarah Redmond, 20, in 1872. The couple had three sons (Robert T., born in 1873; Walter S., born in 1879; and Rowley, born in 1893) and two daughters (Allie, born in 1882 and Olivia, born in 1889). The three sons (ranging in ages from 18 to 38) and one daughter (Ollie Mae) were living at the time of their father's death but one daughter (Allie) had died three months earlier.

In 1996 the grave of Oliver Gunnels, 62, at Springwood Cemetery (Section A, plot 54) is covered by a stone with the words:

OLIVER S. GUNNELS

DEC, 5, 1848

FEB. 17, 1911

Also buried in the Gunnels family plot are the officer's wife, Sarah ("Sallie") Redmond Gunnels, 68 (who died on Aug. 29, 1921); and three of his children, Allie, 28 (who died on Dec. 8, 1910), Rowley S. Gunnels, 31 (who died on March 29, 1931), and Robert T. Gunnels, 71, (who died on July 21, 1945). The family plot also includes the grave of John O. McTindal, 30 (who died on March 20, 1938). He was the son of Allie Gunnels McTindal.

The 1921 obituary for the widow indicated that she (and Oliver Gunnels) was survived by her three sons of Greenville and by one daughter, Mrs. J.L. (Ollie Mae) Batson of Greenville. The 1945 obituary for the officers' eldest son, Robert Terry Gunnels, indicated that he was born in 1873 in Abbeville County and spent most of his life in Greenville. He was survived by his sister, Mrs. J.L. (Ollie Mae) Batson and two nephews. The third son, W.W. Gunnels, lived in New York City most of his life.

Sgt. Gunnels' daughter, Mrs. Ollie Mae Gunnels Batson, 80, died on June 2, 1970. She was preceded in death by her husband Greenville Fire Chief James Luther Batson, 71, who died of a heart attack at the scene of a fire on Dec. 26, 1951. Batson joined the Greenville Fire Dept. in 1904 and "served with the first paid firefighting unit in Greenville." He was a 47-year veteran of the Fire Dept. and was the third fire chief in 18 months to die of heart failure. James Oliver Batson, 64, the only child of James Luther and Ollie Mae Gunnels Batson, died on Dec. 25, 1976, and was survived by his daughter, Dawn Elizabeth Batson.

Allie Gunnels married John H. McTindal and the couple had two sons, Alvin and John O. McTindal. When the children were young, the family moved to Hamlet, N.C. John O. McTindal died at 31 on March 20, 1938. His obituary in the *Greenville News* indicated that he had no children and was survived by his brother Alvin, of Asheville, N.C.

Dr. Wilbanks could locate no living descendants of Sgt. Oliver Gunnels in 1996. Perhaps someone who reads this narrative will contact Wilbanks with news of the whereabouts of the descendants of Gunnels?

The name of Oliver S. Gunnels is inscribed (East Wall, Panel 21, Line 13) on the National Law Enforcement Memorial in Washington, D.C.

A plaque bearing his name is also displayed at the S.C. Criminal Justice Hall of Fame in Columbia.

SOURCES: *Greenville News*, Sept. 13, 1906, Feb. 18,19,20,21,25,26,27,28, 1911, Aug. 30, 1921, March 30, 1931, March 22, 1938, July 22, 1945, Dec. 28, 1951, June 3, 1970, Dec. 27, 1976; *Fire Fighting in Greenville, 1840-1990* by Wm. D. Browning, Jr.; Springwood Cemetery records; and 1900 and 1910 census of Greenville County.

#8 JOHN FLEMON LINDSEY
Deputy Sheriff
Shot and killed during arrest attempt on Oct. 5, 1914.

THE EVENT

Deputy Sheriff John Flemon Lindsey, 33, of Dunean Mill, was shot and killed during an attempt to arrest a husband in a domestic dispute on Oct. 5, 1914. His killer was convicted of manslaughter at his second trial and sentenced to 15 years in prison.

Flemon Lindsey was a "mill deputy" meaning that he was paid by the mill but deputized by the Sheriff of Greenville County. He was called to a home in the Dunean mill village around 5:00AM on Monday, Oct. 5, 1914, to arrest a man causing a disturbance at the home of his estranged wife.

W.S. Chadwick, 38, had been employed until July at the Dunean mill as a "loom fixer" but later "deserted" his wife and family and was living in Woodbury, GA, when he wrote to his wife to tell her that he was coming to visit and threatened her. Upon arrival in Greenville on an early morning train, he went to his wife's home at 13 Blake Street in the Dunean mill village and knocked on her door at 4:00AM. Mrs. Chadwick's brother, Alfred T. Abbott, answered the door and admitted Chadwick on the promise that he would not cause trouble.

However, when Chadwick began to shout and threaten his wife, he was pushed out the door by Abbott

Greenville County, South Carolina Deputy Sheriff, John Flemon Lindsey, 33, was shot and killed at the Dunean Mill Village during a "domestic" call on Oct. 5, 1914. His name is on the National Law Enforcement Memorial in Washington, DC.

and Mrs. Chadwick locked the door behind him leaving him on the front porch. Chadwick, angry at being locked out of the house, began to try to break the front door in with an axe and, after failing to do so, tried the axe on the back door. When he returned to the front porch, Mrs. Chadwick sent her young son out the back door to get Deputy Lindsey.

Lindsey arrived at Mrs. Chadwick's home around 5:00AM and, seeing a man on the front porch, walked up to him. Mrs. Chadwick, who was standing inside the house at a window talking to her husband, later testified as to what happened after Lindsey came to the porch to confront Chadwick.

"Well, what's the trouble? Consider yourself under arrest! Have you a gun ... (then) the deputy placed both of his hands around Chadwick and was feeling of his hip pockets. (*Greenville News,* 11/13/1914)

Chadwick responded, "Yes I have a gun and a good one!" and pulled a .38 calibre revolver from his coat pocket and shot Lindsey in the face. The bullet entered through the eye and came out the back of his head. Chadwick then fled the scene. Several people in the house and neighborhood saw the confrontation but because it was dark and foggy, their vision was somewhat impaired.

Abbott "aroused" some of his neighbors and the Sheriff's office was notified. In a short time a posse was searching for Chadwick. When he was not quickly found a description of the fugitive was sent to nearby counties and to rail stations. Enraged citizens of Dunean mill and law enforcement officers raised a total of $400 for a reward for the arrest of Chadwick. Greenville County Sheriff Hendrix Rector and several of his deputies as well as the "Rural Police" headed by Chief Reuben Gosnell and the Greenville City police scoured the countryside for Chadwick. Most went without sleep for the two days of the search.

Chadwick "struck a straight line for the mountains," traveling a great deal at night and sleeping in the day until he reached Brevard, N.C. He was captured on Wednesday, Oct. 7 (two days after the murder), at Brevard, N.C. where he was arrested by surprise as he walked through the rail yard. Officers found a revolver hidden in a sock and 20 cartridges hidden in a shirt sleeve "evidently carried for the purpose of battle." Chadwick admitted to shooting Lindsey but said that it was an accident, a defense he would later "perfect" for his trial.

Chadwick was taken to the state penitentiary for safe-keeping as he refused to waive extradition from N.C. to go to Greenville fearing he might be lynched by friends of the popular deputy. Sheriff Rector compromised by taking him to Columbia in return for Chadwick's waiving of extradition.

THE PERPETRATOR

W.S. Chadwick, 38, was a former Baptist minister in some small churches in Greenville County and had been a fireman on the railroad. However, in recent years he had been a "loom fixer" at local mills.

Chadwick's trial on murder charges began on Nov. 11, 1914, with Chadwick being defended by Sam J. Nichols of Spartanburg. Solicitor Proctor Bonham prosecuted the case for the state assisted by Col. Alvin H. Dean of the law firm of Cothran, Dean and Cothran, "the latter being employed to assist in the prosecution by the family and by private subscription taken by the Dunean mill operatives."

The one-day trial was described by the *Greenville News* as "spectacular" in that Chadwick took the stand and claimed that the gun discharged accidently when he took it out to give it to Lindsey. He claimed that Lindsey grabbed the gun, causing it to fire. Three local psychiatrists examined Chadwick but the defense decided not to utilize that testimony though the state contended that Chadwick had a "fit" in the jail that scared fellow inmates.

The state countered with the argument that the threats to Mrs. Chadwick from her husband in GA indicated that he had malice toward her before he arrived and that Lindsey stopped the bullet that was intended for Mrs. Chadwick. Col. Alvin H. Dean compared the actions of Lindsey to "one person saving another's life by giving a part of their life's blood."

The most sensational aspect of the trial came when Mrs. Chadwick testified that she feared her husband and that he had "tried to get her to bring young girls into their home to board and asked her to assist him in bringing about their ruin for his own pleasure."

The trial, attended by a large number of "mill people," ended in a mistrial on Nov. 13 with the jury deadlocked, seven jurors holding out for murder and five voting for manslaughter. A second trial began on March 17, 1915, before Judge DeVore. Sam J. Nichols of Spartanburg and H.C. Miller of Greenville represented Chadwick while Solicitor Proctor Bonham and Colonel Alvin H. Dean again prosecuted the case for the state.

The only new element in the second trial was the introduction of several witnesses by the defense to show that the night was very dark and the "foggy-misty" conditions precluded witnesses from seeing the "bulk" of a person's body and from recognizing anyone at a distance. The two-day trial ended on March 20 after all-night deliberations by the jury. The jury was deadlocked for a time (again between murder and manslaughter) but finally agreed—on the seventh ballot—at 7:00AM on March 20 to a verdict of manslaughter.

Judge DeVore sentenced Chadwick the day the verdict was announced to 15 years at hard labor at the state penitentiary "or upon the public works of the county." The judge "congratulated" Chadwick on "getting off so light" and told him the jury might have just as easily found him guilty of murder.

The S.C. Dept. of Corrections has no records of inmate releases until the 1950's and thus the length of time served in prison by Chadwick is unknown.

THE OFFICER

John Flemon Lindsey was born on Dec. 29, 1880, in the mountains of Greenville County, S.C. to J. Thomas Lindsey (born on March 14, 1858) and Huldah Harrison Lindsey (born on Dec. 29, 1865). He was one of nine children and had four brothers (William F., Bennie, J. Thomas, and Henry G.) and four sisters, (Mary Caroline, Minnie, Martha, and Liddy).

Flemon grew up in the mountains of the Dark Corner of Greenville County but little is known of his early life (e.g., which schools he attended) other than that his father, J. Thomas Lindsey, 33, was shot and killed on Nov. 20, 1891, when Flemon was 11. An account of the killing can be found in the *Greenville Mountaineer* and in Mann Batson's book on the Dark Corner. Flemon (he is called "Fleming" in the two accounts) and his father, Thomas, were pulling a wagon "with an extra ox" at the foot of Glassy Mountain when Thomas got into a dispute with Isaac Ballew as he passed by. Later that day the two men met again and Ballew shot and killed Lindsey.

He did not wait to see if Lindsey was killed, but ran on, and that night came to Greenville and surrendered himself the next day. The jury was out only a comparatively short while and returned a verdict of not guilty.

(*A History of the Upper Part of Greenville County, SC*, by Mann Batson, pp. 470-1, quoting the *Greenville Mountaineer*, March 22, 1893)

Ballew claimed that Thomas Lindsey had threatened to shoot him and "had taken his gun out of the wagon" and that he shot him in self-defense.

Flemon Lindsey, 19, married Mary Ann Lindsay around 1899 and the couple was one of the first to reside at the Dunean mill village. He was deputized as a "mill deputy" in 1913 by his close friend, Sheriff Hendrix Rector (who was Sheriff of Greenville County from 1913-1919 and was killed in the line of duty in 1919). Deputy Lindsey was well known at the Dunean mill village as evidenced by the large number of village residents who attended the two murder trials of W.S. Chadwick.

John Flemon Lindsey, 33, was survived by his widow, Mary Ann Lindsey, 30, and six children: Hattie, 14; Garson, 11; Henry Haskell, 6; Bryson, 4; Claude, 3; and Daisey, 10 months. He was also survived by his mother, Huldah Harrison Lindsey, 48, and by eight siblings: William F. Lindsey, 32; Bennie Lindsey, 30; Mrs. James Henry (Martha) Howard, 28; Mrs. Charlie E. (Mary Caroline) Lindsey, 25; J. Thomas Lindsey, 23; Minnie Lindsey, 17 (later Mrs. John W. Emory); Henry G. Lindsey 15; and Liddy Lindsey, 12 (later Mrs. Early D. Harrison).

All of Flemon's siblings are buried in the Dark Corner including seven (William F., 1952; Bennie, 1956; Mary Caroline Lindsey, 1968; J. Thomas, 1958; Minnie Lindsey Emory, 1971; Henry G., 1973; and Liddy Lindsey Harrison, 1971) at Mt. Pleasant Baptist Church cemetery on Highway #101. His father (11/ 20/1891) and mother (11/27/1943) are buried at the Mountain Hill Baptist Church cemetery.

The grave of John Flemon Lindsey is easily found in the southwest corner of the Highland Baptist Church cemetery on Highway 414 in Tigerville. This small church cemetery also includes the graves of Constable James Holland Howard, killed by "moonshiners" in 1924, and Clarence Howard (son of James Holland), killed by a moonshiner in downtown Hendersonville in 1930.

A four foot tall stone monument with the name (Lindsey) marks the family plot at the Highland Baptist Church cemetery where the deputy is buried. The slain deputy's grave marker reads:

JOHN F. LINDSEY

DEC. 29, 1880

OCT. 5, 1914

John Flemon Lindsey was the first to be buried in the family plot at Highland Baptist Church cemetery and was followed by his wife Mary Ann Lindsay who died of pneumonia on Jan. 9, 1920, at the age of 36; and his son, Henry Haskell Lindsay, who died on Aug. 2, 1917, at the age of 9.

Hattie Lindsey married Ernest Smith, had four children, and died on Oct. 22, 1987, at the age of 87. Garson Lindsey had three children and died on March 20, 1991, at the age of 88. Henry Haskell Lindsey died on Aug. 2, 1917, at the age of 9. Claude Lindsey had one child and died on May 16, 1985, at the age of 74. All the children but Garson lived all their lives in Greenville County.

In 1996, Daisey Lindsay Tyner, 82, still lived in Greenville and was the only living child of Deputy John Flemon Lindsey. Two of her four children (John Leon Tyner, 63, of Greenville, and Shirley Jeannette Pyeatt, 60, of Greenville)—the grandchildren of the slain deputy—also lived in Greenville County. Her two other children were Ralph L. Tyner, 56, of Warner-Robbins, GA. and Mary Louise Luchsinger, 50, of New Freedom, PA.

The line of duty death of Deputy John F. Lindsey was forgotten over the years so that the 1996 list of slain Greenville County deputies did not include his name.

Dr. Wilbanks discovered his line of duty death in the pages of the *Greenville News* while researching this book.

However, nothing was known of the descendants of Deputy Lindsey until June 12, 1996, when Daisey Lindsay Tyner, the youngest daughter of Deputy John F. Lindsey, responded to an article in the *Greenville News* about Dr. Wilbanks' research which requested information on John F. Lindsey and other "lost" slain officers.

Sheriff Johnny Mack Brown, upon learning of the "forgotten hero," John F. Lindsey, added his name to the list of slain Greenville County deputies and sent documentation to the National Law Enforcement Memorial in Washington, D.C., so that his name would be inscribed on that memorial in 1996. The name of John F. Lindsey will also be displayed on a plaque at the S.C. Criminal Justice Hall of Fame in Columbia in 1996.

SOURCES: *Greenville News*, Oct. 6,7,8,9,21,30, Nov. 11,12,13,14, 1914, March 15,16,17,18,19,20,21,30, 1915, Jan. 10, 1920; Cemetery index for Greenville County; grave markers at Highland Baptist Church cemetery; 1910 S.C. Census for Greenville County, E.D. 16, Sheet 11); Greenville criminal court case #7675 at S.C. Archives in Columbia; genealogical records provided by Frances Howard; and interview with Daisey Lindsay Tyner.

#9 JAMES E. HOLCOMBE
Greenville Police Dept.
Shot during arrest attempt on May 11, 1915 (died on May 30).

THE EVENT

Greenville Police Chief James E. Holcombe, 53, was shot by a deranged man "while in a fit of supposed insanity" on May 11, 1915, when the Chief and another officer "stormed" the house after the occupant had shot a fellow officer through a window. The Chief was expected to recover from his gunshot wounds but died unexpectedly on May 30 while still in the hospital. The killer was severely wounded by another officer and later died of his wounds.

On Tuesday, May 11, 1915, Walter White, of 9 Gates St. in Carolina Mill village, became angry at his wife and had become so threatening that his wife and three young boys had fled the house. White had a reputation as a "crazy man" who had been in an asylum and was also considered "shiftless" as he did not work and allowed his hard-working wife to support the family through her work at the Carolina mill. A remark by his wife that she would bet $50 that he would be back in the asylum in a week apparently "set his wild passions on edge" and led to his wild and threatening behavior.

White's wife called the police and Call Officer Martin B. Bridges and Policeman Gilreath were sent to the home around 2:00PM to "get White out of the house." The two officers were unsuccessful and "sent word for help." Police Commissioner Henry T. Mills was at the station

James E. Holcombe

when the call came in and offered to carry the "reinforcements" (Chief Holcombe and Sgt. Cooksie) to the White home in his automobile. The Holcombe family recalls that Chief Holcombe would not have ordinarily gone out on such a mission but the subject was known to him and the Chief thought he would be able to talk the man into giving himself up.

Chief Holcombe, Sgt. Cooksie, and Officers Bridges and Gilreath talked with White through windows as he "walked up and down in the house with his pistol in his hand." White told the officers that he "would die before he would come out of the house. The officers told White that the only charge against him was for disorderly conduct and a friend was willing to "go his bond" for that offense.

White then requested that his wife be brought to the house to talk to him. The wife arrived and talked with White but the conversation only made him more angry and she was removed from the scene. The officers at the scene considered several "schemes" to get White out of the house during the three-hour seige (from 2:00PM to 5:00PM) including a plan to have firemen "send a stream of water through the window and thus run him out."

At 5:00PM, as the officers stood outside the house discussing their dilemma, White suddenly, and without warning, fired his pistol through a back window at Officer Bridges and struck him "just below the heart." Chief Holcombe then decided to "storm" the house but, true to his reputation, he did not ask other officers to do what he would not do, and thus the Chief led the "charge" and tried to break through "the front entrances" with the aid of Sgt. Cooksie.

Just as Chief Holcombe kicked in the front window, White fired point blank at him, striking the chief in the left thigh and breaking the bone. The chief fell and was shot in the other thigh as he fell and again through the right arm, and a bullet passed through his hat while he lay upon the ground. In the meantime Sergeant Cooksie entered the adjacent door and ran through the connecting door upon White, who turned to fire at the officer; but Sergeant Cooksie was faster and truer with his gun and he shot White down, striking him in the front part of the left thigh and breaking the bone. White fell upon the bed and threw down his pistol and held up his hands, begging the officer not to shoot again. The officer stopped shooting and dragged him out upon the front porch. ....

The work of Sergeant Cooksie in entering the house alone and facing White is worthy of the highest praise as was his ability to control himself and not shoot White to death. Sergeant Cooksie believed that Chief Holcombe was dead, having seen him fall from the porch to the ground, but he did not consider this stating that after he fired once and saw the gun leave the hand of White, he knew that there was no further danger and did not wish to shoot White any more. (*Greenville News,* 5/12/1915)

Police Commissioner Mills carried the two wounded officers to the city hospital while Sgt. Cooksie carried White "to the city hall and then to the hospital in the patrol wagon." During the nineteen days (May 11-May 30) he was hospitalized, Chief Holcombe was in good spirits though he was "suffering considerable from the wound in his thigh." He underwent surgery ("his broken hip bone was perfectly set") but his physicians expected a full recovery.

On Sunday night, May 30, at 10:00PM the Chief rang for the orderly who became alarmed at his condition and called for a nurse. "Vigorous treatment was administered and medical aid summoned" but the efforts of the nurses were futile as Holcombe lived for only ten minutes and was dead before any doctor arrived. The death was caused by a blood clot resulting from the gunshot wounds.

The death of Chief Holcombe came as a shock to family members as he was expected to recover. Two days before his death he was sitting up in bed in the hospital smoking a cigar and expecting to be discharged soon. He was even planning a rabbit hunting trip with his brother-in-law, Tom League.

THE PERPETRATOR

Walter (or Walker) White, age unknown, lived in Carolina mill village with his wife and three boys (ages 9-12). He did not work and had been in a mental hospital. However, the index for the 1910 census does not list a Walter White and a wife and children as living in S.C.

Walter White was still hospitalized for his injuries when Chief Holcombe died on May 30 (nineteen days after the shooting). The May 8, 1921, *Greenville News* said White "died later as a result of wounds" inflicted at the murder scene. There is no record in the criminal court log book of his being charged or tried. However, there is also no death certificate for a Walter White during this time period.

THE OFFICER

James Earl Holcombe was born on May 10, 1862, in the "upper section of Greenville County on the Saluda River" to W.T. and Harriet B. Thompson Holcombe. His parents were also born in Greenville County.

He came to Greenville as a young man and worked as a carpenter. In 1896, at the age of 34, he was "elected a member of the police force" and served as a Greenville officer for 19 years except for a "time when he served as jailor under Sheriff Jeff Gilreath." He was elected Chief of Police in 1911 on the promise that he would "clean up" Greenville.

It was said that in a city of this size it would be impossible to drive out the lewd women, and almost impossible to put the lid on the sale of liquor. The chief however, supported by the police commission, set resolutely and quietly to work. Within a short time and even in the days of government moral leprosy in this state, he did not relax his efforts to keep the parasitic blind tiger, and the scarlet woman out of Greenville. (*Greenville News*, 5/31/1915)

As to his personality and working style, the newspaper reported that Chief Holcombe

was a silent, cool man, very affable when once he was known, and a man whose integrity was respected. He said little to those who transgressed, and was exceptionally skillful in handling them. He was slow to use force. He came into power at a time when it would have been easy for a man to shut his eyes, and let matters be. But he chose a harder course than this and never swerved therefrom. (*Greenville News*, 5/31/1915)

James Holcombe married twice. He had three children by his first wife, Eleanor (Anna) Rochester Holcombe. His second wife was Margaret Beulah "Maggie" (League) Tinsley.

James E. Holcombe, 53, was survived by his widow, Margaret Beulah "Maggie" Tinsley Holcombe, 31, and their 6-day-old infant daughter, Beulah Marie Holcombe; and by three other children from his first marriage (to Eleanor Rochester Holcombe), William Clarence Holcombe, 33, of Norfolk, VA, Mrs. W.A. (Maud) Eskew, 21, and Bessie Holcombe, 17. He was also survived by two sisters, Mrs. H. Earle Langley and Mrs. C.C. Marchbanks of Greenville; by a brother, W.T. Holcombe of Greenville County; and by a half-brother, Assistant Chief of Police C.M. Thompson, who became acting chief during the hospitalization of Chief Holcombe.

The funeral for Chief Holcombe was perhaps the most elaborate ever seen in the history of the city. At the tolling of the city hall bell, a procession of family members, fellow officers, city officials, and others marched from the morgue to the Pendleton St. Baptist Church for the funeral service. "Not even the beautiful flowers, which covered the casket and were banked around the pulpit, spoke in more eloquent words than did the presence of the citizens for whom Chief Holcombe gave his life in devotion to duty."

The church could not hold all members of the procession and many mourners had to stand in the street during the service. Several ministers spoke at the service and the eulogy was delivered by the chief's pastor, Dr. B.D. Hahn of the Pendleton Street Baptist Church. Dr. Hahn spoke of the necessary role of police officers in society and of the Christian faith of Chief Holcombe.

Dr. Hahn told the mourners that the Chief, while in the hospital, told him that he "wanted nothing done to White, believing that he was insane." The pastor also spoke of the extraordinary courage of Chief Holcombe and said that "no battlefield held out a braver example than did the chief when he met his death wound." He also said a prayer for the Chief's widow, who had been in a state of shock and unconscious since her husband's sudden death and was "at the point of death."

After the funeral service, the procession of mourners marched to Graceland Cemetery for the burial service which was conducted by Dr. Hahn and the other ministers at the funeral service. The burial site was also covered with flowers.

The gravesite of Chief Holcombe is easily found at Graceland Cemetery in 1996. The grave is marked by a five ft. tall stone monument with the name "Holcombe" and is only six graves from that of Sheriff Hendrix Rector (killed in the line of duty on July 4, 1919) and only 50 feet from the grave of Greenville Officer A.M. Blair (killed in the line of duty on Oct. 5, 1919). The 18 inch stone marker below the Holcombe monument marks the only grave in the family plot and reads:

JAMES E. HOLCOMBE
May 10, 1862
May 30, 1915
His words were kindness, his deeds were love,
his spirit humble, he rests above

The Chief's second wife, Margaret ("Maggie") Beulah League Tinsley, was born in Greenville County and was the daughter of Commodore Butler and Robert Malvina "Bobby" Holland League. She was a widow with two sons (Harold and William Clarence "Bill" Tinsley) when she married Chief Holcombe. Maggie later married Robert F. "Bob" Ross, a Greenville contractor. She died in Ocala, FL, in 1967 at the age of 83 and is buried there.

The Chief's infant daughter, Beulah Marie Holcombe, married Joseph Oliver "Jack" Robinson. She spent her retirement years near Hernando, FL, and died there in 1993 at the age of 77. She was survived by two adopted daughters, Mary Beth Robinson and Marie Robinson. Mary Beth Robinson Prater lived in Tampa in 1996 with her husband, Jess, a retired dentist. Marie Robinson Windsor lived in Orlando in 1996.

The Chief's son, William Clarence Holcombe, was killed on June 17, 1943, during service in World War II. He had two children (the grandchildren of Chief Holcombe), William Clarence Holcombe, Jr., born on August 11, 1924, and Ina Rose Holcombe, born on May 30, 1927. Ina Rose Holcombe married Douglas Aldridge Smith on May 5, 1945. They had a son, William Holcombe Smith, born on March 8, 1946, and a daughter, April Jordan Smith, born on Feb. 26, 1949. William Holcombe Smith married Ann Norris and they had three sons (great, great grandchildren of Chief Holcombe), William Holcombe Smith, Jr., born on June 1, 1970; Douglas Langston Smith, born on Jan. 13, 1972; and Matthew McCall Smith, born on Oct. 13, 1973. From a second marriage, William Holcombe Smith and Susan Lay Smith had one daughter, Sarah Elizabeth Smith, born on August 15, 1988.

One of the Chief's daughters, Bessie Holcombe Nelson, and her husband, Jim Nelson, owned and operated a grocery store across from the Pavilion in River Falls, SC. They had two children, Jimmy and Mary Nelson (Cox). A second daughter, Maud Holcombe Eskew, had several children and died in 1971 at the age of 77.

In 1996 many descendants of Chief Holcombe remained in the Greenville area. One granddaughter, Ina Rose Holcombe Smith, 69, of Greenville still possessed a gold-headed walking stick that belonged to her grandfather. The inscription on the cane reads, "Presented to Chief Holcombe by the Greenville Police Department, Christmas, 1911." Other descendants in the Greenville area included grandson Charles Thomas Eskew, 83; Frances Elizabeth Eskew Whitfield, 58; Jack Parker Eskew, 62; George Maxwell Eskew, 72; and Mary Hartin.

The name of James E. Holcombe is inscribed (incorrectly as J.F. Holcombe) on the National Law Enforcement Memorial (East Wall, Panel 40, Line 11) and a plaque bearing his name is displayed at the S.C. Criminal Justice Hall of Fame in Columbia. A photograph of Chief Holcombe is displayed in the lobby of the Greenville Law Enforcement Center.

SOURCES: *Greenville News,* May 12,13,31, June 1,2,3, 1915, May 8, 1921; Death certificate of James E. Holcombe at S.C. State Archives; 1900 and 1910 Census of Greenville County; interviews with descendants Ina Rose Holcombe Smith, Charles Eskew, Mary Hartin, and Lillian Eaton.

#10 JAMES ARTHUR STEWART
Deputy Sheriff of Greenville County
Shot & killed during domestic disturbance on Aug. 26, 1917.

THE EVENT

James Arthur Stewart, 33, a rookie deputy sheriff at Woodside mills, was shot and killed on Aug. 26, 1917, during a "disturbance" at a boarding house in Greenville. The man who shot him during a struggle was sentenced to life in prison only 14 days after the murder in an example of "speedy justice."

Deputy Stewart was on the street in Woodside mill village around 7:30PM on Sunday night, Aug. 26, 1917, when he was approached by a man who told him there was "trouble" at the boarding house owned by Jesse Lewis. The Lewis house was well known to Stewart and everyone in the community as one which had "lewd women staying there" (it may have been a house of prostitution). According to a former mill deputy, Stewart had been "watching the Lewis house and getting evidence against it."

The complaint which brought the deputy to the house apparently came from a woman at the house who complained that Tom Scott, 26, was drunk and had been causing a disturbance by being rowdy and cursing. Scott apparently became angry that someone had called the police and went on the porch and began accusing a man sitting in a chair there of being the one who made the call. The man attempted to get up from the chair but Scott pushed him down and slapped him.

Stewart witnessed the push and slap and approached Scott and told him that he was through "causing trouble" and told him to "go on home." Scott became angrier and said that he would not go home and that "no one could make him." At this point the deputy hit or pushed Scott knocking him to the floor. The two became engaged in a struggle as Scott told Stewart that they were friends and "should not be doing this." During the struggle, a third man, Walter Coon, grabbed Stewart, (later) claiming that he wanted to break up the fight. As Coon grabbed Stewart he said, "I'll take charge of *you*, Stewart." Two witnesses would later testify that Coon had a knife in his hand when he grabbed Scott.

However, as the "three were in grapple," Scott took the deputy's gun from its holster and shot him four times. One of the bullets also wounded Coon. Coon then staggered away and eventually wound up at the city hospital. Scott stayed at the house, and "after a while," "went up to Stewart, turned him over and said, 'You're not dead, for your eyes are open.'" He then went back into the house and threatened to kill "some more" if they didn't find his hat. When a woman asked Scott why he had shot Stewart he replied, "I've taken enough of his damned foolishness."

THE PERPETRATOR

Police called to the home arrested Scott on a charge of murder and Coon was arrested at the hospital. Police also arrested a total of eleven men and women and held them overnight in jail as witnesses for the inquest to be held the next day.

As the inquest began on Monday, Aug. 27, "hundreds of spectators tried to gain entrance and the halls and street outside were filled for several hours."

Sheriff Hendrix Rector assisted the coroner during the three-hour inquest in which several witnesses told of the fight and shooting at the Lewis boarding home. The jury deliberated for 30 minutes before ruling that Stewart "came to his death by gunshot wounds at the hands of Tom Scott and Walter Coon."

In keeping with the "swift justice" common in those days, the trial of Scott and Coon was held on Friday, Sept. 7, 1917—only 13 days after the death of Stewart—and lasted only 16 hours. The trial before Judge Mendel L. Smith began at 10:00AM in the "small court in the federal building" and the courtroom "could not hold the crowd and the halls outside were filled with spectators who craned their necks to try to hear parts of the evidence."

After one hour devoted to jury selection, testimony took the rest of the day (14 hours) and the case went to the jury around midnight. The jury deliberated for over two hours before returning its verdict at 2:25AM on Saturday, Sept. 7. Scott was convicted of murder with a recommendation for mercy and Coon was convicted of manslaughter.

The state presented fifteen witnesses while the defendants themselves were the only witnesses for the defense. Solicitor J.R. Martin, with the assistance of James H. Price and D.W. Smoak, prosecuted the case while Scott was represented by "Messrs. Lanford and Richardson" and Coon was represented by J.J. McSwain and R.A. Cooper. "A brilliant array of legal talent was engaged in the trial and an interesting battle of wits went on all day."

Dr. W.B. Belk was the first witness for the state. He conducted the autopsy on Stewart and testified that he found five bullet wounds from a .38 calibre pistol. Four of the wounds were in the front and side of the body and one was in the back. The death was caused by a bullet that "passed through the heart." There were two powder burns (indicating point blank range), one in the side and one in the back. The other witnesses testified as to what happened during the confrontation between Stewart, Scott and Coon.

There was also some testimony that there was "bad blood" between Stewart and Scott. Sheriff Hendrix Rector testified that Scott met him ten days earlier, congratulated him on being elected to office, and "complained of the deputy at Woodside being a damn rascal." One witness suggested that Scott may have been angry at Stewart because he thought Stewart was trying to steal "his woman" at the boarding house.

Walter Coon, a native of Newberry County, had come to Greenville only a few days before the murder to work at the Carolina mill. He conceded that he "knew the reputation of the house was bad" and testified that "he had a woman" at the boarding house. However, he maintained that he was only trying to breakup the fight between the deputy and Scott. He denied he had a knife when he grabbed Stewart.

Tom Scott, 26, was born in Pelham in Greenville County and conceded that he knew the reputation of the boarding house and that he had a woman there and "on some occasions had stayed all night." He conceded that he had been drinking and claimed that Stewart started the fight by attacking him first and that he tried to break it up by telling the deputy that they were friends and shouldn't be fighting. He also claimed that Stewart's gun fell from the holster to the ground and that he picked it up and fired when he thought he saw a knife.

The sentencing of Scott and Coon took place the day after the trial on Saturday, Sept. 8—only 14 days after the murder. Judge Mendel L. Smith sentenced Scott to "hard labor for life on the public works of the county" (not to state prison) for the conviction of murder with a recommendation of mercy. Coon was given a sentence of three years on the manslaughter conviction.

The criminal court file for Scott and Coon in the State Archives in Columbia indicates that Scott was paroled for "good behavior" on Dec. 23, 1924, after serving only 7 years. No record of time served for Coon on his three year sentence was found in the file. The S.C. State Dept. of Corrections does not have records of inmate releases until the 1950's and thus there is no record of how long Coon was incarcerated.

THE OFFICER

James Arthur Stewart, 33, was born on Jan. 9, 1884, in S.C. to William and Malissa Adeline Ward Stewart. The 1900 S.C. census listed William Stewart, 43, (born in N.C.) as living in the "Greenville Township" with his wife, Marlene, 38, (born in S.C.) and their children, James Arthur, 16 (in 1900), Henry, 14, Edna, 12, Jesse, 10, Julia, 8, Lou M., 6, Bertha, 4, and Ollie, 2.

James Stewart, 24, married Florence Matilda Canup, 23, around 1908 (according to the 1910 census). Florence was born in Hayesville, N.C. The couple lived in Woodside Village. James was a weaver and cotton mill worker at the mill and his wife was also employed there. A son, Lewis Ciscero, was born in 1909, a second son in 1911, and a third son in 1913. However, the latter two died in infancy.

Stewart's law enforcement career began when he was 32 and only nine months before his death. He was appointed a deputy sheriff at Woodside Mills in December of 1916. However, Sheriff Rector said that Stewart "was regarded as a faithful, efficient worker and popular officer of the peace maker type."

"Mill deputies" were quite common in Greenville County in the early years of the 20th century. An article in the *Greenville News* in 1927 indicated that when Sheriff Carlos A. Rector replaced the slain Sheriff Sam D. Willis, he appointed five deputies to his "regular staff" and five mill deputies.

James Stewart was survived by his wife, Florence, and one child, Lewis Ciscero, 8 (born on July 21, 1909); by his mother, Mrs. M.A. Stewart; by three brothers, Jesse, J.H. and Dacus; and by three sisters, Ollie Daisy Stewart, Mrs. Edna Bomar and Mrs. Bertha Eaggres. Stewart's daughter, Lila Mae, was born three months after his death.

Funeral arrangements were handled by "Ramseur-McAffee company, undertakers" with the viewing being held at the deputy's residence at No. 5 Fourth Street, Woodside Mills. The funeral service was held at the "Woodside church" and was "brief but impressive."

The burial was at the Woodside Cemetery where a service was conducted by the Junior Order United American Mechanics "of which order the deceased was a member. Six brother mill deputies acted as pallbearers." The "last resting place" was covered with "flowers, fragrant and beautiful...attesting the esteem in which Mr. Stewart was held."

In 1996 the grave of Deputy Stewart is still visible at Woodside Cemetery in Greenville though the cemetery is somewhat "hidden" a block west of Woodside Ave. on W. 9th St. (about a block from Parker Middle School). There are only about 40 graves in the cemetery and many have been vandalized. The Officer's grave is marked by a 3 ft. tall stone monument with the words:

J.A. Stewart
Jan. 9, 1884
Aug. 26, 1917
He was a kind and affectionate husband,
a fond father and a friend to all

Two of Deputy Stewart's children who died in infancy (before their father's death) are also buried in the Stewart family plot at Woodside Cemetery. Jesse Stewart, 10 months, died on July 19, 1912, and Earnest Stewart, 19 months, died on July 16, 1914. Their grave markers note that they were the children of J.A. and Florence Stewart.

James' widow, Florence Canup Stewart, 94, died on May 27, 1979, in Greenville and was buried at Graceland (since Woodside was no longer accepting new burials and was "unkept").

James Stewart's only son, Lewis Ciscero Stewart, 81, died in Greenville on March 17, 1991. He was a retired textile worker and security guard and was an Army veteran of World War II. Lewis Stewart was survived by a son, Jerry M. Stewart, 63, of Piedmont; a stepson, K.W. Moore, 62, of Tigerville; and a daughter, Mrs. Larry (Delores) Appleton, 51, of Powdersville; and by 16 grandchildren and 9 great grandchildren. He was buried at the Enoree Baptist Church Cemetery in Travelers Rest.

Lila Mae Stewart Coward, 78, of Greenville, was the only child of Deputy Stewart still living in 1996. She had two sons, Ted, 49, and David, 51. David had a stepson while Ted was not married.

The name of James Arthur Stewart was not on the list of slain deputies maintained by the Greenville County Sheriff's Office in 1995. However, when provided by Dr. Wilbanks with the documentation used to compile this narrative, Sheriff Johnny Mack Brown added his name to the list of deputies killed in the line of duty and submitted the documentation to the National Law Enforcement Memorial. The story of the discovery of the "forgotten hero," James Stewart was told in a *Greenville News* article about Dr. Wilbanks' research on June 12, 1996.

In 1996 the name of James Arthur Stewart will be added to the National Law Enforcement Memorial. The S.C. Criminal Justice Hall of Fame in Columbia will also add his name to the list of officers killed statewide and will display a plaque bearing his name in 1996.

SOURCES: *Greenville News*, Aug. 27,28,29, Sept. 2,8,9, 1917, June 19, 1927, May 28, 1979, March 18, 1991; Death certificate of James Arthur Stewart at S.C. State Archives; 1900 S.C. census, Greenville County, ED 29, Sheet 13, Line 21; grave markers at Woodside Cemetery; Greenville criminal court case #8192 at State Archives in Columbia; and interviews with Jerry M. Stewart and Delores Appleton.

#11 HENDRIX RECTOR
Sheriff of Greenville County
Shot & killed by citizen after argument on July 4, 1919.

THE EVENT

Sheriff Hendrix Rector, 37, was shot and killed at a downtown garage by a local citizen after a personal dispute on July 4, 1919. The killer was charged with murder but two trials ended in a mistrial.

Sheriff Rector and Jake Gosnell, 45, "had been friends since childhood" as both were raised in the "mountainous section" of Greenville County. Rector hired Gosnell as a deputy when he was elected in 1913 but the two later became bitter enemies.

At 12:05PM on Friday, July 4, Sheriff Rector stopped by Briscoe's garage "on West Court street, a short distance to the rear of the county courthouse," and saw his bitter enemy, Jake Gosnell, in the garage, along with W. Bunyan Keller, a former deputy and jailer. Keller and Gosnell were about to leave to leave for Greer to attend the afternoon 4th of July celebration when they went to the garage to get some grease for Gosnell's car. The mechanics had found something wrong with the car and were both under the car making the repair.

Sheriff Hendrix Rector, 37, was shot and killed at a garage after a personal dispute on July 4, 1919. He served eight years as a Greenville officer before being elected Sheriff in 1912. His name is inscribed on the National Law Enforcement Memorial in Washington, DC.

Rector said, "Good morning Jake." Gosnell did not respond to the greeting but Keller said, "Good morning, Sheriff." Rector replied, "Fine, Bunyan, how are you?" Rector, seeing that Gosnell had "snubbed him" responded angrily, "G— d— you, I don't care whether you speak or not. I thought I would show you I would speak to you." Keller later testified Gosnell got up from a kneeling position beside his car, which was being repaired, and said, "I don't want to speak to you or have anything to do with you" and started to kneel back down.

Rector walked a short distance past Gosnell and, "stopping and turning his body slightly toward him" said, "You dirty —— —, I don't care whether you speak or not." Keller would later testify that as Rector turned toward Gosnell he had a cigarette or cigar in his left hand and had his right hand "in his belt or hitched in his suspenders."

At this point Gosnell drew his .32 caliber pistol and fired four shots "in rapid succession" at Rector as the two stood eight feet apart. Rector dropped to the floor, with his pistol still in his pocket. He had been shot in the head, side, and shoulder. Rector was rushed by ambulance to the City Hospital but was dead on arrival.

Gosnell then said to his wife, "Get in the car Ann," apparently preparing to leave the garage. Keller told Gosnell that he could not leave but he repeated the command to his wife and started to get into his car. At this point Keller "restrained him and took charge of him" and took him to the county jail. After the shooting, Mrs. Gosnell said to her husband, "Lord, have mercy! Jake, you oughtn't to have done that."

Gosnell was held in the local jail for only a short period before being "secretly removed" to the jail in Spartanburg to avoid any effort that might be made to lynch him for the murder of the popular sheriff. Officials were concerned as the news of the killing of the sheriff "spread like wildfire" over the entire area and the "holiday crowd which thronged the city was joined by hundreds who came from mountain, hillside and plain to gather around the scene of the shooting" and the undertaking establishment where the body was taken from the hospital. There was "some talk of mob violence, but no apparent effort to put it into execution."

THE PERPETRATOR

Jake Gosnell, 47 (born on Feb. 8, 1872), and Hendrix Rector "had been friends since childhood" having both been raised in the mountainous section of Greenville County. When Rector was elected sheriff in 1913 he hired Gosnell as a deputy "but friendship soon gave way to rivalry and hatred." After leaving his post as a deputy sheriff Gosnell operated a farm several miles from Greenville "near Camp Sevier."

At the time of the shooting Gosnell had been for a year a deputy collector of internal revenue for the United States government. His work had been "confined to curbing the manufacture of illicit whiskey" in the counties of Greenville and Pickens and "had been successful in destroying a number of illicit distilleries and arresting not a few persons for operating them." He was one of several deputies who made "whiskey raids" in the Upstate.

Gosnell, 47, was married and had several children and "a large family connection in the county." His cousin, Reuben Gosnell, was a former "chief of the rural police" and was then a magistrate's constable in Greenville.

Dr. W.C. Black performed an autopsy on Rector the day of the shooting but was requested to perform a second autopsy on Saturday night to determine the "exact angle" at which the bullets entered the body of Rector. The request was made by Acting Chief J.H. Allison with a detailed statement of the result of the second autopsy to be given to Allison and to attorneys for both the prosecution and defense early in the week.

However, before the second autopsy report was available, an inquest was held the next day (on Saturday, July 5) at the county courthouse. The inquest was held by Magistrate J.L. Ballenger since Coroner J. H. Allison, who normally was in charge of inquests, had, under the law, assumed the post of sheriff upon the death of Rector. Solicitor J. Robert Martin presented the case for the state assisted by James H. Price, P.A. Bonham, and David W. Smoak. Alvin H. Dean and C.G. Wyche were present to "look after Gosnell's interests." The courtroom "was packed to the doors, with standing room not available for a part of the crowd that tried to gain entrance."

The only witness called at the inquest was W. Bunyan Keller, the friend of

Gosnell's who was with him at the garage at the time of the shooting but who had to arrest him after the shooting. Keller had been "walking toward Rector and Gosnell when the shooting took place" and was between Rector and Gosnell. Keller testified as indicated in the above narrative of the shooting. (The two mechanics heard none of the conversation between Rector and Gosnell and did not see the shooting.)

Upon being cross-examined by the defense, Keller conceded that he saw a pistol in Rector's hip pocket as he fell. "He would not say positively just where Rector's right hand was when the shooting by Gosnell began." After hearing the evidence of Mr. Keller, the "jury of inquest" ruled that Rector "came to his death by gunshot wounds at the hands of Jake Gosnell" and recommended that he be tried for murder.

The trial of Gosnell was first scheduled for late August, 1919, but was delayed several times by motions by the defense. The first trial ended in a mistrial and a second trial was held in Pickens County on a change of venue in 1921. A mistrial again was declared.

In Feb. of 1924, almost five years after the murder of Sheriff Hendrix Rector, Jake Gosnell, returned to Pickens County from his duties in New York as a "federal prohibition enforcement officer," to face a potential third trial. The *Greenville News* reported that Gosnell "had been attached to prohibition forces in New York, on the Canadian border and elsewhere over the country, becoming one of the most widely known members of the dry unit" and that he had served as the "personal guard of Izzy Einstein, the celebrated sleuth of the prohibition unit."

Many expected the third trial to be even more sensational that the first two trials that resulted in mistrials.

A brilliant and imposing array of legal talent is lined up again in the case. Solicitor Smoak, who has earned the reputation of a relentless and brilliant prosecutor is assisted by the well known firm of Bonham, Price and Poag, of Greenville. A group of attorneys, among which are some of the best known in the Piedmont section will appear for the defense. There are Dean, Cothran and Wyche of Greenville, Carey and Carey of Pickens and others. (*Greenville News, 2/18/1924*)

However, the third trial was postponed due to pre-trial publicity that the judge felt prejudiced the case. The *Pickens Sentinel* in its weekly publication of Feb. 14 carried an editorial by F.V. Clayton that Judge E.C. Dennis believed was calculated to influence potential jurors. Editor Clayton had forecast the acquittal of Jake Gosnell and called the trial a waste of the taxpayers' money. On Feb. 25, 1924, Judge Dennis convicted Clayton of contempt of court for publishing the editorial and fined him $10.

The temporary postponement of the trial due to the contempt proceeding apparently led to a reconsideration by the state as there is no record that a third trial was ever held. Apparently the state decided against a third trial and dropped the charges against Gosnell.

Jake Gosnell died at the age of 74 on Dec. 10, 1946, in Pickens County. No obituary appeared in the *Greenville News* at his death. A cemetery index for Pickens County indicated that he was buried beside the Pickens View Wesleyan Church.

THE OFFICER

Hendrix Rector, 37, was born in Glassy Mountain township in Greenville County, S.C., on May 30, 1882, to John W. and Rebecca Barton Rector. His father, who was also born in S.C., served in the Confederacy during the Civil War, and was a "well-known farmer" in the Glassy Mountain "section." His mother was the daughter of Jefferson and Sallie Turner Barton and was born near Cleveland's Mill.

At the age of 14, Hendrix was "left fatherless and worked for the education he acquired at the North Greenville Academy." He came to Greenville as a young man of 26 and was hired in 1904 as a police officer by the Greenville Police Dept.

Officer Rector quickly became well known through two incidents that occurred within ten days in 1911. First, on Feb. 17, 1911, he attempted to arrest a young woman for "scandalous conduct" when he was attacked by two of her friends ("ruffians") and "severely beaten on the head and shoulders with heavy bludgeons." The woman and her friends then barricaded themselves in their home defying a "cordon of police" before surrendering. A headline in the *Greenville News* said that the "Young Call Officer Fought Desperately with Gang of Toughs" while the article praised him for his bravery.

Ten days later (Feb. 27, 1911), Rector again made headlines when he helped solve the murder of Greenville Officer Oliver Gunnels by "rescuing" the body of a man lynched in GA from a medical college (where it had been sold), allowing the corpse to be returned to Greenville so that it could be identified as the killer of Officer Gunnels.

Sheriff Johnny Mack Brown, in his 1984 history of the Greenville County Sheriff's Office, noted that Hendrix Rector, was tried and acquitted of murder charges early in his career.

The incident had taken place many years earlier when Rector, then a West Greenville City Policeman shot to death a black man at the West Greenville Train Depot. Rector alleged that he surprised the man while he was attempting to break into the train depot. Rector said that the man turned and attacked him with a knife before he shot him. Rector's only injury was a tear in his police jacket. Rector was acquitted by the jury during the murder trial. ("The Greenville County Sheriff's Office: Origins and History" by Johnny Mack Brown, 1984, p. 37)

The recently "famous" Hendrix Rector, 30, ran for Sheriff of Greenville County in 1912 and was elected after "one of the most bitterly contested elections ever held in Greenville county." He was re-elected in 1916 in the first primary over five opponents for a second four-year term and had already announced for a third term at the time of his death.

Sheriff Rector was particularly active in destroying illicit distilleries and arresting the operators. Interestingly, this was the same type of work for which his enemy, Jake Gosnell, was known. He was personally very popular, "especially with the people who live in the mountainous section of the county and in the cotton mill villages."

The *Greenville News* described Sheriff Rector as "probably the most active man in politics in Greenville county not only on his own behalf, but for others whose cause he espoused." He was regarded as the leader of what came to be known as the "Reform Party" and often spoke on behalf of other "candidates who have run for office as members of that faction."

The *Greenville News* editorialized about the tragic death of Hendrix Rector on July 6 and said that he had a "talent for making and holding friends" but also had a "talent for making enemies and that unfortunate talent, from all accounts, was instrumental in bringing on his untimely end." The newspaper also said that Rector "had risen by pluck and merit from humble origins and surroundings to the highest office in the gift of the people of his county" and was an "active, fearless, aggressive officer."

The Sheriff was also known for the "warmth and largeness of his heart to the many who found their way into it." Evidence of this generosity is seen in that Rector, during the time he was sheriff, "sent several of his nephews and nieces through school and took them to live with him in his home."

Hendrix Rector married Evie Fleming, the daughter of Bailus and Mary Pittman Fleming. Evie "spent her early life in upper Greenville County where she was born and reared." The couple had no children, "except an adopted son, Linwood." The family lived at a home about a mile and a half from the city on the Laurens Rd.

Hendrix Rector was survived by his wife, Evie, 34, and adopted son, Linwood; by four brothers, Rome Rector, a farmer living near the city; Jeff M. Rector, with the U.S. Army in Camp Merritt, N.J.; James Henry Rector, a well-known farmer of the upper part of the county; and Carlos A. Rector, deputy collector of internal revenue in Columbia. He was also survived by one sister, Birdie Rector, and his "aged" mother. Rector also had a "number of more distant relatives" who lived in the northern part of the county.

Funeral services for Hendrix Rector were held on Sunday, July 6, at Graceland Cemetery. The service at graveside was conducted by Rev. S.T. Matthews, pastor of the Central Baptist Church (where Rector was a member). A quartet sang hymns and the Cedar Camp Woodmen of the World "with their usual ceremonies lowered the casket into the grave."

> As the casket was being lowered, a dove was released and flew away into the distance, symbolic of the flight of the soul. After the funeral, many passed by the grave to look upon the unopened casket and the many wreaths. (*Greenville News,* 7/6/1919)

Plans were to open the casket after the service so that the crowd could view the body but the fainting of Mrs. Rector during the prayer led those in charge to keep the casket closed.

Pallbearers at the burial service were the sheriffs of six surrounding counties (Anderson, Pickens, Spartanburg, Newberry, Laurens, and Florence). All city and county officials attended along with hundreds of citizens who crowded around the canopy where the immediate family was seated. The service was also attended in mass by local members of several organizations to which Hendrix Rector belonged (e.g., Woodman of the World, Knights of Pythias, Elks, and the Tallulah Tribe No. 33, Improved Order of Red Men).

In 1996 the grave of Hendrix Rector is easily found at Graceland Cemetery as it "sticks out" into the main roadway running north from the cemetery office. The 6 ft. tall stone monument reads "RECTOR" and includes the words:

HENDRIX RECTOR
May 30, 1882
July 4, 1919
Woodman of the World
I Have a Smile My Friend
To Greet, Hearty and
Pleasant for All I Meet
Hidden from None
His Heroic Deeds Will
Not be Forgotten

Others buried in the family plot include his mother, Rebecca B. Rector (May 14, 1852-Feb. 9, 1939); his wife, Evie V. Rector (Feb. 8, 1886-Aug. 8, 1947) and three of his siblings, Virgie Rector (1888-1942), Jefferson McCray Rector (1880-1961) and (Sheriff) Carlos Rector (Sept. 17, 1884-Sept. 30, 1966). Evie remarried (to J.M. Rector) and died in Greenville in 1947 at the age of 61. She had no children and was survived by one sister (Tessie Barton) and three brothers (W.D., H.F., and Carl Fleming).

Sam D. Willis was appointed by the Governor to fill the term of Sheriff Rector but, in 1920, Carlos A. Rector, the brother of Hendrix Rector, was elected sheriff. Carlos Rector was defeated in the next election by Sam Willis but was appointed by the Governor to succeed Willis after his murder in 1928. He was defeated for re-election by former Deputy Cliff Bramlett who promised to find the killer of Sheriff Willis.

Sheriff Bramlett did find the killers—who turned out to be Carlos Rector and a deputy. Rector was sentenced to life in prison but was pardoned by Governor Olin D. Johnston in 1939. Rector ran for sheriff again in 1940 but was over-whelmingly defeated. He died in Greenville at the age of 82 on Sept. 30, 1966.

Hendrix Rector had no direct descendants. However, several nephews (the children of Hendrix's brother, James Henry Rector) lived in the Greenville area in 1996 including Carlos Rector, 74, Redo Rector, 78, Proctor Rector, 71, and Alvin Rector, 84.

The name of Hendrix Rector is inscribed (East Wall, Panel 34, Line 13) on the National Law Enforcement Memorial in Washington, D.C. His name is displayed on a plaque at the S.C. Criminal Justice Hall of Fame in Columbia.

SOURCES: *Greenville News,* Feb. 18,21,27, 1911, July 5,6,7,8, Sept. 3, 1919, Feb. 13,18,19,26, 1924, Feb. 13, 1939, Aug. 9, 1947, Oct. 11, 1966; Death certificate of Hendrix Rector at S.C. State Archives; *Greenville: The History of the City and County in the South Carolina Piedmont* by Archie Vernon Huff, Jr., 1995, p. 321; "The Greenville County Sheriff's Office: Origins and History," by Johnny Mack Brown (unpublished manuscript in Greenville Library); and interview with Carlos Rector.

#12 JOSEPH L. KITCHENS
#13 ALFORD M. BLAIR
Greenville Police Dept.
Shot & killed while raiding a dice game on Oct. 5, 1919.

THE EVENT

Joseph L. Kitchens and Alford M. Blair, plainclothes detectives of the Greenville Police Dept., were shot and killed on Oct. 5, 1919, when they raided a dice game in Bucknertown, a negro section of northwestern Greenville. The killer escaped a massive manhunt and, six months later, killed a police officer in Lynchburg, VA. He was executed in VA in 1921 for the latter murder.

Det. Kitchens, 43, was a 16-year veteran of the Greenville Police Dept. and the state constabulary and Det. Blair, 43, was a 11-year veteran of the Greenville Police Dept. The Greenville Police Dept. had only 29 officers in 1919 and two replacements were "elected" by the Board of Police Commissioners several days later to replace the slain officers.

Around 1:00AM on Sunday, Oct. 5, 1919, Detectives J.L. Kitchens, A.M. Blair and Sgt. Cooley received a tip that several negroes were gambling illegally in a house in Bucknertown (a negro section of Greenville). The house was half a block off West Park Ave. and one block from Townes Street. The three officers decided to raid the game that involved (by different accounts) from 8 to 10 men. One account suggested that there may have been two different games in two different rooms of the house.

Det. Alford M. Blair, 43, a 16-year veteran of the Greenville, South Carolina, Police Department, was shot and killed on Oct. 5, 1919, when police raided a dice game in a black section of the city. Blair's name is inscribed on the National Law Enforcement Memorial in Washington, DC.

The three officers decided that Blair would go to the front of the house and Kitchens to the back while Cooley was stationed at the side windows to stop any escape via the windows. As Cooley peeked through the drawn blinds of a window he saw the card game in progress and then heard a "crash at the front door" as Blair attempted a forced entry. Almost immediately shots were fired from inside the house toward the front door and the lights were extinguished.

Almost instantaneously, "a negro man," Ezelle Hawkins, leaped through the window where Sgt. Cooley was stationed and was captured. The man told Cooley that the man inside doing the shooting was Joe Turner. Cooley then heard a man calling for help saying that he was shot and dying. Cooley told Hawkins to call the police station for help and then rushed to the rear of the house and found

Officer Kitchens lying face down on the floor of the room where the gambling had been in progress.

Seeing with his flashlight that Kitchens was shot in the stomach, he took the wounded officer outside to the rear of the house to await an ambulance. Sgt. Cooley heard the dying Kitchens say that he hated to die and leave his wife and children and said that a prayer was on the dying man's lips as he was being carried to the City hospital in a "public service automobile."

A negro woman informed Sgt. Cooley that another officer (Det. Blair) was lying dead on the street near the front of the house. It appeared that Joe Turner, the "shooter," had exited the house through the front door and was chased by Det. Blair who may have tried to shoot the escaping man but his gun "locked" ("failed to revolve") and would not fire. Det. Blair had told Sgt. Cooley several days before his murder that the "barrel of his revolver would not work and that he intended having it repaired."

During the chase, Turner turned and fired a shot at Blair, hitting the officer in the chest. The shot penetrated Blair's heart and he died "instantly."

Det. Kitchens was taken to the hospital but died shortly after arrival. His body and that of Det. Blair were taken to the "Ramseur-McAfee undertaking establishment" where autopsies were performed by Dr. W.C. Black. Dr. Black found that Kitchens received two fatal bullet wounds, either of which would have caused his death. One bullet entered the back, two inches to the right of the backbone and passed through the body. The other bullet penetrated the left shoulder, entered the neck, and lodged somewhere near the collarbone. Blair died from one bullet wound which entered the left breast and penetrated the heart.

An inquest was held on Sunday afternoon and the coroner's jury, after testimony from several witnesses, including Dr. Black, ruled that Joe Turner was responsible for both deaths. However, during the search it was thought that two or more men may have been involved in the shooting of the two detectives and numerous negroes were stopped and questioned. Credibility for the "two-man killer" theory was gained when Red Frazier, a negro man in Anderson, was shot and killed on Oct. 11 by two white men after boasting that he had been a partner of Joe Turner's in the Greenville murders. The multiple killer theory was also strengthened when police questioned Tom Walker, a negro man who was wounded in the shootout. Walker said that several men in the house had guns and may have fired at the officers.

Evidence unearthed by officers in a visit to the house yesterday, as to the location of the bullet holes in the walls and the arrangement of the furniture used by the gamblers strengthened the theory advanced that one man did not shoot both Kitchens and Blair. (*Greenville News,* 10/8/1919)

Greenville Police Chief J.D. Noe was called at home and told of the shooting and immediately went to the police station to organize the manhunt. Though it was after midnight, the news of the shooting spread like wildfire and six hours later (by 7:00AM) more than 2,000 men had joined the search team. The search force swelled to 3,000 men by Sunday afternoon as "the entire countryside was alive with searchers." The search team of armed citizens was led by Greenville police and sheriff's deputies with rifles and shotguns. The search team was partly inspired by a reward of $650 for the capture of Joe Turner (a beginning police officer made only $100 a month in 1919).

The authorities also made "lynching precautions" since the two slain officers were very popular and the posse might decide to lynch Turner if he were captured. The newspaper described the posse as "orderly" but the mood of the posse might have changed if Turner had been caught.

Bloodhounds were brought in to track the fugitive. The search team first concentrated on the "swamps and woodlands" between Greer and Simpsonville as it was fairly well established that Turner boarded a train in Greenville shortly after 7:00AM on Sunday and got off at Suber, a small station not far from Greer.

THE PERPETRATOR

Joe Turner, 26, was described as 6 ft. tall and 150 lbs. and had a "reputation of being a disreputable character, inclined to rowdiness at all times." It was also reported in the local newspaper that most Greenville negroes avoided Turner because of his bad reputation and that he had been involved in "other trouble" earlier in Greenville. He had apparently come to Greenville from Anderson a few months before the murder. He had been fined $50 in Anderson for carrying a concealed weapon and had been in jail there in July on a peace warrant for threatening remarks he had made "about some white people at the Brogan mills."

Several supposed sightings of Joe Turner were made and the Greenville News reported that he had been surrounded and that capture was imminent. However, the sightings proved to be only rumors or the captured fugitive turned out to be someone other than Joe Turner. For several days the *Greenville News* ran stories of the police manhunt and the false sightings. On Friday, March 11, the newspaper reported that Turner wounded two men in a railway yard in Charlotte, N.C. but escaped again.

Six months later, on March 25, 1920, Joe Turner shot and killed a Lynchburg, VA, police officer, Det. Arthur Lee Mann, and escaped again. The incident that led to the murder of Det. Mann began innocently as a crowd stopped on Main St. to listen to a man "pick" his guitar. The black guitar player, known as "Jubilee" because of his music, singing and dancing was John Williams (alias Joe Turner). Nearby, Det. Mann and Officer E.C. Wheeler were told that the "entertainer" was carrying a pistol.

Mann and Wheeler stopped Williams and started to search him when the suspect suddenly started to run. However, the two officers caught Williams and the three "scuffled down" to the street. Officer Honig followed behind and saw the suspect locked in a struggle with the other two officers and asked Det. Mann if he should shoot, fearing the suspect was armed. Mann and Wheeler told him not to shoot. During the struggle, Williams was able to free his left arm, pull his .38 caliber Colt revolver and fire several times, "first at Mann and then at Wheeler."

It was dark and the flash from the suspect's gun momentarily blinded Honig. In a few seconds Honig regained his sight. Both detectives were on the ground, neither had a chance to fire before they fell. Honig fired four shots at the fleeing suspect. Mann had been shot in the head, the bullet had entered his head just above the left ear and had come out through the top of his head. (Pelletier, 1995)

Officer Wheeler was not seriously wounded but Det. Mann died at 8:00AM the following morning. Mann, 38, a 9-year veteran, became the first police officer killed in the line of duty in the history of Lynchburg. He was survived by his wife Willie Henrietta Lee Mann and two sons, Bernard, 14, and Arthur L., Jr., 11.

Officer Honig chased the suspect down the street where Williams engaged in another shootout with Officer Harry Smith and then escaped. Bloodhounds were brought in to track Williams but the dogs lost the scent at the railroad track because of a rain storm. A month later, police in Toledo, Ohio, arrested Williams who was returned to Lynchburg for trial.

The *Greenville News* reported on March 6, 1921, that Greenville authorities were convinced that John H. Williams was the same man known as Joe Turner who killed Detectives Kitchen and Blair in Greenville on Oct. 5, 1919. Special Agent S.L. Peck of the Southern Railway obtained a statement from Williams before his trial that he, in fact, was the Joe Turner who killed the two officers in Greenville.

Under his real name of John Williams, "Joe Turner" was convicted of murder, sentenced to death and electrocuted in VA on March 5, 1921. Special Agent Peck, Greenville Police Chief J.D. Noe, and Greenville County Sheriff Carlos A. Rector traveled to Lynchburg before the scheduled execution to interview Williams but were denied an interview by VA authorities. They reported that Williams spent the afternoon of his execution day in "fervent prayer" and then witnessed his execution. "The Greenville police kept as a memento a guitar that had once belonged to a man called 'Jubilee', also known as 'North Carolina Slim'."

THE OFFICERS

Joseph L. Kitchens, 43, was born on April 6, 1876, in Transylvania County, N.C., to J.C. and Mattie Ballard Kitchens. Both his parents were also born in N.C. He moved to Greenville in 1901, joined the Greenville Police Dept. in 1903 and was a 16-year veteran of the Dept. although part of that time he was a member of the state constabulary. "He had been back on the police force for the past two years."

In an interesting note, Officer Kitchens was re-elected to the Police Dept. on Feb. 24, 1911, to fill the vacated position held by officer Oliver S. Gunnels, killed in the line of duty. The newspaper reported that he was one of ten candidates for the position and was considered the best man for the job. Kitchens also served as a special agent with the Southern Railway "before resigning his position to accept a position on the state constabulary force in Columbia." He lost the state position when he and all other members of the state force were "de-established" by a proclamation of the Governor.

The *Greenville News* reported that Det. Kitchens had "been very active against negro gamblers, and was disliked by practically all of that class" and that "only last spring he...was shot by a negro or negroes near Richland Creek," where he had gone to "quell a disorder." His wounds, though painful, were not serious.

The funeral service for Det. Kitchens were held on Monday, Oct. 6, at the family residence on Webster St. The services were conducted by the Rev. J.R. George with six members of the Greenville Police Dept. serving as pallbearers. A burial service at Springwood Cemetery in Greenville was conducted by

Tallujah Tribe No 33, Red Men, "of which the deceased was a member." The newspaper reported that Kitchens was "a thoroughly capable and efficient officer" and "had warm personal friends throughout this section of the state."

Det. Kitchens was survived by a wife, Nora Owens Kitchens, 36, a son, Eugene Woodrow, 10 (born on Oct. 8, 1909), and a daughter, Ella Mae "Jackie" Kitchens, 14 (born on Sept. 16, 1905).

Woodrow Eugene Kitchens, 50, died on Sept. 13, 1960, and was buried near his father at Springwood Cemetery. He was employed at Monaghan Mill and lived in Greenville all of his life except for his tour of duty in France during World War II. He was survived by his mother, Nora Kitchens of Greenville, his sister, Mrs. Floyd M. (Jackie) Johnson of Atlanta, and his widow, Margarette Gentry Kitchens, 37. (Margarette Kitchens Beck, 73, still lived in Greenville in 1996.)

Officer Kitchens' widow, Nora Kitchens, 78, died in Greenville on May 27, 1961, and was buried beside her husband. She was survived by her daughter, Mrs. Floyd M. (Jackie) Johnson of Atlanta and two grandsons and a granddaughter. Ella Mae "Jackie" Johnson died in Atlanta on June 24, 1992, at the age of 85. She was survived by three children: Mrs. Avery (Constance) Bryant, 69, of Greenville; Harold Whiteside, 67, of CAL, and Charles Hall, 65, of Dothan, AL.

Constance ("Connie") Bryant, the granddaughter of Officer Kitchens, was a police officer for the City of Greenville from 1962-1983. In 1996, Connie's four children were Milton Earl Garrett, 56, of Wright City, MO; James Floyd Garrett, 53, of Greenville; Gary Ray Garrett, 47, of Sumter, S.C.; and Charles Harold Garrett, 45, of Simpsonville. She had 12 grandchildren and 13 great, grandchildren.

The graves of Joseph L. Kitchens, his wife, Nora, and his son, Woodrow Eugene are still visible in section G of Springwood Cemetery in downtown Greenville. The family plot is marked by a 5 ft. tall stone monument with the name, "Kitchens," while the officer's grave is marked by a flat stone marker reading:

JOSEPH L. KITCHENS
APRIL 6, 1876
OCT. 5, 1919

The name of Joseph L. Kitchens (misspelled as J. H. Kitchen) is inscribed (East Wall, Panel 16, Line 2) on the National Law Enforcement Memorial in Washington, D.C., and a plaque bearing his name is displayed at the S.C. Criminal Justice Hall of Fame in Columbia, S.C. The misspelling of Kitchens' name was a mistake in all of the coverage by the *Greenville News* but the correct spelling is found on his death certificate and on his grave marker.

Alford M. Blair, 42, was born on Aug. 21, 1878, in Abbeville County, GA, to W.E. and Judie Dodd Blair. His first wife, Lillie McCoy, died in childbirth and he then married Laura Justus with whom he had six children. Blair had been a member of the Greenville Police Dept. for eleven years and, at the time of his death, had already been accepted for transfer to the Greenville Water Works.

The funeral service for Det. Blair was held on Tuesday, Oct. 7, 1919, at the Emmanuel Baptist Church in Mill's Mill by its pastor, the Rev. Mr. Jolly. Six members of the Greenville Police Dept. served as pallbearers. Burial followed in Graceland Cemetery where graveside services were conducted by the Woodmen of the World ("of which organization the deceased was a member").

Alford M. Blair was survived by his wife, Laura Justus Blair, 39; six children, Floride, 14, Lucile, 13, Gordon, 12, Pauline, 10, Myrdice, 5, and Alvin, 16 months; his father, W.E. Blair, 64, of Greenville; his three brothers, Charles of Mills Mill, Henry, of Greer, and George of GA; and two sisters, Miss Illa Blair of Greenville and Mrs. Every Smith of GA.

The widow received her slain husband's salary for a year. However, Alvin remembered that times were very hard after his father's death. She sent her son Gordon to the Connie Mack Orphanage in Greenwood and planned to also send Myrdice and Alvin there but Gordon ran away from the orphanage. Floride and Lucile and Gordon then went to work in the mills (there were no child labor laws then) to help support the family.

In 1996 the grave of Det. Blair is easily found at the Graceland Cemetery in Greenville only about 40 yards from the graves of Sheriff Hendrix Rector (1919) and Greenville Chief James Holcombe (1915). Marking the officer's grave is a 4 ft. tall white monument with the words:

ALFORD M. BLAIR

Aug. 21, 1878

Oct. 5, 1919

HE WAS A KIND AND AFFECTIONATE HUSBAND,

A FOND FATHER, AND A FRIEND TO ALL

Other family members buried in the Blair plot include his widow, Laura Justus Blair, (1971); a daughter, Pauline (April 1, 1909 - Dec. 27, 1922); and a daughter, Lucille B. Briggs (Sept. 22, 1906 - Oct. 7, 1964). Alford Blair's wife, Laura Justus Blair, 91, died on June 13, 1971, and was buried beside her husband. Her obituary in the *Greenville News* indicated that she lived at 306 McGarity St. in the Mills Mill community and had lived in Greenville for 75 years (arriving in 1896).

The survivors in 1971 of Laura (and Alford M.) Blair were two daughters, Mrs. Paul V. (Myrdice) Campbell and Mrs. John M. (Floride) Grindstaff of Greenville, two sons, Alvin M. and James Gordon Blair of Greenville, and 15 grandchildren and 25 great grandchildren.

In 1996 two of Officer Blair's six children were still living. Myrdice Blair Campbell, 82, lived in Taylors and Alvin M. Blair, 78, lived in Greenville. Fifteen grandchildren continue to live in and around Greenville.

The name of A.M. Blair is inscribed (West Wall, Panel 23, Line 1) on the National Law Enforcement Memorial in Washington, D.C. and a plaque bearing his name is displayed at the S.C. Criminal Justice Hall of Fame in Columbia, S.C.

SOURCES: *Greenville News*, Oct. 5,6,7,8,11,12,23, 1919, March 6, 1921, Sept. 15, 1960, June 14, 1971; *Lynchburg News*, March 27, 1920; Appendix listing all U.S. executions in *Legal Homicide: Death as Punishment in America, 1864-1982* by Wm. J. Bowers, 1984; "The History of Lynchburg's Fallen Police Officers" by Heather E. Pelletier (unpublished manuscript in Lynchburg City Library, 1995); Death certificates of A.M. Blair and J.L. Kitchens in the S.C. Archives; Greenville County cemetery index and grave markers at Springwood and Graceland cemeteries; 1910 Census of Greenville County; and interviews with Myrdice Blair Campbell, Alvin Blair, Eleanor Roper, Constance Bryant and Marguerite Beck

#14 GEORGE STAPLES BURROUGHS
Greenville Police Dept.
Shot attempting an arrest on May 6, 1921 (died on May 7).

THE EVENT

George S. Burroughs, 48, a 12-year veteran of the Greenville Police Dept. was fatally shot on May 6, 1921, when he tried to arrest a man creating a disturbance at his girlfriend's house. The killer was captured in 23 hours and was tried, convicted and sentenced to death within 72 hours of the murder (supposedly a record time for the county and state). However, the conviction was overturned and he was sentenced to life after a second trial.

The fatal incident began at 9:00PM on Friday, May 6, when William Thompson, a 30-year old negro man, began cursing loudly and beating on the door of his girlfriend's rooming house demanding to see her. He may have also fired a couple of shots as Mrs. Burroughs heard two shots from her home at 410 Westfield which was only a couple of blocks away from the "murder house" on Westfield Street near the railroad tracks.

Thompson later told police that he had gone to the home to "tend to that man" referring to a "suitor" of his girlfriend. He claimed that he carried a gun to the house because his girlfriend told him that another man had threatened him and he "needed protection." Newspaper accounts stated that Thompson may have been "on dope" because a package of morphine was found at the crime scene.

Officer Burroughs had gone off duty at 4:00PM and was at a store near his home when his 13-year old niece, Viola Holcombe, came to tell him that Mrs. Burroughs had heard two shots coming from a nearby home on Martin St. (at the rear of a store by the railroad tracks on Westfield St.) and that he should investigate. Burroughs went immediately to the house and found a large (6 ft, 200 lb.) negro man whom he did not know on the porch of the house banging on the door and "creating a disturbance."

Officer Burroughs was not wearing his police uniform but did have on his police badge as he walked up to the man, grabbed him, and said, "I've got you, come with me." Thompson asked what he had done to justify an arrest but the officer did not respond. Thompson would later claim that he would have gone with the officer but didn't want to be caught with the pistol in his pocket and thus decided to escape from the officer.

Thompson and Officer Burroughs struggled for a moment and then fell to the floor. Thompson (later) said that he then pulled his pistol from his pocket and hit the officer on the head "a time or two" and that the pistol accidently discharged. Other witnesses would later testify that Thompson first hit the officer with his fists, then with a board on the head, and then with a flower pot before (intentionally) firing his pistol once at the officer. The bullet entered the Officer's abdomen and penetrated the liver and large intestines before emerging above the right hip. Burroughs would later tell police that he tried to pull his weapon during the struggle but that it "hung in his pocket."

After disabling the officer, Thompson jumped from the porch and fled down the railroad tracks. Neighbors alerted the police and attended to the wounded officer until the first officers arrived (within three minutes). Burroughs was rushed by ambulance to the city hospital where doctors examined him and expressed confidence that, though his wound was painful, his condition was "not serious" and that he would recover from his wounds. However, seven hours later, at 4:00AM, his condition worsened and he suddenly died. A later autopsy revealed he died of "shock" brought on by the blow to the head and the gunshot wound.

THE PERPETRATOR

The Greenville police and Sheriff's deputies began a search for William Thompson, 30, only minutes after arriving on the scene. Chief Noe and Sheriff Rector "spread the dragnet over the entire city" but focused on the area where Thompson lived and on other negro sections of the county. Thompson was captured within 23 hours of his escape (at 8:00 PM on Saturday, May 7) but only after a chase from 6:00 PM until 8:00 PM in which Thompson admitted to firing over 40 shots at the pursuing posse, wounding one citizen. Thompson, fearing that he had killed the officer realized that he "had nothing to lose" (i.e., he would face the death penalty) and thus was desperate to escape.

The newspaper reported that Thompson engaged in a "pitched battle" with the pursuing posse at three points and that the posse "exposed themselves to danger time after time" as they ran into the dark pursuing the fugitive who was firing at them. The ranks of the posse would likely have "been doubled or tripled" if the murder had not occurred in the early morning hours and if word had reached town that the fugitive had been spotted and the "final chase" begun.

The chase ended after Sheriff Carlos Rector shot Thompson in the leg. Though the fugitive continued to run for two more miles he was soon caught and arrested by two city policemen and a citizen "near Mountain Creek church on the Mountain Creek road, six miles or more from the city." Thompson was immediately taken to the city jail but was "spirited away" after a short time to another city for "safekeeping" as the authorities obviously feared that a mob might try to lynch the negro for the killing of a white police officer.

On Saturday, May 7, an inquest was held into the death of Officer Burroughs under the direction of Coroner Vaughan. The coroner's jury ruled, after hearing testimony from the attending physician and three "negroes" who witnessed the shooting, that Burroughs was killed by Thompson.

Thompson was returned to Greenville by Monday, May 9, when the Grand Jury convened and returned an indictment of murder against him at 11:00AM. The trial—"said to be the speediest ever held in Greenville county and it is thought possible it is a record for the state"—began at 3:00PM the same day. Judge T.J. Mauldin appointed J. Frank Epps of the local bar to defend Thompson but gave him no time to prepare his case as the voir dire of jurors began almost immediately.

The state presented its case by Solicitor David W. Smoak in three hours (from 3:00PM to 6:00PM) and called witnesses to prove that Thompson was the man who shot Burroughs and that the gun found at his capture was the gun that killed the officer. Dr. Curran B. Earle, the first witness for the state testified as to the nature of the officer's wounds and stated that he died of shock caused by the gunshot wound and blows to the head. Mrs. Burroughs took the stand briefly "clad in deep mourning...supported to and from the witness chair by a lady friend, who remained at her side during the time (she) testified." She told how she heard the two shots and sent her niece to get her husband to investigate.

The defense put on its case in a little over an hour as Thompson took the stand in his own defense and testified that he did shoot Burroughs but that the gun discharged accidently. He denied that he had been "on dope" but did admit to shooting over 40 times at the pursuing posse. Thompson also told the court that he was raised in Elbert County, GA, but had lived in Greenville since 1917. He had been living with his sister at 517 Oscar St. The defense also put on two witnesses who knew the defendant from his work as a truck driver for the Minter Homes Co. in Greenville. They both testified that Thompson was honest and efficient and had a good reputation.

The judge adjourned the case until 8:00PM when the trial resumed with an eight-minute closing argument by solicitor Smoak and a 16-minute closing argument by defense attorney Epps. The judge then instructed the jury on the difference between manslaughter and murder and between murder and murder with a recommendation for mercy. The jury retired to deliberate at 8:45PM.

After only five minutes of deliberation, the jury returned to the court room and handed its verdict to the clerk of the court. "Silence prevailed in the courtroom as several hundred persons stood breathlessly waiting for the verdict." The verdict was guilty without a recommendation for mercy meaning that the judge was required to sentence the defendant to death. Judge Mauldin promptly sentenced the defendant to death and set the execution date as May 27 (in three weeks). Thus ended perhaps the shortest prosecution of a case in the history of the state—72 hours from the death of the officer to the sentence of death.

However, the S.C. Supreme Court granted William Thompson a new trial on the grounds that "he did not get a fair and impartial trial owing to the swiftness of the trial and attitude of the public in regard to the case." Thompson remained at the state penitentiary from May of 1921 until his new trial which began on Sept. 4, 1923, before Judge W.H. Townsend of Columbia. James H. Price and Proctor A. Bonham defended Thompson and offered to plead their client guilty to manslaughter but the state refused. The case was prosecuted by Solicitor David W. Smoak and G.C. Wyche.

The brilliancy with which the legal technique of the case was handled by attorneys for both sides entertained large throngs of interested spectators throughout the trial, and both galleries were packed from the time of Thompson's arraignment to the moment he was sentenced by Judge Townsend. (*Greenville News*, 9/6/1923)

The state argued that Thompson committed premeditated murder in that he attacked Officer Burroughs by hitting him over the head with a flower pot and then shooting him to death. The defense put Thompson on the stand to testify that he did not know Burroughs was a police officer and that the shooting was an accident.

"I didn't shoot him, we were wrestling, I had the gun in my hand and in the fight it went off, both of us had our hands on it."

Thompson denied in the stand that he had struck Burroughs over the head with a flower pot, but testified that in the fight they had knocked down a stand containing some pots. (*Greenville News*, 9/5/1923)

Thompson also testified to "taking a pistol in his pocket" because he wanted protection against another negro "who was also paying attention to the woman." Defense attorneys also argued that Burroughs was off duty and out of uniform and thus had no authority to arrest Thompson. The defense told the jury if Burroughs "was on duty at the time of the killing then convict this man, if not do otherwise." The *Greenville News* said that the trial was "one of the hardest fought legal battles staged in this county in years."

The defense also told the (all-white) jury "that had Thompson been a white man you would not hesitate to acquit him." Thompson was careful in his testimony not to offend the jury and when the prosecution confronted him with witnesses who contradicted him, Thompson simply said, "I won't dispute no white man's word."

The jury deliberated for five hours on Sept. 5 before returning a verdict of guilty of murder but with a recommendation for mercy (avoiding the mandatory death penalty). The judge immediately sentenced Thompson to the mandatory life term in the state penitentiary "or at hard labor on the public works of Greenville." The defense indicated that it was satisfied with the verdict and would not appeal. Thompson left the courtroom "with an expression of gratitude and relief on the countenance that had been impassive throughout his trial."

The S.C. Dept. of Corrections has no records of inmate releases until the 1950's and thus there is no current record as to how much time Thompson served on his life sentence. However, the norm for time served on a life sentence during this time period was around 15 years. Thus it is likely that Thompson was released from prison in the late 1930's.

THE OFFICER

George Staples Burroughs, 48, was born on Feb. 29, 1873, in Anderson County, S.C., to William A. (born Oct. 22, 1848) and Mary Scarborough Burroughs. His father was also born in Anderson County and his mother was born in S.C.

A family bible given by George to his wife, Maggie, in 1906, indicated that his paternal grandparents were James S. and Charlotte Benson Burroughs who were married on June 16, 1845, and had six children: Robert M. (born 1846); William A. (born 1848); Mary E. (born 1850); Thomas G. (born 1852), Martha J. (born 1858), and Charlotte Matilda (born 1860). The *Greenville News* reported that George Burroughs' "home was originally in Conway in the lower part of the state."

Burroughs first became a member of the Greenville Police Dept. in 1908 at the age of 33 and, at his death, was a 12-year veteran of the Dept. He left the force for a year and then returned in 1912 and remained through 1916. For two years he "pursued another occupation" but returned to the police department in 1918, remaining until his death. The funeral for Officer Burroughs was held on Sunday, May 8, at the Burroughs residence on Westfield St. "During the hour of the funeral the city bell tolled slowly in memory of the deceased officer, who was known as one of the most fearless and efficient officers of the city force." The service was conducted by "the pastor of the deceased," the Rev. C.M. Morris of the Hampton Ave. Methodist Church assisted by the Rev. C.C. Herbert, pastor of the Buncombe Street Methodist Church.

Six Greenville police officers served as pallbearers at the burial service which followed at Springwood Cemetery. One of the pallbearers was Officer R.C. Evans who would later be a pallbearer at the N.C. funeral of his close friend, Officer Arthur Lackey, in 1925.

Members of Cedar Camp No. 3, Woodmen of the World, of which, the deceased officer was a member, attended the funeral in a body. The mound was literally covered with floral offerings, bearing evidence to the esteem in which the officer was held by all who knew him. (*Greenville News*, 5/9/1921)

In 1996 the gravesite of Officer Burroughs is still visible at Springwood Cemetery in downtown Greenville. A four ft. tall stone Woodman of the World monument marks the grave of Burroughs at Springwood Cemetery. The grave marker reads:

GEORGE S. BURROUGHS
Feb. 29, 1873 - May 7, 1921
Woodman of the World

Officer Burroughs' widow, Maggie, 47, did not want to live alone after her husband's death so her brother Otto Holcombe came to live with her. George and Maggie had no living children in 1921 though they had raised his 13-year old niece, Viola Holcombe (the daughter of Victor Paul and Mary Lula Smithers Holcombe) from "early childhood." Viola continued to live with Maggie after George's death and until her marriage.

Maggie Elizabeth Burroughs, 84, the Officer's widow, died in Greenville 37 years after her husband on March 3, 1958, at the age of 84. She was buried beside her husband and infant son, Walter Burroughs, who died on Sept. 6, 1896, at the age of one. Her obituary in the *Greenville News* indicated that she was born in Ida County, N.C., to the late Robert and Janie Erwin Smithers and had lived in Greenville for 70 years. At her death, Mrs. Burroughs lived with her niece, Viola Holcombe Stair, 50, of 10 Ladson St. in Greenville.

There are no direct descendants of Officer George S. Burroughs since he and his wife had no children. However, there are descendants through Viola Stair, the niece who was raised by George and Maggie Elizabeth Burroughs. Ruth Viola Holcombe Stair, 67, died on March 10, 1974, at the age of 67 in Greenville and was buried at Woodlawn Memorial Park. She was survived by her daughter, Mary Elizabeth Viola, 45, of Rock Hill, S.C. In 1996 Mary Elizabeth Viola, 67, lived in Rock Hill, S.C. Her two children: were Michael James Viola, 47, of Hollister, CA, and Michele Maria Viola Nichols, 30, of Rock Hill, S.C.

The name of G.S. Burroughs is inscribed (East Wall, Panel 24, Line 10) of the National Law Enforcement Memorial in Washington, D.C., and a plaque bearing his name is displayed at the S.C. Criminal Justice Hall of Fame in Columbia.

SOURCES: *Greenville News*, May 7,8,9,10, 1921, Aug. 14,27, Sept. 5,6, 1923, May 4, 1958; Greenville County criminal court record #9831; Springwood Cemetery directory; Grave markers at Springwood Cemetery; Death certificate of G.S. Burroughs (#6908) at State Archives in Columbia; and interviews with Mary Elizabeth Viola and Lillian Stephenson.

#15 JAMES H. HOWARD
State Constable
Shot & killed while on "moonshine" raid on Jan. 31, 1924.

THE EVENT

State Constable James Holland Howard was shot and killed during a raid on an illegal distillery in the "Dark Corner" of Greenville County on Jan 31, 1924. Howard became the second law enforcement officer killed around Hogback Mountain as U.S. Revenue Agent Rufus Springs was killed in 1878 in a similar raid. Two "moonshiners" were convicted and sentenced to death for the murder of Constable Howard. However, their sentences were commuted to life and both were later paroled and pardoned.

The scene of the homicide was the side of Hogback Mountain in Glassy Mountain Township near Landrum about 35 miles from Greenville. The site, which was five miles from the nearest house, was also described as a "cove" between Hogback Mountain and Chestnut Ridge and as "one of the loneliest spots in the Dark Corner."

On Thursday, Jan. 31, 1924, Reuben Gosnell, 48, a federal prohibition agent with 19 years experience in raiding illegal stills in the Greenville area, led a team of law enforcement officers on a raid of a suspected still on Hogback Mountain.

Pictured above around 1916 are (seated) James Holland Howard, 44, holding his son Bart, 5; his wife, Elizabeth Moon Howard, 40, holding her daughter Mary, 1; and his daughter Hattie, 20, holding her daughter Nell. standing from left to right are his children Broadus Alton, 8; John Holland, 16; Bertha Sallie, 19; Lillie Ella, 17; William Perry, 11; and Clarence G., 13. Not pictured are James Alexander, 21, and Thurmam Basco born in 1918). Constable James Holland Howard was killed in the line of duty on Jan. 31, 1924, by moonshiners on Hogback Mountain, Greenville County, SC. His name is inscribed on the National Law Enforcement Memorial in Washington, DC. Constable Hofward's son, Clarence G. Howard, 28, a chauffeur for the "Federal Prohibition Raiding Squad" was shot and killed by a moonshiner in Hendersonville, NC, on April 22, 1930.

The team of officers included federal prohibition agent E.N. Austin, and "Special State Constable" J. H. (Holland) Howard, 50, and his son, Clarence, 20, who had been deputized to serve as his father's assistant for the raid. Gosnell and Austin were assigned to Greenville County by the sixth division of the federal prohibition force headquartered in Savannah, GA, and headed by W.T Day, Division Chief. Gosnell was the cousin of Jake Gosnell who was tried and acquitted for the murder of Sheriff Sam D. Willis in 1927.

As the "raiding party" walked up Hogback Mountain toward the suspected still, they met two brothers, W.P. and Alexander Plumley (both around 20 years old), coming down the mountain from the direction of the still. The officers could tell by the clothes being worn by the brothers that they had been working on a still and searched both of them, finding a .32 caliber pistol on one. The brothers were placed under arrest and temporarily incarcerated in a "small log corn crib" about a half mile below the still. Gosnell left Agent Austin and Clarence Howard at that site to guard the two prisoners and, with Constable Howard, proceeded up the mountain to the still.

After Gosnell and J.H. Howard left, Austin and Clarence Howard came under rifle fire from a cave 100 yards away across the Pacolet River. The cave was later discovered to be a "lookout" post to guard the "approach up the valley to the still." Several shots struck the crib and "one barely missed" Agent Austin.

When Agent Gosnell and Constable Howard reached the site of the still, Gosnell "crept stealthily around to the head of the ravine to cut off escape in that direction" while Howard prepared to run into the camp and "flush" the moonshiners. After Howard "made a dash" into the distillery, Gosnell heard cursing and then several shots fired. He then saw two men run from the distillery, one going west and one going east. He "gave chase" to the man running east, and "after a race of about 400 yards," captured Holland Pittman, 21, who "drew or tried to draw a loaded .45 caliber pistol which had not been fired."

Gosnell returned to the distillery and found Constable Howard dead, "his pistol lying within two feet of him." Howard was found "in a kneeling posture, shot through the stomach with five bullets, death having come almost instantly." One bullet entered "from the front, and the others from the back." The autopsy revealed that he died of "gunshot wounds penetrating the aorta several times. In 1996 the State Archives at Columbia still maintained the bullets taken from the body of Constable Howard.

Gosnell was later fired upon from ambush as he tried to leave the area. He returned to the mountain later that day with friends of Howard and they removed the body from the mountain.

THE PERPETRATORS

The captured Holland Pittman, 21, was taken to the Greenville County jail. When Holland Pittman's father, Alexander Pittman, 49, learned that his oldest son was in jail and that he was "wanted by the law," he surrendered himself in Greenville. Both father and son were charged with murder. Alex Pittman was described as a "large man of great physical strength."

A coroner's jury was convened at the Jones-McAfee Funeral Home in Greenville the day after the murder (Friday, Feb. 1). Coroner Arthur Vaughn and State Constable Henry Bell had visited the scene of the murder on Thursday. The inquest was postponed until Monday, Feb. 11, when "newly discovered evidence" was discovered that "caused the case to take an unlooked for turn." Agent Gosnell testified that he believed that the man "that got away" from the murder scene was Alexander Pittman and thus he arrested Pittman when he came to Greenville.

Wade Plumley, a "tracking expert," testified that he visited the murder scene on the day of the killing and examined the tracks left by the man who got away. Plumley told the jury:

"I wouldn't swear that a track was Alexander Pittman's unless I saw him make it but I ain't never made a mistake in recognizing one of our folks' tracks yet." Mr. Plumley testified that he was familiar with the track that Alexander Pittman made when walking or running and that he had followed the trail for about three-quarters of a mile and added that it was in the direction that Agent Gosnell had testified the unknown man had gone immediately after the shooting. (*Greenville News*, 2/12/1924)

Testimony was also presented that the Pittmans "inhabited" the "lookout" cave on the side of Hogback Mountain from which shots were fired at Agent Austin and Clarence Howard. A "repeating Winchester rifle" was found in the cave and was the same type another witness described as being carried by Alexander Pittman two days before the killing. However, the Pittmans' defense attorney made the witness concede that there were a number of such rifles in the mountain community.

The coroner's jury surprised law enforcement officials by ruling on Feb. 11 that there was insufficient evidence to connect the Pittmans with the killing of Constable Howard. The jury blamed the Howard killing on "parties unknown to us." After the verdict was returned Solicitor David Smoak requested that Coroner Vaughn "secure a warrant" charging the Pittmans with murder but Vaughn refused saying that he "had no right to take out a warrant unless authorized to do so by a jury."

However, despite the failure of the coroner's jury to fix blame for the Howard murder on the Pittmans, Solicitor Smoak, on Feb. 11, issued a warrant charging them with murder. The Pittmans had been held in the county jail since their arrest on Jan. 31. The defendants "demanded no preliminary" and thus the case went directly to the grand jury. Holland Pittman was denied bond "at any price" by Judge Dennis but Alexander Pittman was released on a $6,000 bond. The *Greenville News* reported that the refusal of bond to Holland Pittman was "the first time in several years that bond had been refused in a homicide case."

The Greenville County grand jury returned an indictment for murder against the two Pittmans on March 11. The case was continued at the request of the Pittman's defense attorney, James H. Price of Bonham, Price and Poag, on the grounds that Senator Proctor, a member of the defense team, was obligated to attend the legislative session in Columbia. The defense request was granted by Judge E.C. Dennis. The *Greenville News* noted that Judge Dennis of Darlington would not be back in the Greenville Court for six years since circuit court judges in 1924 had to rotate among the fourteen circuits in the state (Greenville was in the 13th Circuit).

Solicitor Smoak took a special interest in the Howard murder case because a law enforcement officer was killed and because he expressed a belief in the newspaper that "ninety per cent of the serious crimes occurring" in the circuit were "directly or indirectly the result of free flowing liquor throughout the section."

The trial of Alexander and Holland Pittman began on Thursday, May 15, and concluded on Saturday, May 17, 1924, before T.J. Mauldin. Solicitor Smoak was assisted by J.D. Lanford and Alvin H. Dean while W.E. Bowen and Joseph R. Bryson, represented the Pittmans. The *Greenville News* described the arguments by both sides as "brilliant and eloquent." Prosecutors presented a case based on circumstantial evidence while Alexander Pittman put forth an alibi that he was elsewhere at the time of the murder.

The jury deliberated only forty minutes before returning a verdict of guilty without recommendation of mercy thus mandating the death penalty. "The two Pittmans, with the wife and mother seated between them, heard the verdict without the quiver of an eyelash, their faces as immobile as they have been throughout the trial." The death sentences were upheld by the SC Supreme Court on Sept. 23, 1926.

Death warrants for both Pittman's was signed by Gov. Thomas G. McLeod on Oct. 11, 1926. However, on Oct. 26, 1926, the Gov. commuted the death sentences of both men to life in prison. The Governor's commutation order came in response to letters in support of clemency from Sam M. Wolfe and David W. Smoak who prosecuted the case and from E.N. Austin, a prohibition agent who accompanied Constable Howard on the fatal raid.

The *Greenville News* reported on Oct. 22, 1927, that Eli Pittman, 19, and Wesley Pittman, 17, the sons of Alexander Pittman "were taken to Washington, D.C., yesterday afternoon by United States Marshal R. Kirksey to be committed to the national training school until they are 21 years of age." They were found guilty in federal court of violating the prohibition law and "Federal Judge H.H. Watkins secured special authority to send them to the training school rather than impose prison terms."

Alexander and Holland Pittman were both paroled on Oct. 5, 1933, after being incarcerated for 9 & 1/2 years. They were both pardoned by the Gov. on Jan. 12, 1935.

The Pittmans knew Constable Howard as all were natives of the Dark Corner. In fact, Justice Marion stated that the Pittmans were "unreconstructed adherents of the ancient mountain code" and that they were hostile toward Constable Howard in that they "regarded him not only as a soldier in the ranks of the enemy" but as a "renegade who deserved short shrift at the hands of mountain men on the firing line." Alex Pittman had allegedly made threats against Howard stating that if Howard "ever came on him 'stilling,' he would kill him."

Justice J.H. Marion of the S.C. Supreme Court in affirming the conviction of the two killers provided considerable background to the murder. Perhaps the quotation below gives some hint as to why the death sentences were commuted and why both were later paroled and pardoned.

In the fastness of these mountains, south of Mason and Dixon's line, have lived for more than a century a sturdy, virile white people of probably as pure Anglo Saxon stock as America can boast. Remote, and isolated by the inaccessibility of their mountain homes, for a century or more, they lived in a world apart, practically untouched and uninfluenced by the currents and tides of social and economic progress which flowed and rose and ebbed in the great world beyond their mountain barriers. The gift of the mountains to their children has always been a love of liberty, fostered by the isolation of their mountain life, is doubtless responsible, in a measure for the antipathy of these people to the law of legislative halls and of courts, in no more striking way, perhaps, has this characteristic been evidenced and illustrated than by the tenacity with which they have clung to the conviction, that their right to convert the corn, grown in their valleys and coves, into whiskey, is a God given and an inalienable right. Prior to the adoption of the 18th amendment to the Federal Constitution these people, or many of them, persisted in asserting that right as against the revenue officers of the Federal Government, and since the enactment of the national prohibition law the phenomenal increase in market value of 'moonshine' has doubtless furnished little incentive to depart from the 'tradition of the elders.' Certain characteristics, for which that faith and practice are perhaps largely responsible, are manifested by a marked tendency to secretiveness and suspicion in all social and business contracts with outsiders, and by a strong inclination to settle scores among themselves in accordance with the spirit of a vendetta, a spirit, however, which in fairness, it may be said, competent observers have ascribed, in part at least, to the influence of ancestral traditions reaching back to the days of chivalry, the reformation and the clan. While in a court of law murder is murder and the halo of mountain romance fades into the dull ember hues of sordid tragedy, the foregoing general observations as to the setting of the crime and as to the racial characteristics of the people who figured almost exclusively as dramatic personae in the trial below are not without pertinent bearing in appraising the contentions of the parties with respect to the relevancy and weight of testimony. (quoted in Mann Batson, *A History of the Upper Part of Greenville County, S.C.,* 1993)

In a similar vein, the *Greenville News* in an article headlined, "Mountain Folk Have Code of Honor All Their Own; Dispensers of Hospitality," noted that the Dark Corner was "famous for its blockade whiskey, gun-play and tragedy" and was a "wild man's neighborhood." However, the newspaper noted that the residents of that sector were very hospitable to strangers.

As a general rule people of the mountain are as peace loving as any citizen of a city. They do not fight and kill for the joy, nor the brutality of the deed, but they have an unwritten law. A code of ethics.

Those who operate distilleries, and there are many who do, attend to their business and expect everyone else to attend to their's They are at peace with the world until someone crosses their path which leads to their still. They love their neighbor until he, or she, reports their distilling plant to the officers. (*Greenville News,* 2/17/1924)

Alexander Pittman died on Jan. 4, 1939, at the age of 64. Holland Pittman died on March 25, 1981, at the age of 78. Both are buried at the Mt. Pleasant Baptist Church Cemetery on Highway 11 within sight of Hogback Mountain in upper Greenville County.

THE OFFICER

James Holland Howard was born on Sept. 18, 1872, in Greenville County, SC, to Wade D. Howard (1839-1905), a Civil War veteran, and Narcissus Center Howard. He was the fourth of eight children (Elizabeth, William "Big Bill,", Wade Jackson, James H., Hattie, Julia Ann, Stephen, and Malinda).

The Howard family had been in the Dark Corner for more than 150 years. James H.'s great grandfather, Captain Thomas Howard (1760-1830), fought in the Revolutionary War and, at the age of 16 in 1776, led several men against a party of Cherokee Indians and "Tories" in the Battle of Round Mountain. The Tories had incited the Indians to attack "patriots" (Tory families were protected by a peeled pole wrapped with white cloth) and several whites were "massacred." Capt. Howard, guided by his friend, Skyuka, surprised the encamped Indians by coming up through an unknown "gap" and routed the Indians, killing several. That gap is now known as "Howard's Gap."

In 1996 a memorial on the east side of Highway 26 between Columbus and Saluda commemorates the Battle of Round Mountain, the last formal battle between local settlers and the Indians. The stone monument and plaque describe the bravery of Capt. Howard and the victory they won. Capt. Thomas Howard is buried in a family cemetery just off Highway 11.

"Hol" Howard was a farmer but worked for several years as an unpaid (volunteer) constable fighting the moonshiners. His family had a history of involvement in moonshining and had several confrontations with the law as described in *High Sheriff* a book about the legendary Greenville County Sheriff P.D. Gilreath who served from 1876-1900. Hatred of "law" was greatest in the Dark Corner after 1892 when the S.C. Legislature, at the urging of Gov. Benjamin R. Tillman, passed a law creating the State Dispensary. Many individuals (and even entire towns) openly defied the law.

However, Hol Howard was a representative of the "new order" in that he was a native of and lived in the mountainous "Dark Corner" of Greenville County but was opposed to the moonshining activity of the "old order." He was so convinced that moonshining was the "curse of the mountains" that he was a state constable "serving without pay" (the *Greenville News* described him as a "special state constable"). Howard apparently worked for sometime as a deputized constable and was well known (and highly regarded) by law enforcement authorities in Greenville. However, he was hated as a traitor by the moonshiners.

Constable Howard was thus a citizen volunteer who recognized the danger of raids on "stills" in the Dark Corner but was willing to take the same risks as those paid to enforce the law. In fact, Howard apparently volunteered for the more dangerous job of "flushing out" the moonshiners at the still site on Jan. 31, 1924, and thus (in modern terms) volunteered "to be the first man through the door" at the raid. His devotion to the task and bravery were exceptional in view of his status as an unpaid volunteer.

Constable Howard was a resident of Glassy Mountain Township and was survived by his widow, Margaret Elizabeth ("Lizzie") Moon Howard, 47, and eleven children, seven sons and four daughters: James Alexander Howard, 29; Hattie Howard Leonard, 28; Bertha Sallie Howard Turner, 26; Lillie Ella Howard, 24; John H. Howard, 23; Clarence Grady Howard, 20; William Perry Howard, 18; Broadus Alton Howard, 15; Bart C. Howard, 13; Mary Lee Howard,

8; and Thurman Basco Howard, 5. His oldest son, James Alexander Howard was a ministerial student at Furman University from 1920-1924 and was a "member of the varsity football squad."

The murder of J. Holland Howard had a great impact on the law-abiding residents of the Dark Corner. On Feb. 13, 39 men from the Pleasant Hill, Highland and Mt. Lebanon communities organized the Pleasant Hill Law and Order League "to aid state and county officers in a general clean-up of lawlessness said to be prevalent" in the Dark Corner. Rev. R.L. Barton, principal of Pleasant Hill School was elected president of the organization.

The killing of Mr. Howard was said to be largely responsible for the new spirit of law enforcement which was given expression at the meeting by speeches from J.A. Howard, a son of the slain officer, who is a ministerial student at Furman University, Deputy Sheriffs F.L. Ballenger and P.H. Jones, Holton Morrow, J.L. Hawkins, J. Farnham and W.T. Forrester.

In speeches at the organization meeting the prevalence of lawlessness and the necessity of quelling it was duly emphasized and the citizens called upon juries to be less lenient with law-breakers and upon judges to impose sentences on chain gangs and in the penitentiary instead of fines.

The committees in each community will gather and place evidence of lawlessness in the hands of the president of the league, who will see that warrants are issued for the alleged law-breakers.....Gov. McLeod will be petitioned by the league to place at least two special state constables on duty in the Highland and Glassy Mountain townships sector of the county for a period of at least three months while the league members pledged themselves to act as special deputies at all times and to aid state and county officers in the two townships... (*Greenville News,* 2/13/1924)

The day after the league was organized, federal prohibition agents Reuben Gosnell and E.N. Austin (who accompanied Constable Howard on the fatal raid on Jan. 31), destroyed three stills in the Cleveland township section and described the stills as some of the "largest ever seen" by the agents. The agents praised the creation of Pleasant Hill League but lamented the fact that its scope did not extend to the Cleveland township. Agent Gosnell, who doubted that the state would assign two constables to the Dark Corner, proposed that a "public subscription" be raised to fund two law enforcement officers in the sector.

On Feb. 17, 1924, the *Greenville News* published a letter from Jim Howard, the son of Constable Howard, who expressed the view that illegal stills were the "breeding place of crime" in Greenville County. He also placed blame on the "faithful customers" of the moonshiners and wrote that the "citizen, judge, lawyer or officer that upholds, sympathizes, drinks, or shields (them) in any shape or form" was guilty of "cultivating and fertilizing the breeding places of crime" and were "enemies to humanity, the yet unborn, the home, the churches and the state."

The funeral of J.H. Howard was held at the Highland Baptist Church on Saturday, Feb. 2, 1924. The service was conducted by Rev. O.L. Orr, assisted by T.E. Reid. Burial in the cemetery beside the church followed the funeral service.

In 1996 the grave marker for Constable Howard can be easily found in the Highland Baptist Church cemetery at 3270 Highway 414 in Highland. The grave marker reads:

James Holland Howard
Sept. 18, 1872
Jan. 31, 1924

All but one of Constable Howard's children are buried in the Highland Baptist Cemetery. His wife, Elizabeth Moon Howard, died in 1957 at the age of 81, and was buried beside her husband. Her obituary in the *Greenville News* indicated that she (and her husband, J. Holland Howard) were survived by 28 grandchildren, 30 great-grandchildren and two great-great-grandchildren in 1957.

Buried near James Holland Howard are two children who died in infancy (in 1904 and 1913) before their father's death. The other children buried nearby and their year of death are James Alexander Howard (1988), Bertha Sallie Howard Turner (1962), Lillie Ella Howard (1954), John H. Howard (1980), Clarence Grady Howard (1930), William Perry Howard (1933), Broadus Alton Howard (1966), Bart C. Howard (1992), and Mary Lee Howard (1961). Hattie Howard Leonard (1984) was the only child not buried at Highland.

Clarence Grady Howard, 28, the son of Constable Howard who accompanied his father on the fatal raid in 1924, was killed on April 22, 1930. The *Greenville News* reported that he was a "chauffeur for the Federal prohibition raiding squad" under Prohibition Officer W.W. Owens, when he was shot and killed on main street in Hendersonville, N.C., by Fred Swartz, "alleged prohibition violator." Swartz was later convicted of manslaughter and sentenced to 15 years in prison. Clarence Howard was survived by a widow and two children who lived at Tuxedo. Another son, William Howard Perry also died a violent death in 1933 from a hunting accident.

The most famous son of J.H. Howard was James Alexander Howard, who was a famous Baptist minister who died in 1988 at the age of 93. He preached in over 1,000 revival meetings, was the superintendent of evangelism of the S.C. Baptist Convention from 1940-1961, and President of the S.C. Convention in 1964. He also served as the Chairman of the board of N. Greenville Academy. Rev. Howard retired to his farm near Glassy Mt. in 1961 and wrote *Dark Corner Heritage* (published in 1980) which described his upbringing but did not mention the famous murder of his father.

In 1996 Basco Howard, 78, of Landrum was the only living child of James Holland and Elizabeth Howard. He lived on Highway 414 within sight of Hogback Mt. where his father was killed. Numerous grandchildren, great grand-children, etc. of Constable Howard still live in Greenville County as documented by Frances Howard, his daughter-in-law. One grandson, William Perry, was a magistrate in Greenville County in the 1970's.

Agent Reuben Gosnell died at the age of 72 on June 12, 1948, and was buried at Graceland Cemetery. The State of S.C. no longer has a State Constabulary as it was replaced in 1947 by the S.C. Law Enforcement Division (SLED).

In 1997 The name of Constable J. Holland Howard will be added to the National Law Enforcement Memorial in Washington, D.C. and a plaque bearing his name will also be added to the S.C. Criminal Justice Hall of Fame in Columbia. The line of duty death of Constable Howard was unknown to these memorials before the publication of this book.

SOURCES: *Greenville News*, Feb. 1,5,12,13,14,17,18,21,28, March 1,9,12, May 15-18, 1924, Oct. 27, 1927, April 23, 1930; Hendersonville N.C. *Times-News*, April 22,23, 1930; *A History of the Upper Park of Greenville County, S.C.* by Mann Batson, 1993, pp. 516-518; *Dark Corner Heritage* by James Alexander Howard, 1980; *Hogback Country* by James Walton Lawrence, Sr., 1982; Greenville County criminal court record #A-1089 in S.C. Archives in Columbia; *State v. Pittman,* et al., Supreme Court of S.C., Sept. 23, 1926; Grave markers at Highland Baptist Church cemetery; 1920 census of S.C., E.D. 18, Sheet 1, Line 53; Interviews with Basco Howard, Bill Howard, Frances Howard, E.L. Turner, Will Turner, Ruth Henson, Altha Howard; and information on Clarence Howard provided by Frances Howard.

#16 ARTHUR F. LACKEY
Greenville Police Dept.
Shot during house search on March 3, 1925 (died on March 4).

THE EVENT

Motorcycle Officer Arthur F. Lackey, 33, a 2-year veteran of the Greenville Police Dept. was fatally shot on March 3, 1925, as he searched a house for a man who had earlier that morning shot another Greenville officer. Lackey died 24 hours later from his wounds. The killer died the same day from wounds inflicted by another Greenville officer as he escaped from the house after shooting Lackey.

Arthur F. Lackey

Around 1:15AM on Tuesday, March 3, 1925, Sgt. Cox and Call Officer Henry Ballard "came upon" a Buick automobile stopped on Augusta St. near the Cline alley intersection. Two negro men, Leo Davenport and Bruce Burgess, were standing near the Buick and attempted to dispose of some liquor as the officers approached. Officer Ballard attempted to seize Burgess and Sgt. Cox "collared" Davenport. Cox later reported:

> As I seized his collar, he threw his hand to his hip. I thought he was reaching for a bottle of whiskey. He flashed his gun in my face instead and I pushed him backward with the barrel of the riot gun which I held. As I pumped the gun to get a cartridge in the chamber, he fired point blank. The bullet burned like a coal of fire in my right side. I then fired at him as he dived around the corner of a nearby store. They say I hit him, a buck shot having split his chin and another his nose. If it hadn't been for my gun he would have shot me through the head. (*Greenville News,* 3/4/1925)

Sgt. Cox was taken to the city hospital and survived his wounds. A posse was organized to search for the man who shot him. Riot guns were issued and bloodhounds were requested from Sheriff Craig of Pickens County (the hounds arrived after Davenport was captured). A posse composed of Greenville officers and deputies under Sheriff Sam D. Willis went to Davenport's home at 303 South Calhoun St. and began a search of the home. After the front room was searched Motorcycle Officer Arthur Lackey opened the door to the darkened back room. Davenport was hiding behind a curtain "that had been thrown over some clothes near the wall." As Officer Lackey entered the room he was shot by Davenport who then "bolted through a back door and plunged into the darkness, escaping a second time."

However, Davenport was again shot as he escaped. Officer Edmund England, who had gone to the rear of the home to guard that exit, fired twice at the fleeing fugitive and inflicted a fatal wound. The officer's shot hit Davenport in the right rear side and exited from the right chest. The fatally wounded Davenport was found at 4:15AM at the home of his brother-in-law. He was taken to the city hospital where he died at 9:05PM the next day.

Officer Lackey was taken to the city hospital but died 24 hours later at 2:15AM on March 4. He was conscious and was able to talk with Chief J.E. Smith about his fatal encounter with Davenport. His wife was called to his bedside at 2:30AM. Neither the wounded officer nor the doctors expected him to survive though there was hope for recovery.

THE PERPETRATOR

Little information about Leo Davenport was given in newspaper accounts. His background and age are unknown. Since he died there was no trial though a coroner's inquest did name him as the man who shot Sgt. Cox and killed Officer Lackey.

The police later found the .35 calibre Colt automatic used to shoot Cox and Lackey in a potato patch near his house where it had been buried by friends. Several of the friends were questioned by police and two (John Peden and Bob Grant) were detained for possible charges. Bruce Burgess, the man involved in the first encounter with police that resulted in the shooting of Sgt. Cox, was taken to the city jail on the charge of transporting whiskey. He was "given a sentence of $100 fine or 30 days on the gang."

THE OFFICER

Arthur F. Lackey, 33, was born on July 19, 1891, in Lincolnton, N.C., to J.M. and Sarah Bess Lackey. Both of his parents were born in N.C. His father, James McGee Lackey, the father of eight children, was described at his death on July 27, 1917, as "one of Lincoln County's old and highly respected citizens."

Arthur was raised in Lincolnton and attended prep school at Christ School at Arden, N.C. He then attended William and Mary College in VA and graduated as a textile engineer. While at William & Mary, Lackey received a commission allowing him to join the U.S. Army as a 2nd Lt. in the Cavalry (Troop A) in France during World War I. Lt. Lackey saw considerable combat duty under Major Bullwinkle who later became a U.S. Senator from N.C. First Lt. Arthur Lackey returned to the states in 1919 after the armistice.

Arthur Lackey, 26, married Amy Ethel Sigmon, 17, on Jan. 4, 1918, at Ft. Jackson, S.C. Amy was from Newton, N.C. and the couple met through mutual friends. Their first child, Arthur F. Lackey, was born on Oct. 20, 1918, while Arthur was in the army in France. The child was six months old when his father first saw him upon his return home. A second child, Sara Bess, was born on Jan. 6, 1921. Shortly after his return to the U.S., Lacked moved to Easley, S.C., to work in a textile plant as an engineer. He was a member of the Masonic Lodge (#189) and American Legion in Easley.

Arthur Lackey, 31, joined the Greenville Police Dept. in 1923 and moved his family from Easley to Greenville. He was a 2-year veteran of the Dept. at the time of his death. He was assigned to the motorcycle unit during most of his short career with the Greenville police and helped start the unit that served as motorcycle escorts for funerals. His daughter, Sara, remembers as a child riding in the side car of her father's motorcycle around their Greenville neighborhood.

The body of Officer Lackey was taken from city hospital to the Jones-McAfee undertaking parlors where a viewing was held on March 4. "A host of people" made the "pilgrimage" to the funeral parlor "to pay respect to the memory of one of Greenville's best loved officers." At 6:00PM the casket was carried by several police officers to the Lackey home at 19 Harvey Street.

A funeral service was held at the Lackey home on March 5 with the Rev. A.R. Mitchell, rector of the St. James and St. Andrews Episcopal churches, and Rev. S.T. Matthews, pastor of the Central Baptist Church officiating. All members of the Police Commission were in attendance as were Mayor Richard E. Watson, Police Chief J.E. Smith, Fire Chief Frank Donald and "all members of the force."

The funeral service was conducted with full military and police honors that included the presence of an honor guard, the firing of rifles, and the playing of taps. Over 70 years later Sara Lackey Bost still hates the sound of Taps because of her memory of it being played at her father's funeral. Also, in 1963, while watching the funeral procession of President John F. Kennedy, Sara remembered for the first time in 38 years that a horse with an empty saddle also followed her father's hearse at his 1925 funeral service.

After the funeral service the casket was carried by the police pallbearers to the train station and placed on the northbound Southern train No. 34 bound for Lincolnton, N.C., for burial on Friday, March 6. R.C. Evans, "companion motorcycle officer since Officer Lackey began service" in Greenville, escorted the body to its destination. Six other members of the police department, including Chief J.E. Smith and Assistant Chief L.W. Hammond, left on a later train to attend the funeral in N.C.

At Gastonia, N.C., a delegation of the American Legion post of that city and "the military company to which the deceased belonged at the outbreak of the war" joined the casket on the remaining leg to Lincolnton. The Masonic Order was in charge of the burial services at the Woodside Cemetery in Lincolnton. Six Greenville police officers served as pallbearers at the graveside services.

Arthur F. Lackey, 33, was survived by his wife, Amy Ethel Sigmon Lackey, 24; a son, Arthur, Jr., 6; a daughter, Sarah Bess, 4; his mother, Mrs. J.W. (Sarah) Lackey; three brothers, O.F. and C.O. Lackey of Lincolnton and the Rev. B.M. Lackey of Raleigh, N.C.; and two sisters, Mrs. A.R. Reeves and Mrs. Preston Bynum of Lincolnton.

In 1996 the grave of Arthur Lackey is located in the Woodside Cemetery at the Church of Our Savior in Lincolnton, N.C. (between Gastonia and Hickory on Highway 321). The 42 inch tall stone grave marker reads:

ARTHUR F. LACKEY
July 19, 1891
March 4, 1925
How Desolate Our Home
Bereft of Thee

Also buried in the Lackey family plot in 1996 at the Woodside Cemetery are his father, J.M. Lackey (1917); mother, Sarah Bess Lackey (1938); widow,

Amy Ethel Sigmon Lackey (1932); and six of his seven siblings. His widow died at the age of 31 in 1932 from "Bright's disease."

The Officer's son, Arthur Francis Lackey, Jr., received an appointment to the U.S. Naval Academy through Sen. Bullwinkle but was unable to attend because of a vision problem. He graduated from a business college and worked as an accountant for Clyde Fabrics, Inc. of Newton, N.C., from 1937-1975. He served in Europe in W.W. II and died at the age of 56 in Oct. of 1975. He was buried in Newton, N.C. (in the plot of his maternal grandparents). Arthur and his wife, Elizabeth, had no children. Elizabeth, remained in Newton, NC, in 1996.

Sara Bess Lackey married Eugene Bost in 1940 and lived in and around Newton, N.C. Her husband also served in Europe in W.W. II and later became an executive for a furniture manufacturing company. He retired in 1986.

In 1996 Officer Lackey was survived by a daughter, Sara Bess Lackey Bost, 75, of Conover, N.C.; and three grandchildren, Sara Bost Perry, 48, of Raleigh, N.C.; Elisabeth Bost Matchen, 44, of Burlington, N.C.; and Marshall Eugene ("Mark") Bost II, 40, of High Point, N.C. He was also survived by three great grandchildren, Amy Elisabeth Perry, 25, of Raleigh NC.; Meredith Carter Matchen, 5, of Burlington, N.C.; and Justin Arthur Bost, 3 (named for his great grandfather), of High Point, N.C. All three grandchildren graduated from Newton, NC, High School and later from college (Sara from Meredith College, Elisabeth from Limestone College, and Marshall from N.C. State).

The name of A.F. Lackey is inscribed (East Wall, Panel 47, Line 12) on the National Law Enforcement Memorial in Washington, D.C. A plaque bearing his name is displayed at the S.C. Criminal Justice Hall of Fame in Columbia.

SOURCES: *Greenville News*, March 3,4,5,6, 1925, *Lincoln County (NC) News,* Aug. 29, 1932, Oct., 1975; funeral records of Jones-McAfee Funeral Home in Greenville; grave markers at Woodside Cemetery in Lincolnton, N.C.; and interview with Sara Bess Lackey Bost.

#17 GEORGE MATTHEW MYERS
Deputy Sheriff, Greenville County
Shot & killed during an arrest attempt on Sept. 22, 1926.

THE EVENT

Greenville County Deputy Sheriff George Myers, 47, was shot and killed on Sept. 22, 1926, by a man he attempted to arrest on a domestic warrant. The killer escaped from a mental hospital before his trial and was never captured.

On the previous day (Tuesday, Sept. 21), a woman went to the Greenville Sheriff's office to ask that a peace bond be served on her husband, Ray Wilkie, 30. Wilkie and his wife had been married for four years and had two children but recently Ray had accused his wife of infidelity and had threatened to kill her, her lover, and her mother (who had participated in filing warrants against him).

The infidelity took place after Ray went to Florida when the "Florida fever swept over this section" (i.e., the rush to FL during the land boom of 1926). While in FL, perhaps working as a carpenter, Wilkie heard through his brother that his wife "was keeping company with another man." Wilkie returned to Greenville to confront his wife and she confessed her infidelity after he "administered an oath to her." "Wilkie then gave her a lecture and forgave, he said, for he loved her."

George Matthew Myers. His mother is above his head.

However, Wilkie soon learned that his wife's "relations had been worse than he believed" and he went to confront the "man in question." Wilkie threatened his wife's lover with a gun and the lover "begged and prayed" for his life. In an act of "mercy," Wilkie "gave him a chance. I shot him in the leg and told him that I would give him life."

Wilkie was charged with assault and battery for the shooting of the lover and was also served with a peace warrant from his wife and mother-in-law, Mrs. Carrie Welchel. Wilkie left town for Baltimore and Cincinnati and returned to Greenville on Monday (two days before he shot Dep. Myers) and tried to see his son, Billie, 3, but his mother-in-law would not let him in the house. He returned the next day (Tuesday) and was refused entry again. His wife and mother-in-law then filed the warrant against him later that day.

Wilkie's "ire was aroused to the killing point" when he learned that his wife and mother-in-law had filed the warrant against him the previous day. He planned to shoot his wife and mother-in-law when they came home that night and decided to hide from the police until he could take his vengeance.

Deputy Myers and Deputy R.F. Craigo searched for Wilkie during the day (Wednesday) but were unable to locate him. The two deputies returned to the Sheriff's office and then both (separately) "started home." Myers took the warrant with him thinking that he might spot Wilkie while enroute home. However, Myers was warned by Dept. Craigo to not try and arrest Wilkie by himself as he said Wilkie was a "bad character." Myers picked up J.W. ("Scoop") Kelley, a young man from the Monaghan Mill, on his way home.

Around 5:30PM, as Wilkie and Kelley drove down Hampton Ave. (near the "Piedmont Bonded warehouses"), they spotted Wilkie on the street. Myers stopped the car and, as Wilkie approached, told him he had a warrant for him. Wilkie pulled a gun and "covered" Myers as he approached the car with the gun and told him that he was not going to be arrested (Kelley then got out of the car and fled).

Myers reached for his pistol, which was under his coat, and Wilkie fired two shots at him. Wilkie then began to run. After two shots by Myers were fired at Wilkie, he turned and fired two more shots at Myers, who was still sitting in the vehicle. The "bullets riddled the officer's body, and he crumpled in the seat of his automobile" and "slid down out of the open door on the right hand side—which had been opened by Kelley in getting out."

The autopsy later revealed that two .38 caliber bullets struck Myers, "one entering under the right arm, tearing through the body and directly through the heart, to emerge from the left side. The same ball fractured his left hand." The second shot "inflicted only a flesh wound, entering and leaving the front of his chest." Myers died "in a moment."

A number of witnesses saw the shooting and the Sheriff's office was quickly notified and dispatched three deputies to the scene to search for Wilkie. The three deputies responding were Cliff R. Bramlett, J.R. Rhodes, and J. Vance Patterson.

Wilkie fled first to a drug store on Cedar Lane Rd. and, "at the point of a gun," ordered the druggist, A.E. Brown, to drive him to his wife's home on Donaldson St. (four blocks away). He went into the house seeking (by his later admission) to kill his wife and mother-in-law but they were not home.

Wilkie then went across the street to the home of H.M. Smith and told Smith that "I got one, but not the ones I wanted." Wilkie was ill at this point having taken six tablets of a poison (bichloride of mercury) shortly after the murder as part of his plan to commit suicide after he had killed his "tormentors." Smith persuaded Wilkie to turn over his gun to him as the three deputies approached. Dep. Bramlett, not knowing of Smith's role, ordered Smith to drop the gun and came "dangerously near shooting" Smith when he did not obey quickly the order to drop the gun. Wilkie was arrested only thirty minutes after the murder of Dep. Myers.

THE PERPETRATOR

Ray Wilkie, 30, had married four years earlier, had one living son, Billie, 3, and was "an ex-serviceman." The *Greenville News* called Wilkie an "ex-

Marine." He was a carpenter and was described by the newspaper as "neatly dressed, and of nice appearance. He has a fine chiseled face, with steel blue eyes, and fair complexion and hair."

An inquest was held on Thursday, Sept. 23, by Coroner J.L. Vaughan. After several witnesses had been heard, the jury found that "George M. Myers came to his death as a result of pistol wounds inflicted at the hands of Ray Wilkie." Solicitor J.G. Leatherwood represented the state at the inquest while Wilkie had no attorney. He made no attempt to secure bail. Wilkie was indicted for murder on Oct. 4, 1926.

Wilkie readily confessed to killing Dep. Myers and even told the *Greenville News* that "I only shot him because he was trying to keep me from killing my wife and mother-in-law." He also "spared no bitterness in denouncing his wife" and mother-in-law for causing his troubles.

Wilkie also told reporters that he wanted to die and didn't want to wait around for "the chair." Wilkie expressed no regret for the killing of Dep. Myers but did express regret that he had failed in his suicide attempt. (He had taken too much poison so that his "stomach threw off, rather than assimilated the tablets.")

Wilkie's Greenville County criminal court file (at the State Archives in Columbia) indicated that a hearing was held on his sanity on Oct. 28, 1926. The judge ruled that the state had "failed to show anything to contradict" the defense claim of insanity, and on the motion of the defense attorney, sent Wilkie to the state "asylum" (i.e., mental hospital) in Columbia for 30 days for "observation and treatment."

After being there 30 days Wilkie escaped one night when the suicidal patient he was in a room with tried to hang himself by strings of bedclothes. In the excitement, the day and night guard on Wilkie was relaxed, and he escaped. (undated issue of *Greenville News*)

There is no record that Wilkie was ever apprehended after his escape though there were numerous alleged "sightings" of the elusive Wilkie over the years.

Through the years since the 1926 escape, Wilkie has been trailed with a vengeance. One time a tipster said Wilkie was in Washington, D.C., but it wasn't the man. Another tipster said Wilkie was serving in the Army but that proved a bum steer.......Wilkie has been reported in places from South American to Washington, D.C. (undated issue of *Greenville News*)

The criminal court file for Wilkie includes the notation that he escaped from the mental hospital and correspondence with a Washington, D.C., man in October of 1935 (nine years after his escape) who claimed that he could find Wilkie if given the reward for his capture. Greenville County Sheriff B.B. Smith, who was sheriff from 1933-1936, assured the D.C. man that the $250 reward was still available.

There is no record in the file that Wilkie was ever captured though there was some information about his background. Ray F. Wilkie, who served in the U.S. Army in France during World War I, was court martialed in France and was convicted of threatening two sergeants with a loaded pistol. He was discharged from the service on May 7, 1919, and confined for two years at hard labor.

THE OFFICER

George Matthew Myers, 47, was born in Greenville ("on the White Horse Road") on Jan. 27, 1879, to William Matthew Myers and Frances Almina "Fannie" Brooks Myers. George was the oldest of eleven children with the others being Mary Elizabeth, Hugh Thompson, William Cullen, Daisy Belle, Willis Key, Albert Anderson, Frances Ellen, Bertie Louise, Lila Covington, and Grace Hendricks. The slain deputy's ancestors came to S.C. before the Revolutionary War and his grandfather, George Matthew Myers (1837-1863), attended Furman University for four years before fighting for the Confederacy in the Civil War. He was a 1st Lt. with Company H of the 8th Regiment of S.C. and was wounded several times before being killed at the Battle of Gettysburg.

George Myers lived on a farm until he moved to Greenville in 1906 at the age of 27. Myers and his wife and three children lived at the Presley Grove township in Greenville County.

George Myers, 21, married Tecora Lee Payne, 19, on Dec. 20, 1900. However she died at the age of 27 on Sept. 25, 1908, and was buried at the Grove Station Baptist Church with her family. George and Tecora had three children: Herman Matthew Myers (born on 9/27/1902); Carl Samuel Myers (born on Oct. 10, 1904); and Wilton ("Bill") Payne Myers (born on Oct. 19, 1906).

George later married a widow, Mary Ann Collier Berry, and they had four children: Ansel Butler Myers (born on 8/25/1910); Mary Louise Myers (born on 9/29/1912); Frances Alma Myers (born on 8/10/1915) and Arthur Wilson Myers (born on 8/12/1918). His second widow survived him and died at the age of 75 on Nov. 15, 1952. She was buried at the Shiloh Methodist Church in Bowman, S.C.

George Myers "operated" a store on Pendleton St. for one year before serving as a constable for Magistrate Stradley from 1907 to 1909. He then "became attached" to the state constabulary under the administration of Gov. Martin F. Angel, serving in Charleston "most of the time" from 1909 to 1911. In 1911 he joined the Greenville Police Dept. and served seven years (until 1919).

Myers ran for sheriff of Greenville County in 1920 but was defeated. He rejoined the Greenville Police Dept. in 1921 "when the force was reorganized and J.E. Smith was made chief." In 1925 Sgt. Myers "headed the plain clothes squad." He served until 1925 and was made Sgt. of the vice squad in 1923, a position he held until the left the Dept. again in 1925.

On Sept. 16, 1925, Myers became a deputy sheriff under Sheriff Willis assigned at Monaghan mill. The *Greenville News* described Myers as a "veteran police officer and constable with a brilliant career of daring and service."

During his long career as an officer, he showed himself one well deserving the name. Fearless, but efficient, he passed through many experiences from which he barely escaped with his life, only to be felled finally by bullets fired by an alleged offender of the law.

While a state constable in Charleston, Deputy Myers accidently shot himself by dropping his pistol. The bullet struck him in the body and ranged upward, tearing through vital organs.

With the Greenville police he passed many hair-raising experiences. Once he was forced to take the life of a man, the victim being Kid Davis, escaped negro convict, who attacked the officer with a razor while on Echols street in 1922.

Again he met a negro and a razor in the dark and the assailant was repulsed with a bullet from Deputy Myers' pistol. The wound was not fatal, however. (*Greenville News,* 9/23/1926)

The "viewing" was held at the Jones-McAfee funeral parlor on Friday, Sept. 23. While the officer "lay in state" at the undertaking parlor, "scores of Greenville people, friends, acquaintances, fellow officers....passed by the open casket."

The funeral for George Myers was held at the Welcome Church near Gantt station. The casket was escorted from the funeral home to the "little country church" by a detachment of policemen from Greenville and from the "force of Sheriff Camp, of Anderson County." Dr. D.B. Hahn, pastor of the Pendleton St. Baptist church, officiated at the funeral and was assisted by Rev. J.S. Jolly.

The graveside services in the cemetery adjoining the Welcome Church were conducted by the Ridenburg Council No. 3 Junior Order and the United American Mechanics (organizations of which he was a member). The pallbearers were "deputies in mill villages of Greenville." "Beautiful wreaths and flowers, tendered in deep sympathy from organizations and individuals, blanketed the casket."

George Matthew Myers, 47, was survived by his wife, Mary Ann Collier Berry Myers, 49, two daughters, Frances Alma, 11, and Mary Louise, 14, of Greenville; five sons, Herman Matthew, 24, of Asheville, N.C., Carl Samuel, 21, Wilton Payne, 21, Ansel Butler, 16, and Arthur Wilson, 8, of Greenville; six sisters, Mrs. V.L. Johnson of Piedmont; Mrs. C.L. Gosnell, Mrs. A.T. McWhite, Mrs. W.R. Whitmire, Mrs. James H. Granger and Miss Ellen Myers of Greenville; and by two brothers, Hugh Thompson and Willis Key Myers of Greenville.

In 1996 the grave of Dep. Myers can be found at the old Welcome Baptist Church cemetery on White Horse Rd. next to the Pizza Hut near the intersection of Highway 81 South (Old Anderson Rd.) and Highway 25 (White Horse Rd.). A four ft. stone monument with the inscription, "MYERS," marks the family plot where the officer is buried. His grave marker reads:

GEORGE M. MYERS

Jan. 27, 1879

Sept. 22, 1926

Deputy Myers was buried next to his father, William M. Myers (April 16, 1858-June 6, 1905) and his brother, Albert Anderson Myers (Oct. 29, 1890-Nov. 16, 1918). His brother's grave marker notes that he was killed in France in World War I. The officer's mother, Fannie Brooks Myers, died at the age of 74 in 1932 and was buried beside her husband and two sons.

In 1996, three children of George M. Myers were still living. Carl Myers, 91, lived in Greenville; Frances Alma, 81, lived in Greenville; and Wilton Payne ("Bill") Myers, 89, lived in Spartanburg. Also, three grandchildren of George Myers (Carl Myers, Jr., Carolyn Myers Posey, and William Matt Myers) lived in Greenville County in 1996. On the second Sunday of each August, Don Whitmire (a nephew) hosts a Myers family reunion at his home in Greenville.

The name of George Matthew Myers is inscribed (East Wall, Panel 54, Line

19) on the National Law Enforcement Memorial in Washington, D.C. A plaque bearing his name is displayed at the S.C. Criminal Justice Hall of Fame in Columbia.

SOURCES: *Greenville News*, Sept. 23,24,26, 1926; death certificate of George Matthew Myers in S.C. Archives; Greenville Criminal Court case of Ray Wilkie (A-1794) in S.C. State Archives in Columbia; Cemetery indexes for Greenville County; and interview with Don Whitmire (who provided genealogical information on the Myers family).

#18 SAMUEL D. WILLIS
Sheriff
Shot & killed in "hired hit" on June 11, 1927.

THE EVENT

Sheriff Samuel D. Willis, 36, was shot and killed at his home shortly after parking his car in his garage on June 11, 1927. Two years later a former sheriff and his deputy were convicted of hiring a negro hit man (who was also convicted) to kill Willis. All three served prison terms.

Sheriff Willis was returning to his home at 219 E. Stone Ave. (in 1996 the site was occupied by a branch of the Wachovia Bank) just after midnight on Sunday, June 11, 1927, when he was "ambushed" as he got out of his automobile. Mrs. Willis, who was inside the house, heard her husband drive up and then heard the shots. She would later testify that she saw a negro walk by her window just after the shooting.

The sheriff was shot four times from a distance of six feet, once in the head, and three times in the left side, "one piercing the heart and two others entering the abdomen." A later autopsy revealed that the bullets were "copper-jacketed" and two "exploded shells" were located at the front of the garage. The sheriff was apparently shot as he walked out of the garage as his body was found at the corner of the garage "near the concrete runway." The later autopsy revealed that he had "four wounds, two through the heart, one straight through the head, and a fourth through the left

Greenville County sheriff Samuel D. Willis, 36, was shot and killed on June 11, 1927. He was a combat hero of WW I and became the youngest sheriff in South Carolina. His name is on the National Law Enforcement Memorial in Washington, DC.

forearm into the body. Two .32 calibre bullets, "steel jacket type," were found in the body. "Death was immediate."

Investigators would later conclude that he was shot from "ambush" and that the sheriff may have "heard something" before the shooting as he had left the key in the ignition of his car and the door open as he exited the car with his holstered pistol in his left hand. The sheriff always kept the holstered gun on the car seat beside him and "took it in his hand on leaving the garage to enter his home".

Several people heard the shots in the "thickly settled part of town" and neighbors found the body of the sheriff at the left rear of the automobile. He had apparently died instantly. The sheriff's office was notified and deputies rushed to the scene.

A "throng" of people was crowding around the shooting scene within minutes destroying whatever tracks or scent might have been left by the killer. Bloodhounds were brought by Sheriff John Craig of Pickens but the dogs lost the trail of the killer after 300 yards when he apparently got into an automobile.

A massive investigative team was soon at work searching for clues and interviewing neighbors. Gov. John G. Richards dispatched six state officers (including Carlos A. Rector) to aid in the investigation. The investigation was led by Greenville Chief J.E. Smith, state constable W.W. Rogers, and Chief Deputy Cliff Bramlett from the Sheriff's office. Since "thousands of persons" gathered around the Willis home and the sheriff's office, there was some concern that a lynching might occur if the rumors of a negro killer were confirmed. At 1:00AM on Sunday (only an hour after the murder), Gov. Richards called out the Butler Guards, the local militia, to prevent any possible mob action. A reward fund of $2,800 was established from state and local funds.

On June 17, 1927, Gov. Richards appointed Carlos A. Rector, 42, to fill the unexpired term of Sheriff Willis. Rector was a native of Greenville County and began his law enforcement career in 1916 serving as a "revenue agent" from 1916-1921. He had also served as a magistrate and constable. His reputation as a foe of the "whiskey interests" (destroying over 3,000 distilleries and arresting thousands of persons") led to his election as sheriff in 1920 at the age of 35. His older (by two years) brother, Hendrix Rector, preceded him as Sheriff of Greenville County and was killed in the line of duty on July 4, 1919.

Carlos Rector had been sheriff from 1920-1924 after defeating Willis in an election. Willis defeated Rector in the 1924 election. Rector had been a state constable on the staff of the Gov. in Columbia at the time of his appointment to succeed Willis in 1927.

THE PERPETRATORS

The *Greenville News* stated that the murder of Sheriff Willis was "well planned, coolly executed and completely covered" and thus officers "were prone to believe that the deed was done by a white man rather than a negro, as at first suspected. However, investigators had not discarded the theory of a hired negro gunman."

The newspaper reported that investigators had "four main theories" but the most feasible, at first, appeared to be the theory that the motive for the ambush killing was a "hired hit" by a "liquor ring" (the "whiskey interests") in revenge for or to prevent future arrests for the making or distribution of illegal liquor. Sheriff Willis had made over 3,000 arrests for liquor offenses and had a reputation as being "hard on the liquor element."

However, there was also a rumor (among the "cyclone of gossip and rumor") that a "domestic difficulty" may have led to the murder. Two days later (at 9:30PM on June 14) investigators, after having talked with over 100 persons, arrested the slain sheriff's closest friend, Deputy Sheriff Henry Townsend, for the murder. Townsend was taken to the state prison at Columbia and held "in communicado."

The theory was that Willis and his wife, Ethel, and Townsend were involved in a "love triangle" and that Townsend had killed Willis to eliminate his rival. Townsend was taken secretly to the state prison in Columbia "for safekeeping." The *Greenville News* reported on June 16 that investigating officers surmised that

Sheriff Willis "driving into his garage surprised Mrs. Willis and Deputy Townsend...who were in the light sedan already in the garage. Realizing that Willis had seen the pair in a compromising position, Townsend "shot his way out" as Mrs. Willis fled into the house. The newspaper even published a sketch of the alleged shooting of Willis by Townsend with Mrs. Willis fleeing.

Henry Townsend was not only a deputy under Sheriff Willis but was considered his closest friend. They had "fought side-by-side" in France during World War I and the two worked together in a salvage company which the Sheriff owned at the time of his death. After Townsend's arrest, Mrs. Willis refused to speak to reporters and declared that she would make her statement to the grand jury "provided only grand jurors were present." Mrs. Townsend and her young son, Henry, Jr., left for Greenwood to live with her sister until the case was completed. She told reporters that her husband was at home with her at the time of the Willis murder and that he was innocent of the charges.

Both defendants were released on $3,000 bond until the trial which began two months later. The grand jury returned a true bill against Mrs. Willis, 31, and Townsend, 31, on Aug. 22, 1927, and the sensational 15-day trial began on Thursday, August 25, 1927, with the selection of the jury (12 white men). Both defendants were confined in the jail at night during the trial and the jury was sequestered for the duration of the trial.

The case was tried before Judge Milledge L. Bonham, 73. Solicitor J.G. Leatherwood, Attorney General John M. Daniel, Mendel L. Smith of Camden and David W. Smoak of Greenville prosecuted the case while Col. Alvin H. Dean, James H. Price, C.G. Wyche, and Proctor A. Bonham (son of the judge) represented the defendants.

The courtroom was packed each day with 205 seats being made available to the public. The balcony, normally reserved for "negroes," was filled with whites only. During the trial the *Greenville News* reported that an "unhealthy situation" had resulted from the spitting of "tobacco chewers" who attended the trial. The audience was urged not to "expectorate."

The trial broke a record for longevity as the previous record was eight days for the "second trial of the Hesters." The trial was described as the most "sensational" in the history of the county and the *Greenville News* published pages of trial testimony each day.

The state's case was based on circumstantial evidence and relied heavily on the claim that Mrs. Willis and Townsend were having an affair and that Sheriff Willis saw them in the garage in a "compromising position" when he returned home leading to his being shot by his wife or Townsend. Several witnesses were presented by the state who claimed to have seen Ethel Willis and Henry Townsend together and "that they had been unduly intimate, and that they had held sundry indiscreet trysts at various times." The state contended that the couple had "for a period of some duration been holding illicit trysts in a 'bawdy' house on the old Camp Sevier reservation." Another witness testified that Deputy Townsend came over "right regular" to the Willis home when the Sheriff was not there.

One witness claimed to have seen them together earlier that evening in a car in downtown Greenville. Coroner J.L. Parks testified that he saw Mrs. Willis and Townsend lying on a bed "pretty close" shortly after the murder while another claimed that Townsend gave her "a big juicy kiss". Chief Deputy Bramlett testified that Townsend had told him he was having an affair with an unidentified married woman and that "there would be a killing" if the affair was discovered.

The state also claimed that physical evidence linked the "couple" to the murder as testimony was presented that tracks in the garage "were apparently of a size and shape as to conform to those of Mrs. Willis and Townsend." Coroner Parks contradicted Mrs. Willis' claim that she had been in bed at the time of the murder as he found her bed "made up" shortly after he entered the home after the murder. The state called a total of 45 witnesses.

The defense team told the jury that the police zeroed in on Mrs. Willis and Townsend early on in the investigation and ignored any evidence that did not point to the couple. They also claimed that the police who gathered the evidence disliked Townsend and were jealous of his close relationship with Sheriff Willis. The defense also presented evidence that the man seen fleeing from the murder scene was a negro, not a white man, and that Townsend had an alibi for that evening and could not have been the man seen fleeing the scene. The alibi was confirmed in part by Townsend's 62 year old father, an ex-policeman, who testified that his son never left his home the night of the murder.

Strangely, during the trial police arrested J.B. Willis, a 30-year-old black man, who told several people that he had killed the sheriff. Also, Townsend had just been released from the hospital after surgery and the defense claimed that he was physically incapable of making the "run" attributed to him by the prosecution shortly after the murder.

The defense presented a female neighbor who testified that she made the tracks claimed by the state to be those of Mrs. Willis. Another witness testified that the bed was made up after the murder when the family was told that the body of the Sheriff would be brought into the house. The defense also presented the Sheriff's sister, Gertrude Ellis, who testified that there were no "improprieties" between Ethel and Townsend. Throughout the trial Mrs. Willis was supported by her family and by the family of Sheriff Willis who, apparently, were unanimous in their belief that she was innocent. Her four young children did not attend the trial.

The defense called 66 witnesses but neither Townsend nor Mrs. Willis took the stand in their own defense. The *Greenville News* reported concern over the "heavy cost" of the trial that included $1,250 in meals for the sequestered jury and a "dollar a day" for the more than 100 witnesses called during the trial. In closing arguments the state suggested that Mrs. Willis actually "shot the sheriff" as her lover watched.

The 15-day trial ended on Thursday, Sept. 8, 1927, when the jury took only an hour to return a verdict of not guilty for both defendants. It should be noted that after the later trial of Carlos Rector and J. Harmon Moore, Judge Dennis castigated the two men at their sentencing for the "horrible" crime of trying to blame the killing of Sheriff Willis on two innocent people (i.e., Mrs. Willis and Henry Townsend).

The *Greenville News* reported that Greenville "returned to normal" after the trial. Interest in the case had been so intense that three downtown merchants had posted signs forbidding any of their clerks from talking to customers about the trial. "Activity in civic and public organizations was nearly paralyzed." Most meetings were postponed until after the trial.

Carlos Rector, who failed to solve the murder of his predecessor, lost his re-election bid in 1929 to Cliff Bramlett, who had been a deputy under Sheriff Willis. Bramlett had campaigned on a promise that he would arrest the person *really responsible*" for the Willis murder. Sheriff Bramlett assigned Deputy Sheriff George King to the Willis murder. King learned that a black man had been approached about killing Sheriff Willis for money. That man refused to make the "hit" but King learned that another black man, Blair Rooks, 32, had suddenly come into a good deal of money. Sheriff Bramlett and King confronted Rooks and he confessed to ambushing and killing Willis.

Rooks led Bramlett and King to the location where he had thrown the murder weapon and the gun was found "although in rusty condition." Laboratory tests confirmed that the gun found fired the bullets taken from Willis' body. Rooks claimed that he was paid $500 by Sheriff Carlos Rector and Deputy J. Harmon Moore to kill Sheriff Willis. "This information spread like wildfire throughout the county and residents were astonished."

Carlos Rector and J. Harmon Moore were arrested the next day (in August of 1929). Moore had been a special constable without pay for Sheriff Rector from 1921 to 1925 and the two were close friends. Moore had also been a "chaingang boss" in Oconee County before moving to Greenville in 1916.

The indictment of Rooks indicated that Moore and Rooks met at "divers times" before the murder and that Moore "did hire and procure" Rooks to commit the murder (thus Rooks was charged with accessory before the fact of murder) and that Moore after the murder "harbored" Rooks, "paid him," and "helped him escape" (thus he was charged with accessory after the fact of murder).

Moore's first trial began on Jan. 17, 1930, but a mistrial was declared on Jan. 20 when the judge ruled that "a certain member of the jury had not followed court instructions over a week-end recess." Defense Attorney J. Frank Eppes claimed double jeopardy since the jury had already been sworn in and the mistrial was "without sufficient legal necessity." However, the judge denied the defense claim.

The state announced its intention to try both Rector and Moore in the spring (1930) session of the court but the proceedings were halted when a judge quashed the indictment against both men "because several members of the grand jury were not registered electors." The two were indicted by a new grand jury on Oct. 28, 1930. Both were released on $5,000 bond. The trial was first scheduled for late Oct., 1930, but was continued until December.

The seven-day Rector/Moore trial began on Tuesday, Dec. 2, 1930, before Judge E.C. Dennis of Darlington. Solicitor J.G. Leatherwood prosecuted the case assisted by C.G. Wyche. The defense team consisted of Mendel L. Smith, David W. Smoak, J.D. Lanford, J. Frank Eppes and Plumer C. Cothran. Rector and Moore were both charged with murder and the state sought the death penalty on those charges. They were also charged with being accessories before and after the fact.

The state contended that the Rector/Moore conspiracy to kill Sheriff Willis began on Feb. 15, 1927 (four months before the murder). The star witness for the state was Blair Rooks, the 32-year-old "negro laborer," who testified that he was hired by Rector and Moore to kill Sheriff Willis. He claimed that he was approached "several times" with the proposal before agreeing to "make the hit."

The Saturday afternoon before the killing, he said that Moore got him to drive him to town, that Moore purchased two pints of whisky and showed him the Willis home after they reached the city. That night he went to the home and waited beside the garage, shooting the sheriff as he came out of the building after parking his car there about midnight.

.... as the sheriff came out of the garage he fired once with his left hand, and as Sheriff Willis started to fall he stepped up and fired several more shots with his right hand. Neither spoke a word, he testified. He estimated distance between them at the first shot as about 15 feet.

Turning, he walked down the driveway and proceeded to the right on Stone Avenue, taking the first street to the right and going up the hill. At top of the hill someone turned on the lights of a car on his left, so he turned to the right, proceeded down the hollow, across Richland creek, and went to the house where Moore was. (*Greenville News*, 13/3/1930)

Rooks also testified that Moore helped him dispose of the murder weapon and that he later tried to hire him to kill Sheriff Cliff R. Bramlett. Several witnesses testified to earlier efforts by Rector and Moore to hire a hitman to kill the Sheriff.

In an ironic twist, Ethel Willis Medlock (she had remarried on May 9, 1929), and Henry Townsend, who had not testified at their own trial, were called to testify at the Rector/Moore trial about the "circumstances surrounding the slaying." The state tried to rebut the charge by the defense that Mrs. Willis and Townsend were the actual killers of the sheriff and that the state had charged Rector and Moore in a "frame-up" to "save face" after failing to convict them.

Ethel denied that the tracks left at the murder scene were hers and also denied that "she was a good shot with a pistol." Ethel also testified that the day after the funeral of her husband she telephoned Gov. J.G. Richards and indicated that she was interested in replacing her husband as sheriff but hoped that if she were not appointed, the job would go to Henry Townsend. She also testified that Carlos Rector had "enmity" for her husband.

Henry Townsend testified that he had been at home in bed at the time of the murder and had taken a taxi to the murder scene after receiving a call from Mrs. Willis that her husband had been killed. He denied "any improper relations between him and Mrs. Willis."

The state presented the pistol used to kill Willis which was found "in a clump of briars near Sterling College" where Rooks led them after confessing that he had thrown the gun away.

The defense presented an alibi witness for Moore. Carlos Rector took the stand in his own defense and denied that he even knew Rooks. Moore also took the stand in his own defense and "made a blanket denial of all charges." He testified that he was at a road construction camp ten miles north of Greenville the morning after the murder and not in the city as Rooks had testified. Several witnesses supported the alibi of Moore. Moore conceded that he knew Rooks as he was foreman of a road construction "gang" that included Rooks but never tried to hire him to kill the sheriff.

The defense gave the jury "20 reasons why the story of Rooks could not be believed" and suggested that Ethel Willis and Henry Townsend were the real killers and that their testimony had not explained some of their actions on the night of the murders. The defense also asked the jury not to believe the testimony of a negro laborer over that of a former (white) sheriff and his deputy.

The jury deliberated for over 23 hours over two days before convicting Rector and Moore of accessory after the fact of manslaughter on Wednesday, Dec. 10. The jury appeared to have been deadlocked at one point but asked the judge if the two could be found guilty of accessory after the fact of manslaughter and not murder. The judge told the jury that this verdict was legal, and within an hour, they returned with that verdict.

Both Rector and Moore were sentenced to 10 years in prison. Judge Dennis noted that accessory after the fact of manslaughter was subject to imprisonment from three months to ten years. At the sentencing Judge Dennis addressed Carlos Rector:

"When I heard that your name had been linked with this case, I did not believe you were guilty. Even when the trial opened I did not believe it but when the testimony had been concluded, I was convinced that you did have something to do with it—both of you did. ....

I am taking it for granted that you are guilty for the jury says you are.

In this country we have come to taking murder lightly. In fact, we frown with more horror upon the one who steals than he who kills. But there is a difference between the killer and the assassin.......As horrible as the killing of Sheriff Willis, I think it was more horrible for you to use your high office as sheriff and deputy, to try to place the crime upon two innocent people." (*Greenville News*, 12/13/1930)

The *Greenville News* indicated after the Rector/Moore trial that the "disposition" of Blair Rooks' case "would await developments in the Rector-Moore case, as the state may wish to use the negro as witness in the future if a new trial is held." Court records indicate that psychiatric exams were ordered for Rooks by Judge J.K. Henry on Sept. 24, Oct. 8, Oct. 31, Nov. 14, and Dec. 3, 1929, by Dr. J.L. Anderson. He spent most of this time at the S.C. State hospital in Columbia. Later newspaper articles indicated that Rooks pled guilty and was sentenced to life in prison. The *Greenville News* reported as late as May 10, 1932, that Rooks was still in prison but his date of release is unknown as the Dept. of Corrections has no records from the 1930's.

The conviction and sentence of Carlos Rector and J. Harmon Moore was upheld by the S.C. Supreme Court on July 2, 1932. The transcript of the trial ran to 1,500 typewritten pages according to court stenographer John Gilbert. "This was probably the most voluminous record of testimony in the history of criminal court."

According to the case file at the State Archives in Columbia, J. Harmon Moore was furloughed from prison on April 14-24, 1933, and was paroled on July 16, 1936. He was pardoned ("for the purpose of restoring his citizenship") on Jan. 9, 1939, by Gov. Olin D. Johnston.

On March 10, 1938, Gov. Olin D. Johnston paroled Carlos Rector "during good behavior" with the Governor "to be the sole judge of what he meant by good behavior." On Jan. 7, 1939, the Gov. pardoned Rector, restoring his citizenship.

Rector ran for Sheriff again in 1940 but was "overwhelmingly defeated." Carlos Rector died at the age of 82 on Sept. 30, 1966, and was buried at Graceland next to his brother, Hendrix Rector (the sheriff killed in the line of duty in 1919).

Henry Townsend, 45, was killed in a traffic accident on Oct. 28, 1935. He was survived by his wife, Minnie Henderson Townsend, and a son, Henry S. Townsend, Jr., 14. His wife died on May 4, 1956, at the age of 65.

THE OFFICER

Samuel Douthit Willis, 36, was born in Greenville County, S.C., on April 11, 1891, to Gideon T. and Julia Hollis Willis. His father (born in 1839) was one of the "oldest and most highly respected citizens of the county" and was a Confederate soldier (in the Hampton Legion, Co. E) who served throughout the Civil War. His mother (born in 1853) was the former Julia Hollis of Spartanburg.

Young Willis was educated at "Oaklawn school" and Central High School in Greenville. After high school he was employed by the Arnold Company and later "became connected with the mercantile firm of Henderson and Ashmore." His last job before becoming sheriff was with the Piedmont Shoe Company.

Willis, 19, joined the Butler Guards, the local militia, on Nov. 29, 1910, as a private. During his eight years with the unit he was promoted to corporal, sgt., second Lt., first Lt., and captain. His service as second Lt. began while the Butler Guards were on duty at the Mexican border in 1915. The Butler Guards were called to duty by Gov. Manning on April 12, 1917. On April 16, the 147 men left by train for Camp Styx in Lexington County. Willis' promotion to first Lt. was by competitive examination while the Guard was stationed at Camp Sevier in Laurens in the spring of 1917.

First Lt. Samuel Willis, 27, assumed command of Company A, 118th Infantry, in France in June of 1918 and "continued in active command" for ten days after the "breaking of the Hindenburg line by the Thirtieth Division, of which the Butler Guards were a part." Lt. Willis was wounded on Oct. 8, 1918, and was sent to a hospital at the front "for a time." Willis was promoted to captain after the armistice by Major W. Workman who made an exception to a general order which denied any post-war promotion except for "rare circumstances." Capt. Willis was "commissioned in recognition of service at the front," assumed command of the Guard again, and returned home from France to Camp Jackson where he was discharged on April 30, 1919.

Shortly after his return home on June 19, 1915, Willis married Ethel Gray of Americus, GA. He was appointed Sheriff of Greenville County by Gov. R.A. Cooper after the murder of Sheriff Hendrix Rector in July of 1919. Sheriff Willis became, at the age of 28, the youngest sheriff in the state. He ran for a full term as sheriff in 1920 but was defeated by Carlos A. Rector.

The funeral for Sheriff Willis was held on Monday, June 13, at the Triune Methodist Church. The gray casket, topped by a metal plate bearing the inscription, "Daddy," was carried from the Willis home to the church by the pallbearers. A crowd estimated at over 5,000 "packed" the church and "adjacent streets" for the eulogy (apparently broadcast over a loudspeaker). The service was attended by the "heavily veiled" widow who was "attended" by her brother-in-law, H.I. Tuck, of Norfolk, VA, and by Deputy Sheriff Henry Townsend.

Rev. H.O. Chambers, surrounded by a massive arrangement of "floral offerings" delivered the eulogy focusing on his contention that the murder was an assault not on a man alone but "upon the laws of the community." He said that he would not deliver a traditional eulogy as "this man's life was his greatest eulogy."

The burial at Springwood Cemetery was attended by over 5,000 persons "spread over several acres of territory about the grave" in perhaps the largest funeral ever held in the county to that date (or perhaps since). The Hejaz Shrine Temple, of which Willis was a member, "had charge" of the burial service at graveside. Also participating in the service were the members of Recovery Lodge no. 31, A.F.M. (a fraternal order).

Samuel D. Willis was survived by his widow, Ethel, 31; by four daughters, Virginia, 11, Julia, 6, Ethel, 4, and Marion, 2; his mother, Mrs. G.T. (Julia Hollis) Willis, 74; three sisters, Mrs. J.T. (Amelia) Blassingame, Mrs. H.E. (Grace) Stewart, Mrs. H.P. (Rose) Goodwin, and Mrs. C.A. (Gertrude) Ellis of Travelers Rest, and Mrs. E.R. (Lydia) Hutchings of Miami, FL; and a brother, W.C. Willis, who was a deputy under his brother "in active charge of collection of delinquent taxes."

Mrs. Willis, after the funeral, helped "handle the affairs" of the Sheriff's office as she was very knowledgeable of her husband's work. She gave serious consideration to the urging of friends that she "offer herself" to the Governor as the successor to her husband but decided not to do so.

In 1996 the grave of Sheriff Willis is easily found in Section G of Springwood Cemetery in downtown Greenville. The grave marker reads:

SAMUEL D. WILLIS
April 11, 1891
June 11, 1927
Capt. Co. A
118 INF 30th Div USA

Other family members buried in the Willis plot are his mother, Julia Hollis Willis, 82, (died Sept. 3, 1935); his father G.T. Willis, 82, (died Sept. 17, 1921); his widow, Ethel Gray Willis, 88, (died April 13, 1984); his daughter, Ethel Gray Willis, 37, (died Sept. 30, 1960); his sister, Rose Willis Goodwin, 96, (died on Aug, 13, 1978); his sister, Amelia Willis Blassingame, 81, (died Dec. 19, 1953); and his brother-in-law, J. Thomas Blassingame, 57, (died June 21, 1927—10 days after Sheriff Willis).

The Sheriff's widow, remarried (becoming Ethel Gray Willis Medlock) and moved to Atlanta, GA, in 1929. After her second husband's death in 1939, she moved to Americus, GA, and then to High Point, N.C., where she died on April 13, 1984, at the age of 88. She was buried at Springwood Cemetery in Greenville beside her first husband, Samuel Willis.

Also, by 1996, three of his four daughters had died. Ethel Gray Willis, 37, died in NYC in 1960, and was buried in Greenville beside her father. Julia Willis Denny (later Farnsworth) lived most of her life in Columbia, S.C., and died in 1979 at the age of 58. She was survived in 1996 by her son, Kenneth Denny, 46, of Durham, NC; a daughter, Gray Farnsworth, 31, and a son, Bland Farnsworth, 30, both of Columbia, S.C.

Virginia Willis Mortimer lived most of her life in High Point, N.C., and died in 1990 at the age of 74. She was survived in 1996 by five children: Lee Mortimer, 49, of Durham, NC; Margaret Mortimer, 47, of Atlanta; Beth Mortimer Foy, 45, of Cincinnati, OH; Allen Mortimer, 39, of Chattanooga, TN; and Judy Mortimer Meyler, 43, of Greensboro, NC.

Marion Willis Shealy, 70, of Columbia, SC, was the only surviving daughter of Sheriff Willis still living in 1996. She had one child, Julia Hess Mackey, 40, of Columbia.

In 1996 Sheriff Samuel Willis was survived by nine grandchildren and nine great, grandchildren. One great grandson, Samuel Mortimer of Chattanooga, was named after his great grandfather. Sheriff Willis had no direct descendants living in Greenville County in 1996 but a nephew, Henry Goodwin, did live in Greenville.

The name of Samuel D. Willis is inscribed (East Wall, Panel 39, Line 1) on the National Law Enforcement Memorial. A plaque bearing his name is displayed at the S.C. Criminal Justice Hall of Fame in Columbia. The Willis family did not know Sam Willis' name was on a national monument in Washington, D.C., until contacted by Dr. Wilbanks in June of 1996.

SOURCES: *Greenville News*, May 6, 1919, June 12,13,14,15,16,17,18,19, Aug. 23, 26-31, Sept. 1-10, 1927, Sept. 19, Oct. 27,28,29, Dec. 1-13,20, 1930, May 10, 1932, Oct. 29, 1935; Greenville County Criminal Court record #A-2685, #A-2995 and #A-3360 in Greenville and in State Archives in Columbia); Death certificate of Samuel Douthit Willis at S.C. State Archives; Springwood Cemetery directory; *Greenville: The History of the City and County in the S.C. Piedmont* by Archie Vernon Huff, Jr., pp. 281,322-323; "The Greenville County Sheriff's Office: Origins and History," unpublished manuscript by Johnny Mack Brown in Greenville Library; and interview with Marion Willis Shealy.

#19 DOCK M. GARRETT
Convict Guard
Killed by inmate during escape attempt on Sept. 19, 1929.

THE EVENT

Dock M. Garrett, 54, "a convict guard," was hit over the head with a shovel and killed by an inmate during an escape from his road work gang. The killer was executed in 1931.

Dock Garrett was struck on the back of the head with a shovel by an inmate in a "chaingang delivery" around 9:30 A.M. on Thursday, Sept. 19, 1929. The attack and attempted escape occurred at the "O'Neal section" north of Greer while Garrett was supervising a detachment of eleven prisoners near Pack's Mountain. The camp was under the supervision of Capt. Walter Willimon.

Garrett was standing and "looking away" with his hands in his pockets when he was struck and "fell on his face in the hard dirt." After Garrett was knocked unconscious, "one of the prisoners snatched his pistol" and six of the eleven "made the break for freedom." Two of the convicts who did not try to escape walked a mile in "double chains" to get help for Garrett.

Garrett was found a short time later by co-workers and rushed to the City Hospital in Greenville. He was admitted to the hospital around 11:00AM and died at 5:00PM. "he never fully regained consciousness, but at times appeared semi-conscious." The autopsy indicated that Garrett died of a "laceration of right side of brain, cerebral hemorrhage, fracture of skull, occipital and orbital plates."

The six inmates who escaped after Garrett was mortally wounded removed their leg shackles with an axe and hammer when they were only 75 feet from the murder site. They then split into two groups after getting away from the camp. One, 14-year-old Henry Townsend, who was serving a 300 day term for train hoboing, returned to the camp and surrendered claiming that he had not wanted to run off but the "others had forced him to do so." He identified the killer as Norman Blakely, "a 16-year-old negro."

Blakely and Henry Moon were captured shortly after the escape by Wade Barton, proprietor of Barton's store in the Terry Creek section (near the Buncombe Road) when the two men entered his store. Barton recognized them as escaped convicts even though they had "discarded their stripes and secured overalls and blue shirts." They had cut off their leg irons with an axe used by the chaingang to cut bushes. Blakely was taken to the Greenville County jail while Moon was returned to the chaingang.

A massive manhunt was organized to find the other three escapees identified as Charlie Enlow, Jess White and Jim Fleming. "Scores of persons, including deputy sheriffs dispatched from the office of Sheriff Cliff Bramlett, camp guards and enraged citizens of upper Greenville county" began a manhunt north and northwest of O'Neal to the North Carolina line. Bloodhounds borrowed from Sheriff John Craig of Pickens County aided in the search. A reward of $2,500 was offered for the arrest of the three convicts.

Enlow spent the night on Hogback Mountain which was 8 miles away but was caught the next day. After a five-day search it appeared that Jess White and James Flemming had escaped from the state.

THE PERPETRATOR

An inquest into the death of Dock Garrett was held on Saturday, Sept. 21, in the main courtroom at the courthouse. Henry Townsend, a "negro boy serving a 30-day sentence for trespassing" testified that he saw Blakely strike Garrett on the back of the head with a shovel and then reach over Garrett's body and take his gun before fleeing. The coroner's jury ruled that Blakely was responsible for Garrett's death.

Blakely was convicted of murder at his first trial in October of 1929 and sentenced to death but the original indictment was thrown out "on the ground that it was drawn faultily" and that "the grand jury which returned a true bill was not legally constituted." The S.C. Supreme Court granted Blakely a new trial on Oct. 20, 1930. The Greenville County grand jury returned a new indictment for murder against Blakely on Oct. 28, 1930. The second trial (which lasted only one day) ended on Monday, Nov. 3, 1930, and again resulted in a conviction and death sentence.

Solicitor J.G. Leatherwood argued for the state that Blakely committed a premeditated murder "for the purpose of effecting an escape from the gang on which he was serving a sentence." Dr. T.R.W. Wilson gave a report on the autopsy and told the jury that the "guard's head was shattered by a heavy blow from the rear." Deputy Sheriff E.L. Craigo testified that while he and Deputy Mack Parson had been hidden in the county jail, Blakely had shown Blair Rooks (who was awaiting trial for the murder of Sheriff Sam Willis) how he killed the guard.

C.S. Bowen and Lionel E. Wooten, attorneys appointed by the court to defend Blakely set up the defense that he was driven to the crime by frequent whippings and at the suggestion and command of older negroes on the gang who wished to escape and wanted to see the guard injured or killed....

Blakely took the stand to testify that he killed Garrett because older and larger negroes told him to do it to escape being whipped. He said he had been flogged several times. (*Greenville News*, 11/4/1930)

Two other convicts testified that beatings of chaingang convicts was common. The jury returned a verdict of guilty or murder with no recommendation to mercy and Judge E.C. Dennis of Darlington sentenced Blakely to death. A second appeal delayed the execution of the death sentence set for Dec. 19, 1930. However, the appeal was denied on Jan. 19, 1931, and Judge John S. Wilson set the execution date for March 27, 1931.

Norman Blakely, 18, was executed at the state penitentiary in Columbia on May 26, 1931. In his last statement before execution he admitted that he had killed Garrett and declared his faith. He became the sixth man executed in S.C. for a Greenville County crime after the state took over executions from the counties in 1912.

Garrett's daughter, Mrs. Calvin G. (Annie May) Howard and his brother, J.H. Garrett, witnessed the execution. The headline in the *Greenville News* stated: "Blakely Pays in Chair for Garrett Death; Greenville Negro Jovial to Last Moment, Laughing in Shadow; 18 See Execution." Blakely's body was returned to Greenville for burial.

THE OFFICER

Dock M. Garrett, 54, was born on June 15, 1875, in S.C. to Lewis and Eliza Bramlett Garrett. Both his parents were also born in S.C. His mother's obituary in 1927 indicated that she was a lifelong resident of Greenville County.

The 1920 S.C. census indicates that Dock M. Garrett, 46, was a farmer living in the Austin Township in Greenville County with his wife, Lillie M. Cox Garrett, 46, his son Junius G., 22, and his daughter Annie May, 16. His wife, Lillie Cox Garrett, 55, preceded him in death by three months as she died on June 28, 1929. Her obituary indicated that she was a life long resident of Greenville County and, at her death, lived at the family home on Hudson St., Sans Souci. She was the daughter of Isaac and Mary Moore Cox and grew up in the Austin township.

Dock Garrett's obituary in the *Greenville News* in 1929 indicated that he was survived by a son, Junius G. Garrett, 31, and a daughter, Mrs. Calvin G. (Annie Mae) Howard, 25; by one grandchild of Greenville; by three brothers, J.H. Garrett of Piedmont, T.N. Garrett of Laurens, and W.F. Garrett of Simpsonville; and by two sisters, Mrs. S.A. Fowler and Mrs. J.N. Clarke, both of Simpsonville.

The funeral service for Dock Garrett was held at the Mackey mortuary on N. Main at Elford. Services were conducted by the Rev. John N. Wren, assisted by the Rev. J.R. Moore and the Rev. Ben D. Davenport. "A large crowd of friends and relatives including persons with whom Mr. Garrett had worked since he became connected with the county about 10 years ago were present." Burial followed in the Standing Spring church cemetery near Simpsonville.

In 1996 the grave of Dock Garrett is easily found at the Standing Spring Baptist Church cemetery on Standing Spring Road near Simpsonville. The 3' by 4' stone monument that marks his grave reads:

DOCK M. GARRETTE

June 15, 1875

Sept. 19, 1929

It should be noted that the spelling (Garrette) on the marker is different from the spelling in the newspaper accounts and on the death certificate (i.e., Garrett). Buried beside Dock Garrett are his wife, Lillie Cox Garrette, 55 (who died on 6/28/1929); his father, R.L. Garrett, 80 (who died on 2/18/1912); and his mother, Eliza Bramlett Garrett, 91 (who died on 10/21/1927). Her obituary in the Oct. 22, 1927, *Greenville News* indicated that she was survived by four sons and two daughters (the siblings of Dock Garrett), J.H., Dock M., N.D. and William Garrett, Mrs. Susan Clarke and Mrs. S.A. Fowler of Greenville County; and by 28 grandchildren, 82 great-grandchildren and 7 great-great-grandchildren.

Junius Garrett never married and died in the 1940's. He was buried at the Standing Springs church cemetery in an unmarked grave by his father. However, there are living descendants of Dock Garrett through Annie Mae Garrett Howard, 81, who died in Greenville on March 11, 1983, and was buried at Woodlawn Cemetery in Greenville. Annie Mae and her husband George Calvin Howard had one son, George Calvin Howard, Jr., who in turn had two children (the great grandchildren of Dock Garrett), Alan Howard and Janet Howard.

No descendants of Dock Garrett could be located in 1996 though Alan and

Janet Howard were thought to be living in New Orleans. Perhaps readers of this narrative will contact Dr. Wilbanks about the whereabouts of any of Garrett's descendants?

The name of Dock M. Garrett will be added to the National Law Enforcement Memorial in 1996 as his "line of duty death" status was unknown to Greenville authorities until "discovered" by Dr. Wilbanks. A plaque bearing his name will also be displayed in 1996 at the S.C. Criminal Justice Hall of Fame in Columbia.

SOURCES: *Greenville News*, Oct. 22, 1927, June 30, 1929, Sept. 20,21,22,23,24, 1929, Oct. 28,29, Nov. 3,4, 1930, Jan. 20, May 27, 1931; Greenville Criminal Court file (#A-2617 MIC-94-1485); Death certificate of Dock M. Garrett (#15805) in SC Archives in Columbia; Criminal Court file of Norman Blakely (#A-2617) in SC State Archives; 1920 SC census of Greenville County (E.D. 1, Sheet 12, Line 87);and *Legal Homicide: Death as Punishment in America, 1864-1982*, Appendix A, p. 499; and interview with Evelyn Garrett.

#20 PERRY PARIS
Deputy Sheriff
Killed by auto during foot chase of bootlegger, Oct. 24, 1930.

THE EVENT

Greenville County Deputy Sheriff Perry Paris, 36, was hit by an auto as he chased a bootlegger across the "Spartanburg highway" on Oct. 24, 1930. He became the first known Greenville County law enforcement officer to be killed in an on-duty traffic accident. The driver of the auto that struck Paris was charged with murder but the charges were eventually dropped.

Deputy Paris "had gone to a Tourist camp" on the Spartanburg highway about 3 miles west of Greer "late Friday" (Oct. 24, 1930) with Deputy Fleet Craigo and two Spartanburg constables, F.H. Johnson and C.L. Harrison, to arrest a man on a liquor charge.

The four officers arrested the man and were taking him to one of their cars when the prisoner suddenly "bolted." He crossed the road and fled through a corn field on the opposite side of the road. The three other officers started to pursue (on foot) while Paris "got in his automobile and rode down the road toward Greer in an effort to head the man off."

Greenville, South Carolina Deputy Sheriff, Perry Paris, 36, was killed by an auto during a footchase of a bootlegger on Oct. 24, 1930. His name is inscribed on the National Law Enforcement Memorial in Washington, DC.

Paris drove 100 yards down the road and stopped near a culvert as the chase neared that point. The deputy exited his vehicle and was told by Deputy Craigo that the fugitive had gone under the culvert. Paris had to cross the busy highway to get to the culvert.

The deputy started across and stopped to let a passing auto by. As he started on again a Ford sedan traveling at what officers said was a fairly rapid rate of speed hit him, flinging the body across to the left and against the railing.....The machine, driven by Mr. McGill, of Charlotte, stopped. (*Greenville News*, 10/25/1930)

The body of Paris had been thrown 20 feet by the impact of the collision. The other three officers abandoned the chase for the bootlegger and "rushed to the scene of the tragedy." Paris' "body was picked up limp" and placed in a automobile driven by J.W. Walker, a "Greenville traveling man," who had stopped there and was "hurried" to Chick Springs Hospital. Deputy Paris died on the way to the hospital. The body was then taken to Greenville to the Jones-McAfee Funeral Home.

THE PERPETRATOR

E.P. McGill was held by Sheriff Cliff Bramlett pending the outcome of the inquest to be held at 3:00PM the next day. Coroner Joe Wooten placed seven witnesses on the stand during the inquest. Several pages of testimony from the inquest can be found in the microfilm record of the court case against McGill at the Greenville County courthouse. The *Greenville News* also gave excerpts of the testimony under a story headlined, "Hold E.P. McGill, Charlotte, for Tragic Death of Deputy Perry Paris."

The first to take the stand was Dr. T.R.W. Wilson, who performed the autopsy. He testified that there were "fractures of both legs and the left arm, rupture of the heart, and brush wounds of the face, forehead, and head." The rupture of the heart was caused by a blow that struck the officer in the chest breaking some of the rib cartilages.

T.B. Suddeth, who operated a "filling station" about 75 yards from the scene of the accident testified that Paris was in the center of the road when he was struck by the car that "was traveling at a fairly rapid rate of speed." Constable C.L. Harrison, part of the "chase team," testified that the auto was "making 40 or 45 miles an hour" when it hit Paris. He also said that the auto driven by McGill was traveling in the wrong lane.

The verdict of the coroner's inquest was not reported in the Oct. 26 newspaper article (or the following day) but court records indicate that the verdict was that "Paris died from injuries sustained when he was struck by an auto driven by E.P. McGill."

McGill was indicted for murder on the "first Monday in December" (Dec. 1, 1930) for "feloniously, willfully and with malice aforethought" striking Paris with his auto. There is no indication in the record why the grand jury thought the actions of McGill were "willful" and with "malice aforethought." The case was continued by the court of general sessions on March 9, 1931, and on August 31, 1932, before being nolle prossed in Jan. of 1932 (15 months after the death of Paris).

Little information was provided by the newspapers or court records about McGill other than he was a "young" insurance man from Charlotte.

THE OFFICER

Perry Payton Paris was born in 1895 in the Mountainview community in Greenville County to John Morgan Paris (1857-1939). and Martha Ferguson Paris. Both his parents were also born in Greenville County. Perry's mother died in 1897 when he was three years old and he was raised by his father and stepmother, Alice Ferguson Paris.

Perry grew up in the Oneal township near Mountainview (now part of Taylors) with his four brothers and five sisters. All the Paris children attended the Mountainview School. As a youth and adult, Perry was an avid hunter and fisherman.

Around 1916, Perry, 21, married Cora Howell, also of the Oneal township. Their only child, King, was born on Feb. 24, 1917. Perry Paris was a farmer before he became a Greer police officer in 1919 at the age of 24.

Perry Paris was a "patrolman" in Greer for nine years before his two-year tenure as a Greenville County deputy sheriff began in 1928. During his 11-year law enforcement career, "he had close calls with death while in discharge of his duty" on "several occasions."

The *Greenville News* reported that during his nine years in Greer he "made many friends and was a fearless officer and citizen" and that he "was well known throughout this section, and has many friends that will learn with regret of his untimely death." The newspaper also reported that "Mr. Paris was one of the most efficient and congenial men on the sheriff's force." Sheriff Bramlett "deplored the tragic passing of his deputy and declared he felt a deep personal loss in addition to losing 'one of the best officers I ever knew.'" The sheriff added:

Perry was brave to the very last and never thought of shirking his duty. He was congenial and capable and made friends wherever he went. He took a pride in his personal appearance and was always neat. It's going to be hard to fill his place. (*Greenville News,* 10/25/1930)

The newspaper also reported that Paris was "popular among his associates and throughout the county and that "gloom settled over the sheriff's office last night as the deputies went about their duties with the thought of their comrade's untimely death."

Deputy Paris was survived by his father, John Morgan Paris, 73, and stepmother, Alice Paris, 65, of Oneal township; his widow, Cora Howell Paris, 32, and one son, King, 13, of Greer; by four brothers, Ben Paris, of Greenville, and John Paris, Guy Paris, and James Paris, of Taylors; by five sisters, Mrs. Ida Crain, of Greer, Mrs. Alice Kelly, and Mrs. Dallas Coster, of Travelers Rest, Mrs. J.T. (Miron) Collins, and Miss Lillie Paris, of Taylors; and by a "large family connection."

The viewing of the body before the Sunday funeral was held at the Deputy's home on Fairview Ave. in Greer. The funeral was held at the Washington Baptist Church (five miles north of Greer) on Sunday, Oct. 26. A large crowd attended the funeral including many police officers in uniform. However, the service was not a police or military style service.

The services were conducted by the Rev. Shields T. Hardin, pastor, assisted by the Rev. W.J. Bolt of Inman. "Active" pallbearers included Greer Police Chief W.J. Tapp and "patrolmen" C.F. Liverett, A.A. Finley, Green Taylor and Bob Wood. The "honorary escort" included "members of Sheriff Bramlett's force," Deputy Prohibition Administrator J.A. Clifton, Greer Mayor B.A. Bennett and six Greer "aldermen."

The burial services, conducted by the Masons, followed in the adjoining churchyard cemetery. The slain deputy's widow eventually remarried (becoming Mrs. Cora Sloan) but was buried by his side upon her death in 1985. His father, John Morgan Paris, died in 1939 at the age of 82. His stepmother, Alice Paris, died in 1938, at the age of 73. Both were buried at the Double Springs Baptist Church cemetery on Highway 290 near Greer.

In 1996 the grave of Deputy Paris is easily found in the small Washington Baptist Church cemetery five miles north of Greer on Highway 14. The grave marker reads:

PERRY P. PARIS
B. 1895
D. 1930

The marker also includes the word, "Masonic," as Paris was a member of Bailey Masonic Lodge No. 146 in Greer.

In 1996, King Paris, 79, remained in Greer living in the same house on Fairview Ave. occupied by his father in 1930. King's two sons, Marion Paris, 58, and Larry Paris, 52 (the grandchildren of Deputy Paris) also lived in Greer. Deputy Perry Paris is also survived by four great, grandchildren who live in Greenville County: Myron Paris, 28, and Avery Paris, 25 (the children of Marion Paris) and Shane Paris, 28, and Page Paris, 25 (the children of Larry Paris).

The line of duty death of Deputy Perry Paris was forgotten by the Greenville County Sheriff's office and was not listed on their 1996 list of officers killed in the line of duty. The "discovery" of the "forgotten hero" came as the result of a June 12, 1996, article in the *Greenville News* that reported on Dr. Wilbanks' research on slain Greenville County law enforcement officers. Marie Waters, a niece of Perry Paris, called to report that her "favorite uncle" should have been on the list of slain officers.

Sheriff Johnny Mack Brown then added Deputy Paris to his list of slain officers and sent documentation to the National Law Enforcement Memorial in Washington, D.C., so that his name would be inscribed on that monument in 1996. The name of Perry Payton Paris will also be displayed on a plaque at the S.C. Criminal Justice Hall of Fame in Columbia in 1996. Thus in 1996 a forgotten hero was remembered.

SOURCES: *Greenville News*, Oct. 25,26, 1930; Criminal Court case #A-3126 (MIC 100-855); Cemetery markers at Washington Baptist Church in Greer; and interview with King Paris.

#21 A.B. HUNT
Greenville Police Dept.
Shot & killed by bandits on May 1, 1932.

THE EVENT

Motorcycle Officer Absolom Blythe (A.B.) Hunt, 31, a 2-year veteran of the Greenville Police Dept. was shot and killed on May 1, 1932, by a gang of five bandits in a shootout with three Greenville police officers. Four of the five men were eventually captured but only one, the "shooter," was prosecuted. He pled guilty and received a life sentence in 1936.

A.B. Hunt

Around 10:00PM on Sunday, May 1, 1932, two men telephoned the Blue Ribbon Taxicab Co. from a lunchroom and fruit stand at 712 Buncombe St. in Greenville. The taxi dispatcher and driver became suspicious when the called asked what kind of cars they had. Both feared that the caller might want the cab for some type of crime and also feared a robbery. Several taxis had been robbed and hijacked in recent months. The driver left his money with the dispatcher and drove to the pickup site.

The two men told the taxi driver that they wanted him to take them to Greer (13 miles away). The driver told them he had only one gallon of gas (a precaution against hijackings) but that if they would wait a moment he would go and get more gas. However, the driver went to the police station and told police that he was suspicious of the two men and wanted them to investigate. The police agreed to stop and question the two men. The driver returned to the pickup site and the two "flashily-dressed men" got in the rear of the taxi.

Before the taxi had moved 25 yards, the police car drove up and forced the taxi to the curb in front of the Triangle Service Station. The police car was occupied by Det. John Corea, Det. Cliff Singleton and Motorcycle Officer A.B. Hunt (the only officer in uniform). Greenville Chief of Police J.E. Smith later told the story of the shooting in an article published in a detective magazine.

The three officers jumped out of their car, Hunt running to the right side of the taxi and Singleton and Corea covering the left side. As they did so the negro driver heard one of his passengers mutter:

"It's the cops. We've got to do something!."

Officer Hunt opened the right rear door of the taxi and at that moment the inside of the car lit up as the two passengers commenced shooting at the officers. All three officers returned the fire and wounded both men, silencing their guns. Singleton wounded the larger of the two with his first shot and then disabled the other occupant of the taxi. Corea had been shooting, but one of the first bullets from the taxi's passengers had struck the cylinder of his gun, causing the weapon to jam and rendering it useless. The bullet splattered and a portion of it ripped through the fleshy part of Corea's face.

As he was hit, the larger of the two men in the cab fell out of the right rear door into Hunt's arms. At the same moment Singleton reached in and dragged out the other passenger. (*Master Detective Magazine*, Sept, 1937)

At this point the three officers seemed to have the situation under control but that changed suddenly as a second "bandit car," apparently a back-up, arrived on the scene to rescue the two wounded bandits.

In a flash a maroon coach rolled by, and one man, gun in hand, jumped out and ran toward the cab. At the same moment a machine-gun began spitting lead from the rear window of the coach as it drove slowly up Rutherford Street. The gunman who had left the coach came up behind Officer Hunt, who was still supporting in his arms the wounded gunman who had fallen out of the taxi.

"Copper!" shouted the gunman to Officer Hunt, who was the only man in uniform. "Stick 'em up!" (*Master Detective Magazine*, Sept. 1937)

The gunman fired twice at Hunt at point blank range. One steel-jacket bullet "cut under Hunt's fifth rib on the left side, severed the aorta, and buried itself in the spinal column." Hunt died instantly.

The wounded gunman twisted away from Hunt's falling body and staggered toward the third bandit. Detective Singleton, attracted by the renewed gunfire, dropped his prisoner to the pavement, came around the side of the taxi and fired five bullets straight into the body of the gunman who had shot Hunt. The bandit car rolled back in reverse, and as Corea and Singleton pulled Hunt back out of the line of fire and tried to reply with their pistols to the machine-gun the remaining occupants of the bandit car dragged all three wounded gunmen into their auto and sped away up Rutherford Street, the machine-gun beating a tattoo as they went. The detectives had exhausted their supply of ammunition and were powerless to stop the escape of the thugs. (*Master Detective Magazine*, Sept., 1937)

Officer Hunt was picked up by an ambulance and rushed to the city hospital where he was pronounced dead on arrival. A later autopsy would reveal that the bullet entered his left side, severed the aorta, and lodged against the spine.

Hunt's body was taken to the Jones/McAfee funeral home for an autopsy. Det. Corea was struck on the left cheekbone and right hand but was not seriously wounded and participated for a time in the manhunt before going to the hospital for treatment. Singleton was not wounded in the shootout.

THE PERPETRATORS

A massive manhunt began almost immediately after the shootout as all available Greenville officers and Sheriff's deputies converged on the scene of the shootout. Roadblocks were set up on all highways out of town with orders to stop any car fitting the description of the roadster. Knowing that at least two of the five men involved in the shootout and escape were wounded, police called all hospitals within a hundred miles to be on the lookout for the wounded men.

The police investigation later revealed that from 75-100 shots were fired in the shootout and escape though none of the many bystanders were hit by the gunfire. It appeared that the machine-gun was mostly fired into the air to intimidate the officers and the crowd. Police located fifteen witnesses to the shooting and took them to police headquarters for questioning. Police determined that three cabs had been called that night in an effort to hijack a taxi. Investigators theorized that the gang was in town for a bank robbery and hoped to use the hijacked taxis to escape.

Six hours after the shootout, Ray Bailey, 22, who fit the police description of the fugitive who shot and killed Officer Hunt, was admitted to the hospital at Sylva, N.C. with gunshot wounds. Greenville police drove to Sylva and determined that Bailey was one of the five men involved in the murder of Officer Hunt. Greenville Detectives Singleton and Corea saw Bailey in the hospital bed and identified him as the man who shot Hunt and as the man Singleton shot five times.

Fearing that other members of the gang might try to rescue Ray Bailey from the Sylva hospital, the Greenville police (and later N.C. Highway Patrol officers) set up an armed guard around the hospital. The FBI even joined the "reinforcements" when evidence indicated that the gang resembled one which had robbed the Federal post office at Travellers Rest, S.C.

The five men involved in the shootout in Greenville that took the life of Officer Hunt were apparently part of a "bandit gang" that had been involved in numerous crimes and was based in Yancey County, N.C. "All had criminal records." Investigators believed that the gang had intended to hijack the taxi and use it for a safe-cracking or robbery before escaping in the Ford roadster.

Vernon Bailey, 36, was arrested when he came to visit his brother in the Sylva hospital. Reese Bailey, 26, was captured (on May 6) and was arrested as he slept in a tobacco barn near his home at Burnsville, N.C., by Yancey County officers. He had two pistols, a shotgun and a rifle at his side when arrested. Reese Bailey was familiar with Greenville as he had been a student at Furman University from 1927-1929.

Shortly after the Hunt murder, Ray Bailey was arrested at the Sylva Hospital and charged with murder. Greenville authorities filed for extradition to bring the four men (the three Bailey brothers and a fourth member of the gang) back to Greenville for prosecution.

Ray, Reese and Vernon Bailey were the sons of Gus Bailey of Jacks Creek in Yancey County. The Bailey family, which was "politically and financially powerful in western North Carolina," hired Clyde R. Hoey, "a prominent North Carolina attorney," who petitioned for a writ of habeas corpus for the three Bailey brothers and a fourth member of the gang, Osborne Briggs, 29 (who was married to a sister of the Bailey brothers).

According to the 1930 *Asheville Times*, "no other family in North Carolina has a more interesting and romantic history as that of the Bailey family of Western North Carolina and Eastern Tennessee. The "original" members of the Bailey family emigrated to Virginia in the "early part of the 17th century." A later descendant, Ancel Bailey, settled in Yancey County in western N.C. and his son, John "Yellow Jacket John" Bailey donated the land for the Burnsville city square.

Many of the Bailey ancestors are buried in the Bailey cemetery at Bailey Hill, near Toledo.

A four volume family history of the Baileys by Dr. Lloyd Richard Bailey is in the Burnsville, N.C., public library across from the city square. Dr. Bailey, a professor of Hebrew Bible at Duke University, is a "distant cousin" of the Baileys and is the foremost authority on the history of Yancey County. He is the author of *The Heritage of the Toe River Valley* and *Images of Yancey County* and provided information to this author about the Bailey brothers.

The habeas corpus hearing for the four alleged bandits was held on May 10, 1932, in Asheville, NC, before Judge H. Holye Sink. Solicitor Zeb Nettles of the nineteenth NC judicial circuit presented the case for Greenville authorities and offered as evidence the SC murder warrants and affidavits stating that the four had been identified as members of the gang and were in Greenville at the time of the shootout.

However, Judge Sink ruled for the four bandits (i.e., granted the writs of habeas corpus) and denied custody of them to SC authorities. The fourth (alleged) bandit freed was Osborne Briggs. However, Vernon Bailey's parole (for a manslaughter conviction for the killing of two men) was revoked and he was returned to prison to serve the remainder of his seven year sentence (he had served three before being paroled). Vernon was also wanted for an armed robbery in Buncombe County. Reese Bailey was arrested by Buncombe County officers and charged with highway robbery.

The fourth member of the gang was set free by the judge while Ray Bailey was held pending appeal of the judge's decision. Apparently, SC authorities appealed only the ruling setting Ray Bailey free and the other three bandits were never taken into SC custody.

Another gang member, Peek Royston was captured in Johnson City, TN, in August of 1932, when police found the getaway car used in the Greenville shootout. However, since he had escaped from jail after a federal conviction for a post office robbery, he was taken to the federal penitentiary in Atlanta. Greenville authorities filed a detainer so that Royston would be held on accessory to murder charges in SC after his release from prison in Atlanta.

A second hearing set to consider the release of Ray Bailey was held on June 27 in Sylva, NC, before Judge W.E. Moore. Thirteen officers and fifteen witnesses traveled from Greenville to the hearing. Police Chief J.E. Smith would later state:

This time our case was air-tight. We presented witnesses who swore that they had seen Ray Bailey shoot down officer Hunt; who swore that Bailey had been wounded on Sunday night, May 1st, in identically the same manner that Hunt's slayer had been wounded by Singleton; who swore that Bailey's thumb wound corresponded exactly with the mark of a bullet on the gun dropped by Hunt's slayer. And he had the positive, unshakable identification of Bailey as the slayer, by Detectives Singleton and Corea.

Against this Bailey, appearing gaunt and wan in a wheel chair, presented an affidavit that he had been shot by his best friend, Howell Wilson, and had gone to the remote hospital and given a fictitious name in order to avoid unfavorable publicity for Wilson. Wilson was not present at the trial, although Mr. Hoey presented his affidavit supporting Ray Bailey's statement. (*Master Detective Magazine,* Sept., 1937)

But again, perhaps due to the political influence of the Bailey family in western NC, Judge Moore ruled that insufficient evidence had been submitted to release Bailey to SC authorities. The state of SC filed an appeal against Judge Moore's ruling to the NC Supreme Court. The Greenville coroner's jury, which had been waiting for testimony from Ray Bailey, met without him and recommended that he be held for the murder of Hunt. The August grand jury returned an indictment of murder against Bailey.

In October of 1932, the NC Supreme Court upheld Judge Moore's decision to refuse custody of Ray Bailey to Greenville authorities. SC Attorney General John M. Daniel appealed the ruling of the NC Supreme Court to the U.S. Supreme Court. On May 23, 1933, the U.S. Supreme Court reversed the NC Supreme Court and ruled that Ray Bailey should be turned over to SC authorities for prosecution.

However, Bailey, heard of the U.S. Supreme Court ruling, and "retreated to his impenetrable mountain hideaways" before SC authorities could arrest him. Bailey was able to elude SC police for 2 & 1/2 years though he had several narrow escapes.Each time he was "flushed out" of a Blue Ridge mountain hideaway he would escape in a "treechoked gorge"or "boulder-strewn slope." The closest "near capture" came on Sept. 22, 1935, near Rosman NC when police surrounded a cabin occupied by Bailey. However, he escaped out a cabin window into the darkness.

The hunt ended a week later (in October of 1935) in Gainesville, GA, when Ray Bailey was arrested by local police. However, Greenville police almost "lost" him again as the Gainesville police were holding out for a larger reward from N.C. authorities (who wanted him for a series of robberies) and refused to surrender their prisoner. They finally agreed to release Bailey to Greenville authorities when served with a federal warrant for Bailey's arrest by U.S. Marshal Reuben Gosnell.

Ray Bailey, 26, was taken to the Greenville County jail on Oct. 4, 1935, four years after the murder of Officer Hunt. The state prosecution team was led by Solicitor J.G. Leatherwood and County Solicitor W.A. Bull. Bailey's defense team included attorneys Clyde R. Hoey of Shelby, NC (who was running for Governor of NC at the time), W.C. Mann of Pickens, Redden and Redden of Hendersonville, and W.E. Bowen and C.G. Wyche of Greenville. The defense asked the court for a change of venue to Pickens County arguing that their client could not get a fair trial in Greenville due to the great amount of publicity about the case.

However, on Jan. 13, 1936, Bailey suddenly and unexpectedly accepted a plea offer from the state. He pled guilty to first degree murder with the state consenting to a "recommendation to mercy" so that he would avoid the death penalty. He was sentenced that same day by Judge A.L. Gaston of Chester to "spend the remainder of his natural life in the state penitentiary or on public works of the county." The decision as to whether he would spend the life sentence on the county chain gang or in the state prison was apparently left to County Supervisor J. Ed Means who had not made a decision by Jan. 14.

Bailey still claimed to be innocent and claimed that he was the victim of "false witnesses" but could not fight the case due to a lack of funds (even though he obviously had enough money to hire a team of expensive lawyers). Bailey broke down and "sobbed audibly" during his sentencing.

Bailey remained in prison for 28 years (from 1936 to 1964) though he escaped (temporarily) on two occasions. On July 3, 1950, he walked away from a prison farm at Boykin, SC, where he was a trusty and rode a bus to Raleigh, NC. "He surrendered there, announcing that he wanted to test his conviction in court, but South Carolina officials took him back to the penitentiary in Columbia."

Then in March, 1957, Bailey, escaped a farm detail but left $18,000 in securities at the prison bank. He invested his earnings made in selling leather goods in the stock market. The money, still unclaimed, has been drawing interest ever since.

He was recaptured in West Yellowstone, Montana and returned to prison where he stayed until July, 1964, when his conviction was overturned. (*Greenville News*, Jan. 1, 1967)

In July of 1964, Bailey was freed by a lower court ruling (by State Circuit Court Judge John Grimball) that overturned his conviction on the grounds that he had pled guilty only after the prosecution promised an early parole (after 10 years). Bailey posted a $10,000 bond and returned to the mountains of Yancey County, N.C. The S.C. Supreme Court reversed the lower court decision and ordered Bailey back to prison to complete his sentence but he went into hiding again.

Bailey, 57, was recaptured on Dec. 30, 1966, in Tucson, AZ. Bond was set at $50,000 and Bailey refused to waive extradition. Greenville bondsman Luke Forrester had to forfeit the $10,000 bond to the court as the capture came one day too late. Bailey was returned to prison in Columbia and, after more litigation, was returned to the Greenville County Jail on Oct. 29, 1967, under orders from the S.C. Supreme Court to either try him again or release him.

On Monday, Dec. 2, 1968, Bailey was indicted again by a Greenville grand jury. A jury was drawn the next day by Circuit Judge John Grimball but on Thursday, Dec. 4, 1968, Solicitor B.O. Thomason, Jr. announced that Bailey would not be tried again and nolle prossed the case. Since the prosecutor's dismissal came after a jury had been drawn, the court ruled that Bailey was dismissed "forever" (i.e., could not be tried again).

Solicitor Thomason cited several reasons for his decision to dismiss the case. First, he noted that Bailey, 59, had served 23 years, 9 months and 12 days which was "10 years longer than the average life termer." Second, his investigative team (which included Circuit Court criminal investigator Johnny Mack Brown) concluded that the case would be difficult to try again after 32 years though eye witnesses were still available. Third, the solicitor consulted with members of Officer A.B. Hunt's family who did not oppose the decision to not retry Bailey. Finally, Thomason noted that there was a letter in the court file from the solicitor in 1932 promising Bailey parole after 10 years if he pled guilty. However, Thomason noted that parole was contingent on good behavior and he had not been a model prisoner. His misbehavior in prison included

cutting a guard, breaking into a room, seeking alcoholic beverages, two escapes and then his complete disregard for a court order which ordered him to appear in Greenville for disposition of his case on January 28, 1966. This was in effect a third escape.

"We might add that while Bailey was out of prison under Judge Grimball's legal order, he was charged with disorderly conduct and reckless driving on the Blue Ridge Parkway in North Carolina and was sentenced to 90 days in jail, suspended upon payment of a $100 fine." (*Greenville News*, 12/5/1968)

Ray Bailey's 1968 release was greeted by a "group of well-wishers and relatives, mostly from North Carolina" who crowded around him after the verdict. A free man, he returned to his home in North Carolina.

In 1996, Ray Bailey, 86, still lived in the mountains near Burnsville, N.C.

Vernon Bailey was released from prison in 1963 at the age of 67. He died on Dec. 22, 1983, at the age of 87 and was buried with his relatives on Jacks Creek in Yancey County.

Reese Bailey was convicted of a 1932 robbery in Buncombe County, NC, and sentenced to 7-10 years in prison. He escaped from the NC prison and "shot his way out" of a "G-man trap" in Chillicothe, OH, on Nov. 13, 1936, but was recaptured shortly after. Reese Bailey was also convicted in federal court for a robbery and assault against federal officers in Rosalia, Washington, in 1935. He was sentenced to 20 years in prison and was sent to Alcatraz in 1937. He was later sentenced to life for a 1946 murder and was sent to Leavenworth and Atlanta federal prisons. Reese Bailey was paroled in 1959 and pardoned in 1962 (at the age of 57). When his legal troubles were over he returned to farming in Yancey County, NC.

THE OFFICER

Absolom Blythe Hunt, 31, was born on Dec. 17, 1901, in the Travelers Rest area and was also raised in that section of Greenville County. He was one of nine children born to Benjamin Franklin Hunt and Eulalia Nicoll Hunt, who were also born in S.C.

Previous to his service with the police department, A.B. Hunt had been employed by the Southern railway at Asheville, N.C., for five years. He was a member of the Brotherhood of Railway Trainmen. Hunt joined the Greenville Police Dept. on Oct. 21, 1930, and served first as a traffic officer and then as a motorcycle officer. He was a two-year veteran of the Dept. at the time of his death.

The funeral service for Officer Hunt was held on Tuesday, May 3, at the Liberty Baptist Church (where Hunt was a member), five miles north of Travelers Rest. Over 600 mourners attended the service and overflowed the 350-seat country church so that many had to stand in the churchyard. Most city officials attended as did many police officers from Greenville and surrounding cities. A delegation of police officers from Asheville, N.C., also attended as Hunt had lived in that city for five years before becoming a Greenville police officer.

The eulogy was delivered by the Rev. B. Rhett Turnipseed, pastor of the Buncombe Methodist Church and the Rev. S.W. Jolly, pastor of the Monaghan Baptist Church. Rev. Turnipseed told the audience that "his death shall not have been in vain if it sets in motion the power of the law to put down the gangster rule and the wave of criminality now sweeping our land." Six fellow Greenville officers served as pallbearers and carried the casket from the church to the graveyard outside the building.

A.B. Hunt was survived by one sister, Mrs. Laten Springfield of Travelers

Rest and three brothers, Roy F. Hunt of Greenville, Paul Hunt of Travelers Rest and S.L. Hunt of Asheville. The slain officer was not married and had no children. His father (1931) and mother (1922) preceded him in death.

In 1996 the gravesite of A.B. Hunt is located in the cemetery beside the New Liberty Baptist Church five miles north of Travelers Rest on Highway #25. The grave is marked by a two ft. tall stone monument which reads:

Absolom Blythe Hunt
Dec. 17, 1901
May 1, 1932
Not My Will But Thine Be Done

Four other family members are buried in the Hunt family plot at the New Liberty Baptist Church Cemetery. Officer Hunt is buried beside his father, Benjamin F. Hunt, who died on June 16, 1931, at the age of 71; his mother, Eula Nicoll Hunt, who died on Dec. 8, 1922, at the age of 55; his sister, Leila Hunt, who died on Jan. 6, 1906, at the age of 9 months; and his brother, Thomas J. Hunt, who died on Oct. 18, 1918, at the age of 19.

In 1996 there were no direct descendants of A.B. Hunt as he had no children and none of his eight siblings were still living. However, the slain officer was survived in 1996 by three nephews and six nieces. Among this number were Azalee S. Lindsey of Travellers Rest; Roy F. Hunt, Jr., Ben H. Runion, and Lucille Collins of Greenville; Ruth Heinly of Anderson, S.C.; Bettie Henry of Fairview, NC; Virginia Jameson of Asheville, NC; and Kay Patricia Alford of Houston, TX. Ms. Lindsey's son, Steven L. Lindsey, was a 22-year veteran of the Greenville County Sheriff's Office.

The name of A.B. Hunt is inscribed (East Wall, Panel 61, Line 14) on the National Law Enforcement Memorial in Washington, D.C., and a plaque bearing his name is displayed at the S.C. Criminal Justice Hall of Fame in Columbia.

SOURCES: *Greenville News*, May 2,3,4, 1932, Oct. 5,6,24,28,29, 1935, Jan. 14, 1936, Oct. 11, 1965, Jan. 1, 1967, Dec. 5, 1968; *Asheville Times,* Sept. 21, 1930, May 11, 1932; *Hendersonville Times-News,* May 11, June 28, 1932; "Blasting the Blue Ridge Bandits," by Greenville Police Chief J.E. Smith as told to R.L. Waldrop, Jr., in *Master Detective Magazine*, Sept., 1937; Death certificate of A.B. Hunt in S.C. Archives; Criminal Court case of Ray Bailey (D-5018 MIC 569-807); "The History of the Greenville City Police Department, 1845-1976" by S.M. Batson, 1976, unpublished manuscript in Greenville City Library; Greenville County criminal court record #A4561; Grave markers at New Liberty Baptist Church Cemetery; interview with and family records (and photograph) provided by Azalee S. Lindsey; and interview with and Bailey family records provided by historian Lloyd Richard Bailey of Burnsville, N.C.

#22 EDWIN D. MILAM
S.C. Highway Patrol
Shot & beat to death by two men at a disturbance on Dec. 25, 1934.

THE EVENT

Edwin Deronda Milam, 25, a rookie trooper with the S.C. Highway Patrol, was shot and beaten to death while trying to quell a "disturbance" at a Christmas party outside a church near Mauldin. The two killers were convicted and sentenced to death and were executed in 1935.

Trooper Milam had spent Christmas day (Tuesday, Dec. 25) with his widowed mother, Marie Milam, in Newberry and was returning to Greenville on his motorcycle in the "late afternoon" (it was still daylight). He was flagged down by the leader of the Laurel Creek Colored Methodist Church which was just off the highway a mile north of Mauldin. Milam was told that there was a disturbance at the churchyard by drunk and unruly men and was asked "to quell the fighting and general disorder at the negro Christmas tree celebration." The complainant made it clear that the unruly men were uninvited and the church had no part in the disorder.

Milam rode up on his motorcycle and parked it between the church and the schoolhouse. He walked up to the crowd and said, "You negroes go on home." Witnesses said that Harry Hill, 26, with an open pocket knife in his hand, then said, "You white son of a bitch, we'll go when we are ready." Milam started toward Hill when Cornell Luster, 25, spoke up and said, "You've got no business here. This place is not on the road." Luster then drew a pistol out of his overalls. Hill and Luster were not the only two defying the orders of Milam as "others stalked about threateningly, given courage through drink."

Milam demanded that Luster give him his gun but Luster refused and began to back away from Milam. As Milam approached Luster, Hill began striking at Milam with the knife. Milam did not draw his gun but continued to pursue Luster to disarm him. The rest of the crowd "who wanted no part in it" walked away. Milam and Luster began "scuffling" over the gun as Hill continued to "cut at" Milam.

At some point during the scuffle, Luster fired his gun at Milam and wounded him but the trooper continued to try to disarm him. However, as the two were on the ground with Milam "on top," Hill approached the trooper with a large rock and hit him over the head knocking him unconscious. "After the officer was unconscious and lying face downward, a rock was used to further batter the back of his head." Luster then got up and fired two more shots into the prone, face-down body of Milam and fled. Hill removed Milam's gun and fired a final shot into the body of the prone and defenseless officer and then joined Luster in flight. The "lifeless body" was left near the church and his police motorcycle was hidden behind the church "as the crowd quickly scattered."

The murder caused a "furor" (i.e., racial unrest) in Milam's home-town of Newberry and in Greenville County in general and led to a massive police effort to find the fugitives. Almost every trooper in the state was called to Greenville County and surrounding areas to partici-pate in the search that also involved Greenville city and sheriff's officers, and deputies from surrounding counties. Deputies were called and when they arrived, the crowd was gone and they did not see Milam's body in the gathering darkness. En route back to the city, they met an ambulance that had been called and returned to the scene.

All deputy sheriffs were put immediately on the case. Lieut. G. C. Kinsey, in charge of this area, was summoned and all other patrolmen of the area were put on the case. B.R. Stroup of Columbia, director of the motor vehicle division of the state highway department in charge of the state patrol, came here Tuesday night to direct troopers in the search for the slayers. Within an hour or so after the killing, patrolmen began arriving from all parts of the state and yesterday virtually the entire state force was on the job. City police joined in the search and the radio patrol has been active ever since. City police aided throughout in searching negro houses in the city while deputies and patrolmen combed suburban negro sections and watched all highways leading to and from the city. (*Newberry Observer*, Dec. 28, 1934)

Bloodhounds brought from Pickens and "guided by Jim Poole, aged negro," picked up the trail of the two principal suspects and tracked them to a house in Greenville's "Nickeltown" where the two guns were discovered. Hill and Luster had stopped in Nickeltown to pawn the two weapons for $1.25 and $2.00 (both guns were recovered by police). The search team "rounded up" and questioned more than 50 "negroes" and detained 35 suspects and/or witnesses at the city jail for questioning. Several suspects claimed they were beaten before and during interrogation and so testified at the eventual trial.

Hill and Luster (temporarily) avoided the dragnet and fled north to Asheville, N.C., by car and bus. However, they were both arrested on Thursday, Dec. 27, 40 hours after the murder.

THE PERPETRATORS

Cornell Luster, 25, and Harry Hill, 26, the two fugitives, were arrested in Asheville on Thursday, Dec. 27 (at the same time as Milam's funeral was being held) and were taken to the state penitentiary in Columbia for "safekeeping." The authorities feared a lynching and/or racial unrest if the two were brought back to Greenville.

All those detained during the investigation were released without charges except Thurston ("Bill") Hill, the brother of Harry Hill. Police claimed that Bill Hill lied to officers when first questioned and later helped the two fugitives pawn the two guns in Greenville. He was charged with accessory after the fact of murder in that he, knowing that Hill and Luster had committed a felony, "did harbor, receive, assist, aid and abet" them in their escape from officers." He was tried on that charge after the Hill/Luster murder trial.

Consistent with "quick" trials in the 1930's, the murder trial of Luster and Hill before Judge C.C. Featherstone began in Greenville on Monday, Jan. 21, 1935 (less than a month after the murder), and lasted for three days. The case was prosecuted by Solicitor J.G. Leatherwood assisted by Assistant Solicitor Thomas A. Wofford and D.B. Leatherwood. Hill was represented by L.E. Wooten and D.M. Feild while C.S. Bowen was appointed to defend Luster. An inquest had been held earlier (on Jan. 2, 1935) and found Luster and Hill responsible for Milam's murder.

The courtroom was "packed" and a "a number of persons who could not find seats were ordered to leave the room." The balcony (reserved for "colored" persons) was "jammed with negroes and several special bailiffs were stationed in that portion of the room to keep down demonstrations."

The state introduced confessions by both Luster and Hill taken shortly after they were arrested that "implicated themselves and each other." However, both confessions were recanted at trial as both claimed the confessions were coerced. Luster took the stand to claim that he did refuse to give up the gun and only fired "accidently" during the scuffle with Milam. He denied that he fired the "execution shots" after Milam was unconscious. Hill claimed that he walked away from the "fight" and never struck Milam with a knife or fired a gun at him.

However, the state introduced several witnesses from the scene who contradicted the two defendants. Witnesses testified that they saw Luster shoot Milam before and after he was knocked unconscious and saw Hill hit Milam with the rock, knocking him unconscious, and then fire a final shot at the helpless officer. On cross-examination, defense attorneys claimed that the statements had been given by the witnesses after they were beaten.

Dr. L.W. Boggs testified that his autopsy indicated that the bullet wounds or the fractures were sufficient to have caused death. Boggs also testified that Milam's skull was "fractured in several places and brain tissue was oozing from every wound" and "the skull was so badly crushed that it felt like a bag of bones." Milam also had a bullet wound to the head and other gunshot wounds.

Milam's mother, Marie Milam, was in attendance at the trial and was visibly upset at Bogg's testimony. She was also a witness at the trial and told of her son's visit to her home shortly before his murder.

The 12-man (all-white) jury received the case on Wednesday afternoon (Jan. 23) and deliberated for an hour and two minutes before returning verdicts of guilty of murder for the two defendants. The verdicts were delivered without a recommendation for mercy thus the only option for Judge Featherstone was to sentence the two men to death. After denying arguments for a new trial on Friday, Jan. 25, 1935, the judge sentenced both men to death and set the date of execution for March 22, 1935.

Luster and Hill appealed to the S.C. Supreme Court through their attorneys L.E. Wooten, D.M. Feild, and C.S. Bowen while Solicitor J.G. Leatherwood represented the state. The appeal was denied on Nov. 27, 1935, in a written decision that included lengthy quotations from several witnesses at the trial. On "the week of the executions," Gov. Olin Johnston denied executive clemency "after an investigation of charges that negro witnesses for the state had been beaten before the trial failed to convince him there was ground for clemency."

Cornell Luster and Harry Hill were electrocuted at the state penitentiary on Dec. 20, 1935. Thus the trial was completed within a month of the murder and the executions took place within a year of the murder. They became the eighth and ninth persons executed from Greenville County since the state took over executions in 1912.

The *Greenville News* reported that Hill protested his innocence until the end while Luster confessed to his part in the murder. William Alex Milam, the slain trooper's brother, and "a number of officials" witnessed the executions. Hill was buried only a few steps from the murder scene at the Laurel Creek church. Luster was buried at "Reedy River Baptist church colored, near Conestee," three miles from the murder site.

THE OFFICER

Edwin Deronda Milam was born on Aug. 10, 1909, in Newberry, S.C., to Vance Lee and Marie Waters Milam. Both of his parents were also born in S.C. His family moved to Newberry after the death of his father when Edwin was a child. The *Newberry Observer* at his death reported that Edwin Milam was "well known here, having lived his entire life in Newberry." The newspaper also reported that Edwin Milam "was a graduate of Newberry high school and Carolina Fitting School."

In 1996, Fred Lester remembered that Edwin Milam was known locally in Newberry as "Sheik" for his good looks and was a dashing figure as he rode through town on his motorcycle in his "spotless uniform."

Edwin Milam, 24, joined the S.C. Highway Patrol on July 1, 1934, and thus was a rookie trooper at the time he was killed. At the time of his death, Trooper Milam was single and lived on Laurens Rd. in Greenville. He was described by his superior officers as "an officer and a gentleman" and as "one of the most fearless men on the patrol, always pleasant and more than willing to get along with anybody but always able to care of himself under ordinary circumstances."

Edwin Milam was survived by his mother, Marie Waters Milam of Glen St. in Newberry; by two brothers, Robert Milam, 28, and William Milam, 26, of Newberry; and by one sister, Miss Ella Mae Milam, 22, of Newberry.

Funeral services for Edwin D. Milam were arranged by Jones-McAfee of Greenville and were held on Thursday, Dec. 27, at the home of his mother on Glenn St. in Newberry, S.C. The service was conducted by the trooper's pastor, the Rev. E.B. Keisler of the Lutheran Church of the Redeemer and by the Rev. F.O. Lamoreaux, pastor of the First Baptist Church of Newberry. "All of the state patrolmen of Milam's district" attended the service as did patrolmen from "many from other sections of the state" to pay final tribute to their fallen comrade."

The officer was buried in the Rosemont cemetery in Newberry. In 1996 the grave of Edwin D. Milam is easily found in the Rosemont cemetery on College Street near Newberry College (a Lutheran college, the same faith as Edwin Milam). The Milam family plot is only about 75 feet from home plate on the college baseball field and is marked by a 3 ft. by 5 ft. stone monument with the inscription, "MILAM." The grave marker of the slain trooper reads:

EDWIN DERONDA MILAM
Aug. 10, 1909
Dec. 25, 1943

Others buried in the Milam family plot by 1996 are his mother, Marie Waters Milam (1950); his sister, Eula May Milam (1979); his brother, Robert Landon Milam (1980); and his brother, William Alex Milam (1981) and his wife, Inez Price Milam (1980). William Alex Milam, the last member of the family buried in Newberry, was a graduate of Newberry College, served in World War II, and worked for many years for the S.C. Employment Commission in Newberry. Eula Mae worked for many years in Washington, D.C., and Robert worked for several years as a security guard at a lumber store in Columbia.

None of the three siblings of E.D. Milam had any children and thus there were no direct descendants of the slain officer in 1996. However, a fifth cousin, Robby Milam, 49, lived in Columbia and was a criminalist with the S.C. State Transport Police.

The name of Edwin D. Milam is inscribed (East Wall, Panel 59, Line 10) on the National Law Enforcement Memorial in Washington, D.C., and a plaque bearing his name is displayed in the S.C. Criminal Justice Hall of Fame in Columbia. In 1996 the *Old Newberry District Quarterly* published a draft of this chapter.

SOURCES: *Greenville News,* Dec. 27,28,29,30,31, 1934, Jan. 2,4,17,22,23, 24,26, Dec. 21, 1935; *Newberry Observer,* Dec. 28, 1934, July 4, 1950, Jan. 24, 1980, Jan. 26, 1981; Greenville Criminal court record #A-4561; Cemetery index for Rosemont Cemetery in Newberry; Page 499 of Appendix (List of Executions) of *Legal Homicide: Death as Punishment in American, 1864-1982* by Wm. J. Bowers, 1984; death certificate of E.D. Milam at S.C. State Archives; and interviews with Fred Lester and Robby Milam.

#23 JOHN D. MARTIN
Deputy Sheriff
Shot & killed in an "ambush" on Sept. 12, 1965.

THE EVENT

Deputy Sheriff John P. Martin, 45, was shot and killed on Sept. 12, 1965, at a sand pit after being lured there by a man and his wife on a pretext. He became the first law enforcement officer killed in Greenville County in 31 years (since 1934). The male killer was convicted after a sensational five-day trial and was sentenced to life while his wife and girlfriend got 7 and 9 years as "accessories after the fact."

After midnight on Sunday morning, Sept. 12, 1965, Vernon Clifton Carroll, 24 (born on Feb. 2, 1940), who was drunk on Doriden pills, forced his wife, Peggy Lee McCombs Carroll, 23, to help him lure Deputy Martin to a sand pit to steal his badge and gun. The couple had been drinking at the sand pit beside Freeman's Bridge Road on the South Saluda River above Travelers Rest (between Pumpkintown and Marietta) and just inside Greenville County. Mrs. Carroll later testified that her husband forced her to drive to Marietta to try to talk Deputy Martin into going with her to the sand pit on the pretext of investigating a rock-throwing incident. Her husband would then ambush him there.

Mrs. Carroll located Martin but did not follow her husband's instructions since Martin had someone else with him in the patrol car. Carroll was angry at his wife's failure and accompanied her to Marietta where they saw Martin's car at a service station. Carroll told his wife to make another attempt to lure Martin to the sand pit and this time she was successful. When they arrived at the pit, the deputy began investigating the scene using his car headlights to illuminate the area.

At this point (around 3:00AM) Vernon Carroll got out of his car with a .30 calibre automatic carbine and pointed the rifle at Martin. Martin apparently saw the weapon being pointed at him and both men fired. It is unclear who fired first but Martin did apparently draw his weapon and fire twice in self-defense before being knocked down and killed by six shots from Vernon Carroll's carbine. Martin's head had also been "battered" with a number of "cuts and bruises."

The autopsy would later indicate that six shots passed through his body and made six exit holes. The tears from the bullet wounds made it appear that Martin had also been stabbed as was erroneously reported by the first news accounts of the shooting.

After the shooting Carroll got into the patrol car and drove it from the scene and "dumped it." He and his wife then dragged the body into their 1958 Buick convertible and transported it six miles to a wooded area in Pickens County on Hester Bridge Road, a half mile off S.C. Highway 283.

Vernon Carroll then obtained the help of a girlfriend, Joyce Ann Chapman, 24, to aid in getting rid of some of the evidence of the murder. Around 10:00PM Carroll left town with Chapman bound for Virginia. His wife stayed in their Greenville apartment with their small child.

When Martin's wife, Eva Mae, awoke at 7:00AM and discovered that her husband had not returned home (he usually arrived around 5:30AM while she was still asleep), she called the Sheriff's Office to report his failure to arrive home. Deputies from Greenville and Pickens County began a search for the deputy. The search intensified when W.A. (Bill) Martin, found his brother's patrol car parked 50 yards off the Pumpkintown-Marietta road on a narrow dirt road.

Around noon on Sunday, some berry pickers found the body of the slain deputy in a wooded area about 2.6 miles inside Pickens County on the Hendrix Bridge Road. It had been moved about six miles from the murder scene.

THE PERPETRATOR

Peggy Carroll was arrested at her home on Monday, Sept. 13, the day after the murder. She had been married to Vernon Carroll for one year and the couple had one child. The couple had met when both worked the same shift at Gayley Mill near Marietta. Vernon was unemployed at the time of the murder and was supported by his wife. He also had three children from a prior marriage.

Mrs. Carroll told police that her husband had shot Deputy Martin and had left for Virginia with his girlfriend, Joyce Chapman, 24. Chapman was married but her husband was in the service in VietNam. The police put out an all-points bulletin for Carroll and Chapman and they were arrested late that night (Monday, Sept. 13) near Gate City, VA, after being intercepted by local officers.

Carroll and Chapman waived extradition and were brought back to Greenville by two deputies. Vernon Carroll was charged with first degree murder while his wife was charged with murder and being an accessory before and after the fact. Ms. Chapman was charged with being an accessory after the fact. Police recovered Martin's badge, nameplate and wrist watch from a lake near Furman University and his .38 calibre service pistol "from a spot near Paris Mountain."

Shortly before the Jan. 17-22, 1967, trial of Vernon Carroll, his wife and Joyce Chapman pled guilty to being accessories after the fact and agreed to testify for the state. The murder charge and accessory before the fact charges against Peggy Carroll were dismissed in return for her testimony.

The five-day trial was held before Judge T.B. Greneker of Edgefield. Solicitor B.O. Thomason, Jr., and Assistant Solicitor H.F. Partee prosecuted the case for the state while Herman E. Cox and Fred N. McDonald represented Vernon Carroll. Mrs. Carroll and Ms. Chapman were represented by Sol Abrams. The state sought the death penalty for Carroll. Jury selection from a panel of 39 took two hours on Monday, Jan. 17. Twelve potential jurors were excused because of their opposition to the death penalty.

A total of 30 witnesses, 27 for the state and 3 for the defense, testified during the five-day trial. The jurors were sequestered each night once the trial began. The *Greenville News* described the trial as the "county's most spectacular since the May, 1947, Willie Earle Lynch trial."

The "spectacular" phase of the trial began on the second day when Peggy Carroll took the stand and kept the "approximately 250 spectators, attorneys, and newsmen spellbound as she testified about the slaying" for three hours. Mrs. Carroll, a native of Marietta, told the court that she and her husband were sitting around a fire at the sand pit when her increasingly drunk (on pills) husband told her to go to Marietta to get Deputy Martin to come to the rock pit so that he could steal his badge and gun. She testified that she was afraid of her husband who often beat her and was afraid to disobey him. Her first attempt failed as Deputy Martin was accompanied by Magistrate's Constable Joe Matthews and she returned "empty-handed" to the sand pit.

Shortly after 3:00AM the Carrolls decided to return home but as they drove through Marietta they spotted Deputy Martin's car at a gas station. Peggy testified that her husband "forced" her to go to Martin with the same "ruse" of a rock-throwing incident at the sand pit and convinced him to return to the pit with them. Martin led the procession of two cars to the sand pit. Vernon Carroll loaded his carbine on the way.

Upon arrival Martin began looking around the pit using his car headlights for illumination. Vernon Carroll got out of his car and stood beside the car with the carbine in his hand. He then told Martin to "hold it a minute" and pointed the carbine at him. Both men fired and Martin fell face down on the sand.

Mrs. Carroll testified that her husband ordered her to take Martin's gun and she, though "hysterical and crying," obeyed. Vernon Carroll then drove Martin's car to another spot (off Pace's Bridge Road) and parked it and the couple returned to the sand pit. They dragged the 275 lb. body of Martin to their car and placed it in the trunk. They then drove to a place in Pickens County where they stopped and Vernon drug the body by the feet into the woods.

Peggy testified that after they returned home, her husband forced her and his girlfriend, Joyce Ann Chapman, to take the bloody clothes they had worn during the night and Martin's shirt and hat and burn them. The two women "drove up on Paris Mountain and burned the items, including Martin's wallet and the lining of the trunk of their car which was also bloody." On their way back home, Ms. Chapman threw Martin's nameplate, badge, and watch into a lake near Furman University. When both women were asked in court why they did all these things for Vernon Carroll, they testified, "because I loved him." Both women also said they also feared him and that he had beaten them on occasion.

Dr. Adrian D. Duffy of the State Hospital at Columbia testified that he had examined Vernon Carroll for 30 days after his arrest and that he was sane and knew right from wrong.

The last witness to testify for the state was Dr. W. Marion Waters who performed the autopsy on Martin's body. He testified that Martin died of multiple bullet wounds and that the six bullets passed through his body and thus made 12 holes. He also testified that a paraffin test done on Martin's right hand indicated that he had fired a gun in that hand.

Vernon Carroll took the stand in his own defense on Thursday, Jan. 20, and testified for two and a half hours. He claimed that he took 8-10 Doriden pills a day and could not hold a job because of his almost continuous "drunk condition" caused by the pills.

He claimed that he only wounded Martin in the arm and that his wife shot and killed Martin when he tried to get up off the ground. He further testified that he only wanted to talk with Martin as his wife admitted to him that she had been dating Martin. He claimed that he only fired at Martin in self-defense when Martin saw him with the carbine. He also claimed that he went for medical help but returned only to find that Martin was dead (shot again by his wife who told him "he tried to get up").

Three hours of closing arguments followed Vernon Carroll's testimony. The jury was out for 12 hours before returning a verdict of guilty of murder but with a recommendation for mercy (thus precluding the death penalty). The sentencing of the three occurred the next day (Saturday, Jan. 22). Judge Greneker sentenced Vernon Carroll to the mandatory life in prison and told him that he "had gotten off very light." The judge seemed particularly angry that Martin had tried to smear the reputation of Deputy Martin in addition to killing him in cold blood and stated that there was no evidence that Martin had an affair with Peggy Carroll.

Court records indicated that Vernon Carroll, 5'9" and 150 lbs., had been arrested twice while in the Army at Ft. Knox (9/18/1958) and Ft. Meade (2/17/1959) and for burglary (on 7/18/1959) while in Blountville, TN. He had been sentenced to one year in jail on the burglary conviction. In April of 1996, Vernon Clifton Carroll was still incarcerated in a S.C. prison. His next parole hearing date was set for April 13, 1998.

Peggy Carroll was sentenced to 7 years in prison and Joyce Ann Chapman to 9 years (one less than the maximum allowed). The judge obviously did not buy the defense contention that both women were weak and dominated by the allegedly physically abusive Carroll. Peggy Lee Carroll, 27, was paroled on Feb. 5, 1969, after serving less than 4 years on her 7 year sentence. She was released from parole on July 3, 1973. Joyce Ann Chapman, 28, was paroled on Feb. 5, 1969 (the same day as Peggy Carroll) after serving less than 4 years on her 9 year sentence. She was also released from parole on July 3, 1973.

THE OFFICER

John P. Martin was born on Aug. 9, 1920, in upper Greenville County to James R. and Era Selmon Martin. He grew up with two brothers in upper Greenville County and attended Slater-Marietta H.S.

John Martin served in the Army Air Force (Base Unit 1419) during World War II, serving overseas in Italy, and was discharged as a corporal. After the war, Martin began his police career by serving as a "special deputy" of the Greenville Sheriff's Office. "His wages came from three different sources: from the county as a special deputy; from the Gayley Mills, as a sort of cruising night watchman; and from the town of Marietta, where he checked stores and provided protection for the community during the late-night hours."

John Martin was known around Marietta as "Big John" as he was 6'4" and 275 lbs. He was very well-liked in the community of Marietta, especially by the youth. He was the "only visible police presence in the area after dark."

One neighbor said that Deputy Martin was a "big, kindly man who had many friends. I don't know anyone who disliked him."

Deputy John Martin was held in high esteem by the teen-age boys in the Marietta area. More than once he had helped with advice and counsel young boys who had leanings toward straying into scrapes.

To show their high regard and respect for the big deputy, the teen-age youngsters in Marietta contributed all the money they could earn to buy a floral piece for their hero's funeral.

"It was a huge, beautiful arrangement, star shaped like a deputy's badge. It was four or five feet high. The boys gave their allowances and worked to buy the floral decoration," one mourner recalled.

The residents of the town of Marietta, shocked and saddened by the deputy's untimely death, set up a "John Martin" fund. Shops and stores in the town had containers on counters marked "John Martin" fund. The money was to be turned over to the murdered deputy's widow. (*True Police Stories*, Oct., 1965)

John Martin married Doris Gooch Martin in 1940. Their daughter, Patricia, was born on Feb. 6, 1942., and their son, Robert E., on Oct. 23, 1945. John and Doris divorced around 1949 and Doris took the two children to live in Greenville where she worked at Judson Mill to support her family. Doris Gooch Moss died in 1971 at the age of 50.

Officer Martin, 45, was survived by his second wife, Eva Charping Martin, 51; by his two children from his first marriage, Patricia, 23, and Robert E., 20; by his mother, Era, 73; and by two brothers, Olin Martin, 56, and Wm. H. (Bill) Martin, 52, of Marietta.

The funeral, arranged by O'Dell Mortuary, was held at the Marietta First Baptist Church on Tuesday, Sept. 14. Rev. James Roberts and Rev. Emmett McCall conducted the service. The service was not a police-type funeral although hundreds of uniformed officers were in attendance and the procession from the church to the cemetery was led by numerous police cars with flashing lights. A brief burial service was conducted at the cemetery adjoining the Friendship Baptist Church on Highway #288 just west of Marietta.

In 1996 the officer's grave marker at the Friendship Baptist Church Cemetery reads:

JOHN P. MARTIN
SOUTH CAROLINA
CPL 1419 BASE UNIT AAF
Aug. 9, 1920 - Sept. 12, 1965

Officer Martin was buried in the Martin family plot next to his father, James R. Martin who died in 1953 at the age of 69. His widow, Eva Mae Charping Martin, 67, was buried beside her husband upon her death in 1981. His brothers, William H. Martin (1988) and Olin Martin (1991) were buried in the family plot as was his mother, Era Selmon Martin, 94, who died on Jan. 7, 1987.

In 1996, Deputy Martin's son, Robert E. Martin, 51, still lived in Greenville and worked for a sheet metal company. His daughter, Patricia Martin Harkey, 54, lived in Winder, GA, with her husband Barton. Patricia was a chemist, working for the U.S. Dept. of Agriculture at the Eastern Lab in Athens, GA, in the area of food safety and inspection. Patricia Harkey's children, Elisabeth Marie Harkey, 30, and Barton Harkey, Jr., 23, are the only grandchildren of Deputy John P. Martin. Deputy Martin died shortly before Elisabeth's birth and thus did not live to see his grandchildren.

Deputy Martin's name is inscribed (West Wall, Panel 15, Line 16) on the

National Law Enforcement Memorial in Washington, D.C., though his middle initial is erroneously inscribed as R. instead of P. A plaque bearing his name is displayed at the S.C. Criminal Justice Hall of Fame in Columbia.

SOURCES: *Greenville News*, March 20, 1953, Sept. 13,14,15,16,17,18, 1965, Jan. 17,18,19,20,21,22, 1966, March 3, 1981, Jan. 8, 1987; "Who Killed the Deputy Everybody Loved?" by Mary Lou Culbertson in *True Police Stories,* October, 1965; Records of S.C. Dept. of Corrections; and interview with Mrs. Bill Martin and Patricia Martin Harkey.

#24 CLAUDE V. SOUTHERLIN, JR.
Deputy Sheriff
Killed in auto accident during chase on Dec. 31, 1966.

THE EVENT

Claude V. Southerlin, Jr., 40, the Chief Deputy of the Greenville Sheriff's Office was killed in a traffic accident on Dec. 31, 1966. He became the second Greenville County law enforcement officer known to have been killed in the line of duty in a traffic accident (Deputy Perry Paris was the first in 1930).

The accident that claimed the life of Chief Deputy Southerlin occurred at 12:45PM on Saturday, Dec. 31, 1966, on S.C. Highway 101, approximately 4 miles north of Greer. Southerlin was driving an unmarked patrol car (a 1966 Ford) and was on his way home at the end of his shift when he heard on the police radio from Deputy Joe Worthy (the radio operator) that two other deputies (Joe K. Chastain and T. Pralo Woods) "were having difficulties" in trying to stop a car driven by a woman just north of Greer. Deputy Southerlin, though off-duty, volunteered to go to the aid of the two deputies and asked for the location of the chase. He apparently planned to set up a road block at State Highway 290.

Southerlin was traveling toward Greer with his siren on and red light blinking when he "passed one car and ran up behind a slower moving car." Witnesses said that Southerlin "slammed on his brakes" and the car "went out of control" on the "rain-slick highway" and skidded some 200 feet into the path of an oncoming car (a 1960 Chevrolet). The right front side of the patrol car hit the front of the oncoming car.

On impact, Chief Southerlin was thrown clear of his car and it burst into flames. Passing motorists stopped and pulled the fatally injured law enforcement officer away from the blazing automobile which was destroyed by the fire. (*Greenville News,* 1/1/1967)

Southerlin was killed instantly. He was dead on arrival at the Greer hospital at 1:45PM. His daughter, Diane, 16, who had been dropped off at the hairdresser by her father, phoned her mother to pick her up when he did not return. When both returned home, Dep. Pralo Wood, a relative, came to the home and told them about the accident that killed Claude Southerlin.

The (right front) passenger in the second car, Larry Anders, 20, of Greer, was also killed in the accident. He was a Sr. at Blue Ridge H.S. and was a classmate of Deputy Southerlin's daughter, Diane. The driver of the second car, Mrs. Francis B. Strange, 40, of Greer (the mother of Anders) was taken to the hospital with a broken ankle and facial lacerations. A second passenger, Wayne Anders, 12, who was in the back seat, suffered less serious injuries and was not hospitalized.

Another traffic accident on Dec. 31, 1966, brought the death total for the day to three and the total for the year of 1966 to 68, "a record," according to the *Greenville News.*

THE PERPETRATOR

No one was charged in the death of Deputy Southerlin. A coroner's jury ruled on Jan. 25 that the accident was "unavoidable." Testimony at the inquest by

Deputy Leland H. Lowery indicated that Southerlin "had put new mud and snow tires on his car just a week prior to the crash and these afforded much less traction when braking than conventional treads." The tires plus the fact that the road was wet contributed to the accident.

Mrs. Carol Foster, a passenger in the car passed by Southerlin during the chase testified that the deputy applied his brakes just as he passed the crest of a hill and the car "skidded broadside into the northbound lane into a 1960 Chevrolet. Investigators found almost 300 feet of skid marks at the accident site.

THE OFFICER

Claude Southerlin, Jr., was born on Oct. 12, 1926, in Tigerville S.C., the only child born to Claude V. Southerlin, Sr., and Mary Elizabeth Wood Southerlin. Both his parents were natives of Greenville County. His father was a farmer and also worked at the Southern Weaving Mill in Taylors. His grandfather, Arthur J. Southerlin was a farmer and also operated the Southerlin Grocery store on Woodside Ave. until his retirement in 1938. His great grandparents were Philip P. and Amelia Hightower Southerlin of Tigerville.

Claude's mother, Mary Elizabeth Wood Southerlin, was the daughter of J. Austin and Corrie Barnett Wood, and was a lifelong resident of Tigerville and a 1922 graduate of the N. Greenville Baptist Academy. She worked for many years as a dietitian for the Greenville County School District.

Claude Southerlin was raised in Tigerville and attended the Mountain View School for elementary through high school. As a youth he enjoyed hunting and fishing with his father. He graduated from Mountainview H.S. in 1943 and immediately joined the Army at the age of 17 at the height of World War II. He served for a time overseas in Egypt.

After the war, Southerlin worked first as a guard with Southern Bleachery, a textile mill in Taylors. Then, at the age of 20, he joined the Sheriff's Dept. in 1946 under Sheriff Homer Bearden (Sheriff from 1940-1952) and first served as a radio operator. He left the sheriff's office for approximately four years (1953-1957) during the tenure of Sheriff R.V. Chandler, Jr., and worked at Southern Weaving Mill at Taylors (where his father also worked) as a security guard. He returned as a deputy when Sheriff J.R. Martin was elected in 1957 and was appointed chief deputy by Sheriff Martin in 1962 when the former Chief Deputy, J. Harold Scott, was elected city magistrate. He was a 17-year veteran of the Dept. at his death.

In 1965 Chief Deputy Southerlin was named the Outstanding Greenville County Sheriff's Deputy by the Greater Greenville Chamber of Commerce. The presentation was made at the Law Enforcement-Fireman Event which was held to honor the outstanding fireman and deputy. He served in the Sheriff's office with his brother-in-law, T. Pralo Wood, who was a Greenville County deputy sheriff from 1937-1964. (Wood died in Greenville on April 12, 1995).

During a leave home from World War II in 1944, Claude Southerlin, 18, married Mary Katheryn Carlton, 17. Their only child, Diane, was born Oct. 17, 1949. The family attended the Tyger Baptist Church in Tigerville. Claude was a 32nd degree mason with the Tigerville Masonic Lodge.

Claude Southerlin was survived by his wife Kathryn Carlton Southerlin, 39, and daughter, Diane, 16, of Taylors and by his father, Claude V. Southerlin, Sr., 63, and mother, Mary Elizabeth Wood Southerlin, 59, of Tigerville.

The funeral arrangements were handled by Wood Mortuary of Greer where the funeral service was held on Monday, Jan. 2, 1967. The service, conducted by Rev. Ruford Hodges, Rev. L.R. Duncan and Rev. Sam Avery, was attended by hundreds of uniformed police officers. A police honor guard lined Main Street in Greer at the conclusion of the service. Burial was at the cemetery adjoining the Tyger Baptist Church with the services being conducted by the Masons.

A Letter to the Editor by Solicitor B.O. Thomason, Jr., praised the slain deputy:

I know of no more dedicated or conscientious officer than was the late Chief Deputy Claude Southerlin....He had an uncanny knack for handling criminal investigations, but most important of all, he handled his office in such a way as to inspire confidence in himself and his department. (*Greenville News*, 1/3/1967)

An editorial in the *Greenville News* called Southerlin "a virtual model of a citizen whose most notable characteristics were his restraint in dealing with accused or suspected lawbreakers and his compassion for his fellowman."

In 1996 the grave of Claude Southerlin is easily located in the middle of the Tygerville Baptist Church Cemetery on Highway 414, just east of Highway 25. The grave marker reads:

Claude V. Southerlin, Jr.
Oct. 12, 1926
Dec. 31, 1966

Claude V. Southerlin, Sr., died on Jan. 29, 1973, at the age of 69 and was buried beside his son. His mother, Mary Elizabeth Wood Southerlin died on March 11, 1996, at the age of 89, and was buried beside her son and husband. Several other Southerlin "ancestors" are buried nearby with the earliest burial being 1898.

In 1996 Diane Southerlin Green, 46, and her husband Tom lived in Taylors with their three children, Todd, 22, Jayson, 18, and Tim, 17 (the grandchildren of Deputy Southerlin).

The name of Claude Southerlin, Jr., is inscribed (but misspelled as Sutherline) on the National Law Enforcement Memorial in Washington, D.C. (East Wall, Panel 36, Line 1) and a plaque bearing his name is displayed at the S.C. Hall of Fame in Columbia.

SOURCES: *Greenville News,* Jan. 1,2,26, 1967, March 13, 1996; Cemetery index for Greenville County & grave markers at Tyger Baptist Church Cemetery; and interview with Diane Southerlin Green.

#25 JAMES P. BAGWELL
Greenville County Jailer
Stabbed to death by inmate on Aug. 3, 1970.

THE EVENT

Greenville County Jailer James Perry "Jim" Bagwell, 62, was stabbed to death by an inmate on Aug. 3, 1970. The perpetrator was sentenced to life in prison but later escaped and was killed in Boston.

At 1:05AM on Monday, Aug. 3, 1970, Jailer James P. Bagwell went to a cell at the old "antiquated two-story" County Jail at 32 East Broad St. to remove a prisoner who had been booked on a drunk charge. During the removal, another inmate, John Smith, Jr., 23, started shouting "obscene things" at Bagwell and the inmate being removed. Smith was also "making crazy remarks" and claimed to be ill and thus Bagwell and two other jailers, Garland Edwards and Jeff Raines, decided they would remove Smith from the group cell and put him in an individual cell where he could be examined by a doctor.

James P. Bagwell

Jailer Raines opened the door to let Smith out of the cell he shared with 15 other inmates. As Smith exited the cell he grabbed Raines from behind and put a home-made knife (made from a "support for the mattress and springs") to his throat and threatened to kill him if the other two guards interfered. However, Jailer Edwards grabbed Smith and the two "wrestled" for a moment. Smith tried to stab Edwards but then turned on Jailer Bagwell, stabbing him in the upper left chest. He then tried to stab Raines but the knife was bent.

Two City of Greenville police officers, Jack McCall and W.J. Acker, saw the incident from outside and came inside the jail to help. They were able to subdue Smith in a corridor that runs through the cellblock. Smith was taken to the hospital for emergency treatment of possible head injuries. He was then taken to the maximum security section of the State Department of Corrections in Columbia.

Jailer Bagwell was taken to Greenville General Hospital where emergency surgery was performed. The surgery was unsuccessful and Bagwell died at 4:32AM according to County Coroner Mercer Brissey. Jailer Raines was treated for a stab wound of his shoulder, but was not seriously injured.

THE PERPETRATOR

John "Junebug" Smith, Jr., 23 (born on March 28, 1947), of Rt. 2, Ponder Rd. in Greenville, had been arrested on July 12 and charged with five armed robberies in Greenville since May 22 including two at the Western Union Telegraph Co. and robberies at the Laurens Road Package Store and the Augusta Street Seven-Eleven Store.

After his arrest on Aug. 3, Smith was charged with the murder of Bagwell and with assault and battery with intent to kill against Raines and Edwards. Judge Frank Eppes sent Smith to the S.C. State Hospital for a psychiatric evaluation on Aug. 3 and ordered that he be held in Columbia at the state prison until his trial.

The grand jury indicted Smith for murder on Aug. 30. He was returned from the state prison in Columbia to Greenville for his arraignment and trial before Judge Louis Rosen on Nov. 2, 1970. Solicitor B.O. Thomason, Jr., prosecuted the case for the state and claimed that Smith and two other inmates had plotted an escape and that the two other inmates had been seen with the knife prior to Smith having it. Another inmate testified that he saw Smith running through the corridor after the murder and that Smith had said he had stabbed two men and was trying to escape.

The two guards testified as to what happened at the murder scene as Smith exited the cell and said that Smith grabbed Raines and said he would "cut his head off" and "kill him."

Smith took the stand in his own defense and claimed that, because of his earlier "words" with Bagwell, he expected to be taken from his cell and beaten and "put in the hole" (i.e., solitary) if the jailors returned. He claimed that he armed himself with the knife because he was frightened of being beaten.

Smith testified that after he put the knife to Jailor Raines' throat, one of the other jailors grabbed him from behind and Raines "jerked free." He then said he started swinging the knife to ward off the jailors and one swing of the blade struck Bagwell. Smith argued that he could have easily killed Raines but that he didn't intend to kill anyone as he just wanted to avoid a beating and/or escape. Smith denied that he and other inmates had plotted an escape.

The trial ended on Tuesday, Nov. 3 (election day). After canceling the morning court session to allow everyone to vote, the jury found Smith guilty of murder but recommended mercy allowing him to avoid the death penalty. He was then sentenced to life in prison by Judge Rosen on Nov. 3, 1970. He was received by the prison system on Nov. 18, 1970. The first time Smith was eligible for parole the Bagwell family was notified and objected to his release.

The records of the S.C. Dept. of Corrections indicate that John Smith, Jr., 28, escaped from the maximum security Central Correctional Institution in Columbia on Jan. 23, 1976 (after serving 5 years). Smith remained free for ten years until he was killed (at the age of 38) in a "drug shootout" in Boston on Feb. 9, 1986.

THE OFFICER

James Perry Bagwell was born on Nov. 9, 1907, in Anderson County, S.C., to Adolphus and Emma Pace Bagwell. His ancestors emigrated to N.C. shortly before the Civil War.

James was one of 16 children raised on a farm on the border between

Anderson and Pickens County. He attended school through the 8th grade at the McLemore School near Liberty, S.C. (the building is now a museum on Highway 8). He did not attend H.S. but later took college courses at Clemson University in the early 1950's while he was employed by a textile mill.

Jim Perry, 16, married Vera Patterson, 16 on Nov. 4, 1923. They lived in Liberty with their seven children: Vera Estelle (born on 9/16/1924), James Roy (1/30/1928), Sarah Janette (12/18/1933), Carol Louise (6/14/1940), Clara Diane (6/7/1941), Tommy Adolphus (6/14/1943), and Melody Ann (1/21/1946).

During World War II, James served in Company F, Second Regiment, of the S.C. Defense Force (an organization similar to the National Guard) rather than the armed services because of his age (he was in his mid-30's) and the fact that he had so many children. He was promoted to 1st Sgt. on June 1, 1943, and to 2nd Lt. on Aug. 10, 1943.

For approximately 30 years James worked at Woodside Mill's Liberty plant, first as a mechanic and then as a supervisor. He began his law enforcement career in 1952 at the age of 45 when he joined the Liberty Police Dept. He served that city for five years until 1957 when he became a deputy with the Pickens County Sheriff's Office under Sheriff P.C. Bolding where he served for 11 years. After reaching the age of 60 in 1968, Perry retired from police work and began working as a jailer at the Greenville County jail in early 1969.

James Bagwell was survived by his wife Vera Patterson Bagwell, 63; by two sons, Roy J. Bagwell, 42, of Easley and Tommy Bagwell, 27, of Liberty; by four daughters, Mrs. David M. (Sarah) Ray, 36, of Newberry, Mrs. Joe (Clara) Hunter, 29, of Liberty, Mrs. Wayne (Melody Ann) Gastley, 24, of Easley and Carol Bagwell, 30, of Liberty. He was also survived by six grandchildren and two great grandchildren.

James Bagwell was also survived by seven brothers, Sethie and Luther Bagwell of Liberty, Horace Bagwell of Easley, Cecil Bagwell of Columbia, the Rev. Winfred L. Bagwell of Gaffney, Sam Bagwell of Ramseur, N.C., and John Bagwell of Cateechee; and four sisters, Mrs. Walter (Margaret) Higgins of Johnson City, TN, Mrs. Eula Bracken of Pelzer, Mrs. Ernest (Mary) Tant of Spartanburg, and Mrs. Peter (Ann) Malaga of Columbia.

The funeral service for Bagwell was held on Wednesday, Aug. 5, at the Jones Ave. Baptist Church in Easley (where he and his family were members). The funeral was not a "police-type" funeral although most of the pallbearers were deputies he had worked with in Liberty and though many police officers in uniform attended.

Burial was in the Westview Cemetery at the corner of Summit and Old Norris Rd. in Liberty. In 1996 the grave of James Bagwell is marked by a 3 ft. tall by 5 ft. wide stone monument that reads:

JAMES PERRY BAGWELL
1902 - 1970

The stone monument also includes the date of James' marriage and the words "together forever." His widow, Vera, was buried by her husband's side upon her death at age 84 on April 11, 1991. The couple's daughter, Vera Estelle, was the first to be buried in the family plot upon her death on Jan. 22, 1946.

In 1996, four of the children of James Bagwell (Carol Lois, 56; Clara Diane

Hunter, 55; Tommy Adolphus Bagwell, 53; and Melody Ann Gastley, 50) were still living. Also, in 1996, he was survived by 14 grandchildren with all but two of the grandchildren living in Pickens County. Five of James' siblings were still living in 1996 but only one, Luther Bagwell, 73, remained in Pickens County (the four others lived in Columbia, S.C.).

James' son, Roy Bagwell, 42, was a deputy sheriff in Pickens County but quit the day Dad his Dad was killed in Greenville. A grandson, Robert Ray, was a deputy sheriff in Albertville, AL, for 10 years.

James Bagwell's brother, Sam Bagwell, a deputy sheriff in Randolph County, N.C., was shot and severely wounded in a shootout with bandits in 1972. He later died of heart failure but his death was not declared as "line of duty" since he did not die until two years after the shootout.

The *Greenville News* used the occasion of James Bagwell's death to proclaim the need to speed up the planning process for the proposed new Law Enforcement Center that would include a new jail. The newspaper said that the "inadequate facilities" at the (old) jail "contributed" to the death of Bagwell. An investigation into Bagwell's death by the Public Safety Committee of the Greenville County Council concluded with a recommendation that the county needed a new jail to prevent future incidents.

The name of Jailer James P. Bagwell will be added to the National Law Enforcement Memorial in 1996 and a plaque bearing his name will be added to the S.C. Criminal Justice Hall of Fame in Columbia.

SOURCES: *Greenville News,* Aug. 4, Nov. 3,4, 1970, April 13, 1991; *Easley Progress,* Aug. 5, 1970; *Pickens Sentinel,* Aug. 5, 1970; Incident report of Greenville County Jail; Court file of John Smith, Jr. (#E-2131); Cemetery markers Westview Cemetery in Liberty, S.C.; S.C. Dept. of Corrections prison file for John Smith, Jr. (#63899); and interviews with Ann Bagley Castley, Carol Bagwell, Tommy Bagwell, Luther Bagwell and Capt. Frank Loftis.

#26 WILLIAM FRANK CHASTEEN
Greenville Police Dept.
Shot & killed questioning a suspect on Feb. 21, 1971.

THE EVENT

Greenville Officer William Frank Chasteen, 47, a 17-year veteran, was shot and killed on Feb. 21, 1971, as he questioned a suspect in an alleged earlier shooting. The killer was wounded by Chasteen and his partner and committed suicide when "cornered" by police. Chasteen was the first City of Greenville officer killed in 39 years (since Officer A.B. Hunt was killed in 1932).

Officer Chasteen and his close friend and partner of 12 years, Officer David A. Woodall, 39, had just begun their tour of duty on the midnight shift on Sunday, Feb. 21, 1971, when they received a call from the dispatcher at 12:22AM that there was a disturbance in "Booker's Alley" in the "Greenline area" (a black ghetto in the northeast section of the city).

Upon arrival Chasteen and Woodall were told by a black woman that Richard Brooks had shot her in the neck and run out of the house. The officers knew Brooks, a 26-year-old, 300 lb., black man, from their many years patrolling the city.

Greenville, South Carolina Officer Frank Chasteen, 47, was shot and killed on Feb. 21, 1971, as he questioned a suspect about an earlier shooting. His name is inscribed on the National Law Enforcement Memorial in Washington, DC.

The officers went to Brooks' nearby home but were unable to find him. They then drove back to the home of the woman who had reported the shooting incident and were told that Brooks had been back and had shot her 16-year-old daughter in the arm as she sat outside her house with a 16-year-old boy. The *Greenville News* later reported that the two wounded women were Mary Jane Bowens, 41, who was shot in the head, and her daughter, Linda Bowens, 16, who was shot in the right arm. Brooks and the older woman had apparently been involved in a violent argument over Brooks dating her 16-year-old daughter.

According to a later police investigation, Brooks was "fond of" the 16-year-old Linda Bowens and became enraged when he discovered that she had a date with a 16-year-old boy. When the young couple drove up to Linda's house just before midnight, Brooks fired three shots into the youths' car. Linda ran inside her home and Brooks tried to kick in the door and "began firing shots all over the house." The grandmother hit Brooks twice in the head with a hammer before he left.

As the officers were talking with the woman complainant, a man walked up to the officers and said, "Brooks is standing up yonder on the corner under the street light." The two officers drove their patrol car to the corner and both got out, drew their service revolvers, and approached Brooks who was standing under the street light with a pistol in his right hand. The officers knew that Brooks had often been in court on charges of drunk and disorderly conduct and drunken driving but he had never been violent before.

Chasteen, who was nearest Brooks, said "Give me the gun, big guy." Brooks raised his left hand and wiped the sweat from his face, and at the same time he raised the pistol in his right hand and started shooting Chasteen in the chest.

Things happened so swiftly then that everything seemed like a blur of frenzied movement....

Chasteen was smashed to the ground by the impact of bullets striking him in the chest....The dying Chasteen, on his ground, emptied his revolver with his last strength but the bullets went into the ground. (*Insight*, Nov., 1972)

As Chasteen fell, Woodall began firing at Brooks who started running from the scene. The officer's first shot "knocked down" Brooks but he got up and began running again only to be felled by a second shot. Brooks did not get up after the second "knock down" and thus Woodall, thinking that Brooks was immobilized or dead, ran back to help his fallen partner. He determined that Chasteen was badly wounded and ran back to the patrol car (about 100 yards away) to call for an ambulance.

As he was calling for help on the police radio a witness to the shooting yelled to Woodall that "the man was coming again." Brooks fired at Woodall (hitting the windshield of the patrol car) who could not return fire immediately as he had emptied his gun earlier firing at the fleeing Brooks. Woodall ran around his car to re-load and emerged only to find that the shooter had disappeared.

Officer Woodall returned to his fallen partner and examined him more closely as he awaited the ambulance. He saw that Chasteen had been shot twice in the upper left chest and was probably dead. Other officers arrived about the same time as the ambulance. Chasteen was rushed to the hospital but was dead on arrival.

THE PERPETRATOR

A police search team was organized to locate the gunman. SLED agents brought bloodhounds to the shooting scene and they "sniffed a bloodstained trail" that led (at 3:20AM) to an old grocery store building on Stone Avenue, two blocks from the shooting.

Officers converged on the building and one of them detected movement under the floor. He started to call out, and a single pistol shot sounded underneath the floor. Then silence.

The hunters crawled in and discovered the dead killer. He had fired a single shot into his brain. (*Insight*, Nov., 1972)

Brooks had entered the building by crawling through an open basement window. Realizing that he was "cornered," the killer shot himself in the head. He was found unconscious with his pistol near him. He had been shot four times and died five hours later. The killer was identified as Richard Dean Brooks, 26. The autopsy revealed that he had been "shot three times in his right arm and once in the back before firing the fatal shot into his head."

THE OFFICER

William Franklin "Frank" Chasteen, 47, was born in Piedmont, S.C., on Sept. 23, 1924, the only child of William Henry Chasteen and Willie Lou Odom Chasteen. Frank was raised in Piedmont and attended the public schools there. He left high school short of graduation to join the U.S. Navy in 1942 at the age of 17 and served throughout World War II. Most of his six-year Navy career was spent on a refueling ship in the Atlantic but he also served for a time as a military policeman.

Chasteen returned to Greenville County in 1948 after discharge from the Navy and completed his G.E.D. at the Veteran's School in Greenville. He worked at the Franklin Mill in Greer for several years before joining the Greenville Police Dept. in June of 1954. He was a patrol officer for all of his 17-year career and was a partner to Officer Woodall for 12 years. He also worked off-duty jobs for several years to supplement his meager police salary ($7,600 in 1971).

Officer Chasteen was well-known and well-liked in both the white and black communities. He was known to collect food and clothing from citizens and merchants for delivery to needy persons in the community. In fact, he had even given shoes on one occasion to his killer, Richard Brooks. "Some of the most beautiful flowers at his funeral were sent by black friends."

An editorial in the *Greenville News* noted that Chasteen was an officer well known by the editors and staff members of the newspaper and lamented the lack of respect often given to police officers.

> How ironic that today Frank Chasteen is a fallen hero eulogized by the leaders of the community. On Saturday he was just another policeman whose family sometimes suffered slights simply because he was a cop. (*Greenville News*, 2/22/1971)

Frank Chasteen married Nadeene Smith on May 23, 1947 (before his discharge from the Navy). Their son, Steve, was born in 1949. Frank and his family lived at 118 Windemere Dr. in Greenville and were members of the East North St. Baptist Church. Frank was a 32nd degree Mason and a member of Recovery Lodge 31, AFM.

The funeral for Officer Chasteen was held at the Thomas McAfee Funeral Home in Greenville on Tuesday, Feb. 23, and was conducted by Rev. Billy Huff, pastor of East N. St. Baptist Church. The service was conducted with full police honors, including a police honor guard. The service was attended by hundreds of uniformed police officers from Greenville and surrounding cities.

The funeral procession from the church to Woodlawn Memorial Park in Greenville stretched for five miles as the police motorcycles leading the procession reached the cemetery before some cars left the church. A brief service was held at graveside and the folded American flag from the casket was given to the slain officer's widow.

In 1996 the grave of Officer Chasteen is easily found in the northeast corner of Woodlawn Memorial Park. The grave marker reads:

WILLIAM FRANK CHASTEEN
September 23, 1924
February 21, 1971

The grave marker also includes an emblem signifying that Chasteen was a 32nd degree Mason and a police shield with badge #141. The marker includes the name of his widow, who will be buried beside her husband, and the words, "Together Forever."

Frank Chasteen was survived by his wife of 23 years, Nadeene Smith Chasteen, 44, and his son, Steve Franklin Chasteen, 21, both of Greenville, and his mother, Willie Lou Chasteen (his father died in 1964). Steve Chasteen had just returned from a tour of duty in Vietnam where he had continued the family tradition of service in the U.S. Navy begun by his grandfather and father. Steve had only recently married and was attending North Greenville Jr. College.

In 1996 Nadeene Chasteen, 65, still lived in the family home at 118 Windemere Dr. in Greenville and her son, Steve Chasteen, 47, lived in nearby Taylors and worked at Wal-Mart. Nadeene Chasteen worked as a bookkeeper at Taylors Lumber Company until her retirement in 1994. The family did not receive an anticipated $50,000 federal death benefit from a recently enacted Omnibus Crime Control bill but did receive, a total of $7,500 (one year's salary), $1,000 from the Patrolman's Volunteer Pledge Fund, some insurance money and a substantial sum of money collected from local citizens. The officer's widow was overwhelmed by the "outpouring of sympathy" from the people of Greenville in the form of flowers and cards at the funeral and the money collected. The money enabled the family to pay off its debts and Steve to finish his education.

Also in 1996, Officer Frank Chasteen was survived by two grandchildren, Stephen Paul Chasteen, 23, of Taylors and Stephanie Ann Chasteen, 19, a student at Limestone College in Gafney. Frank's mother, Willie Lou, died in 1991 and was buried in Piedmont by her husband. Officer David A. Woodall retired from the Greenville Police Dept. in 1990 after 35 years of service and remained in Greenville in 1996.

The name of William Frank Chasteen is inscribed (East Wall, Panel 30, Line 9) on the National Law Enforcement Memorial in Washington, D.C., and a plaque bearing his name is displayed at the S.C. Criminal Justice Hall of Fame in Columbia.

SOURCES: *Greenville News*, Feb. 22,23, 1971; *Insight, The Magazine of Greenville County,* Nov., 1972; and interviews with Steve Chasteen, David A. Woodall, and Mark Batson.

#27 FULTON H. ANTHONY S.C.
Highway Patrol
Shot & killed while transporting prisoners on March 10, 1973.

THE EVENT

Fulton H. Anthony, 37, a 13-year veteran of the S.C. Highway Patrol, was shot and killed on March 10, 1973, by a prisoner who was in the back seat of a patrol vehicle that was transporting he and his wife to jail. The highway patrolman driving the vehicle was wounded by the gunfire but was able to shoot and kill the killer. Anthony became the eighth highway patrolman killed in the history of the S.C. Patrol and the second killed in Greenville County (Patrolman E.D. Milam was killed in Greenville in 1934).

Fulton H. Anthony

Around 4:00PM on Saturday, March 10, 1973, S.C. Highway Patrolman R.E. Wallace was on routine patrol on Highway 276 near River Falls, about 15 miles north of Greenville, when he stopped to investigate a 1963 Ford station wagon which was in a ditch. He discovered that the occupants, Clyde Edmond Ogle, 53, and his wife, Virginia Dare Ogle, 33, of Rt. 1, Cleveland, S.C., were intoxicated. Officer Wallace arrested the couple for public drunkenness and "brownbagging" and decided to transport them to the Greenville County jail.

Wallace made a cursory search of the male but did not search the female, as policy required that only females search females and thus the female was not searched "beyond observation." Wallace did not handcuff either Ogle or his wife and placed them in the back seat of his patrol car. He then called his dispatcher and requested that a backup officer meet him to help transport the two prisoners. He then started for the jail.

Patrolman Anthony, responding to the dispatcher, parked his car at the intersection of S.C. 276 and White Horse Road to await the vehicle driven by Patrolman Wallace. Anthony then got into the passenger seat of Wallace's patrol vehicle while Ogle and his wife remained in the back seat.

As the patrol vehicle reached the Greenville city limits (near Stone Manufacturing and Park Place and "Bruce Plaza") around 4:30PM, Ogle removed a "snub-nosed .38 caliber revolver" he had hidden in his "combat-type boots" and fired five shots "through the seat" at Anthony. Four of the shots hit Anthony in the back and one came out his temple. A fifth bullet fired by Ogle "went wild" and struck Mrs. Ogle in the upper right arm. Patrolman Wallace's right hand was also injured from the shots that hit Anthony.

After firing five shots at Anthony, Ogle "placed" the five-shot revolver "against Wallace's forehand and fired, but the gun was empty."Wallace then stopped the vehicle and "rolled out and fired a shot at Ogle, striking him in the chest."

Officer Anthony was rushed by ambulance to Greenville General Hospital with bullet wounds to the back. He was pronounced dead on arrival. The slain officer's wife, Doris, heard of the death of her husband on the radio before she could be notified of the shooting.

THE PERPETRATOR

Clyde Edmond Ogle, 53, of Cleveland, S.C., was killed at the scene by Patrolman Wallace. The Ogles had five children.

Shortly after the shooting, Ogle's wife, Virginia Dare Ogle, 33, was charged with murder in connection with the shooting. Investigators first believed that the gun used to kill Anthony was possessed by Mrs. Ogle since he—but not she— had been searched and that it was then given to her husband while both were in the back seat.

However, investigators from S.C.L.E.D, the Highway Patrol and the Sheriff's office later determined that the revolver had been hidden in Clyde Ogle's boots and was not found by the cursory search by Wallace. The murder charges against Virginia Dare were dropped the following day. The killing of Clyde Ogle by Patrolman Wallace was ruled a justifiable homicide without an inquest.

The murder of Trooper Anthony caused considerable furor over police search policy and led to a state law that *required* police officers to handcuff prisoners being transported in patrol cars. Failure to do so would subject the officer to a fine of $100 and suspension from his duties for 90 days. The purpose of the law was to "take off the hook" officers who wanted to "be nice" or who were dealing with influential or prominent people.

The Highway Patrol and other police agencies also adopted a policy that required that one officer ride in the back seat with handcuffed prisoners and not in the front passenger seat as was the case in the incident that led to the murder of Anthony.

THE OFFICER

Fulton H. Anthony was born on June 28, 1935, in the Griffin Community in Pickens County to Jacob Vernon and Pearl Clark Anthony. He was the oldest of six children (Fulton, Juanita, Leuna, Lillie, Henry and Mary Alice).

Fulton was raised in the Griffin community as the family lived on a farm in the area. He attended Glassy Mt. Elementary School and Pickens H.S., graduating in 1953. He had no time for "activities" in H.S. as he had to work on the family farm and also drove a school bus.

On Aug. 6, 1955, Fulton Anthony, 20, married Doris Smith, 16. Their daughter, Rhonda Lea, was born on July 25, 1962. Fulton worked at Union Bleachery (a textile plant) and Poinsett Lumber and Manufacturing Co. (later Diehl Manufacturing) from 1953 to 1960 before joining the S.C. Highway Patrol at the age of 25.

He was stationed in Union County for 8 months before being transferred to Greenville where he remained for 13 years until his death. He went to "breathalyzer school" and was part of the special tactics team sent to the Orangeburg "riot."

Fulton Anthony was a religious man and, with his wife and daughter, was a member of the Berea Baptist Church for the 13 years he lived in Greenville. He was elected a deacon at the church just before his death.

Funeral services for Fulton Anthony were held at the Berea First Baptist Church on Monday, March 12. More than 200 law enforcement officers from throughout the state were joined by about 800 other persons for the funeral at the church where Anthony had been a member. The church overflowed and some mourners had to stand in the aisles and in the vestibule.

The service was conducted by Anthony's pastor, the Rev. Douglas N. Baker, assisted by the associate pastor, the Rev. Floyd Parker. At the end of the service the mourners stood at attention as six police officers carried Anthony's coffin down the church steps and placed it in the waiting funeral coach.

A 3-mile procession of over 350 cars, including many police cars with lights flashing, made the 20-mile trip to Hillcrest Memorial Gardens, near Pickens. The officers made a semi-circle around the canopy covering the gravesite during a brief graveside service.

The service was not conducted with full police honors as Fulton had told his wife three months earlier (after the death of another S.C. trooper) that if he were killed he wanted only a "regular" funeral. He had even told his daughter that she would not have to go to his funeral if he were killed and she, at 10 years old, remembered that and chose not to attend. She didn't want that memory.

Fulton Anthony was survived by his wife, Doris Anthony, 35, and a 10-year old daughter, Rhonda Lea; by his mother, Pearl Clark Anthony of Pickens County; and by his siblings, Juanita Anthony Campbell, Leuna Kelley, Lillie Davis, Henry Anthony, and Mary Alice Denton, all of Pickens County.

In 1996 the grave of Fulton Anthony is easily found at Hillcrest Memorial Gardens on Highway 8 near Pickens. The grave marker reads:

Fulton H. Anthony
1935-1973

Also buried in the family plot is an infant daughter, Aneta, who was born in 1959 but lived only 12 hours.

In 1996, Doris Anthony, 57, still lived in Greenville as did her daughter, Rhonda Lea, 34. Doris was the executive secretary and office manager at the Berea First Baptist Church. Rhonda graduated from Berea H.S. in 1980, Furman University in 1984, and the Southern Baptist Theological Seminary in Louisville, KY, in 1987. In 1996 Rhonda Lea was a counselor for the Greenville County Alcohol and Drug Commission.

A small bridge on the Poinsett Highway was dedicated to the memory of Fulton Anthony in 1981. The marker at the bridge reads:

March 10, 1973
Fulton H. Anthony
Memorial Bridge
Erected, 1981

The name of Fulton H. Anthony is inscribed (East Wall, Panel 43, Line 10) on the National Law Enforcement Memorial in Washington, D.C., and a plaque bearing his name is displayed at the S.C. Criminal Justice Hall of Fame in Columbia. Doris and Rhonda attended the dedication ceremonies of the Columbia Hall of Fame and hope some day to visit the national memorial in Washington, D.C.

SOURCES: *Greenville News,* March 11,12,13,14, 1973; and interview with Doris Anthony.

#28 RUFUS FRANKLIN LOOPER, III
Greenville Sheriff's Deputy
Shot & killed by robber on Jan. 31, 1975.

THE EVENT

Lt. R.F. (Frank) Looper, III, 34, the head of the six-man narcotics squad of the Greenville County Sheriff's Office, was shot and killed at his father's car repair garage in an armed robbery on Jan. 31, 1975. His father was also killed by the lone gunman who was convicted and sentenced to death. The SC Supreme Court reduced the death sentence to life in prison.

Around 2:00PM on Friday, Jan. 31, 1975, Rufus Franklin Looper, Sr., 57, was working in his car repair garage at 1190 Pendleton Street in West Greenville. His son, Greenville Officer Rufus Franklin Looper, III, 34, was at their home next door to the Looper Garage when he saw a black man enter the garage. Lt. Looper walked over to the garage to check out the suspicious person.

As he entered the garage he was shot once in the head by a lone gunman. Looper fell to the floor of the garage next to the entrance. He drew his service revolver but never fired it and the gun was found next to his body. His father was also shot one time in the head and fell at the back of the garage in front of a station wagon which was in the garage for repairs.

A neighbor heard the two shots and saw a black man, described as about 20 years old, 6 ft. tall, and 150 lbs., running from the garage. She ran to the scene and found the wife/mother of the two vic-

Rufus F. Looper, III

tims "screaming" as an ambulance arrived. Both victims were taken to the Greenville Memorial Hospital. The father died at 5:00PM (3 hours later) and his son, Lt. Looper, died at 9:25AM on Saturday, Feb. 1 (19 hours later). Both died of gunshot wounds to the head from a large caliber pistol.

A massive police search by Greenville officers and sheriff's deputies began almost immediately for the suspect. The S.C. Law Enforcement Dept. (SLED) sent 19 agents, a plane and pilot and bloodhounds from Columbia Friday night to help in the search. Several local officers came in on off-duty time to assist in the investigation. A reward of $3,000 was posted for information leading to the arrest and conviction of the killer of Lt. Looper and his father.

Sheriff Cash F. Williams told the media that he was assuming the shooting was "a narcotics-motivated assassination until proven different" since Lt. Looper was head of the narcotics unit for the Sheriff's Office and since no money was taken from the garage. The sheriff speculated that Lt. Looper may have been shot for revenge by one of the many persons he had arrested on narcotics charges

.THE PERPETRATOR

However, police later determined that the elder Looper's wallet had been taken and eventually focused on robbery as the motive. Charles "Wacky" Wakefield, Jr., 22, was arrested on Nov. 13, 1975 (9 & 1/2 months after the double-murder). He was indicted on Dec. 1, 1975, on two counts of murder while committing an armed robbery, one count of murdering a law enforcement officer in the line of duty, and armed robbery. Three of these charges carried a mandatory death sentence.

Wakefield's trial began on Monday, Feb. 23, 1976 (13 months after the murder), before Judge Frank Eppes. The case was prosecuted by Circuit Solicitor William W. Wilkins, Jr., and Wakefield was defended by Grover S. "Buddy" Parnell. The state presented one witness, Mae McIntire, an employee of the Salvation Army, who testified she was only two feet away from (a black man she identified as) Wakefield as he walked into the garage as she was leaving after receiving a donation for the Salvation Army from the elder Looper. After hearing what sounded like shots, she saw Wakefield running from the garage.

The state also presented evidence from Wyatt Earp Harper, 18, who said that he and Wakefield had planned to rob a liquor store near the Looper home but instead decided to rob Looper. Harper agreed to serve as a lookout and testified that he was given $45 for serving as a lookout during the robbery. He said that Wakefield told him he had shot two people.

The prosecution challenged the credibility of the two major state witnesses claiming that McIntire made up her story as part of a deal with the state to have her son-in-law's 24-year prison term reduced and that Harper pinned the blame on Wakefield in return for the state dropping a murder charge against him. The defense also claimed that Harper was the "shooter" and presented two relatives and a friend who claimed that Wakefield was elsewhere at the time of the murder.

The trial lasted three days and the jury deliberated more than four hours before returning guilty verdicts on all counts on Thursday, Feb. 26. Judge Eppes then pronounced the death penalty mandated by three of the counts.

Wakefield's sentence was later commuted to life and, in April of 1996, he was still incarcerated in a S.C. prison and had served 21 years in prison. His next parole hearing date was scheduled for September 28, 1996.

THE OFFICER

Frank Looper, 34, was born in Greenville on Dec. 30, 1940, the only child of Rufus Franklin Looper Jr., and Vera Mann Looper. His mother was born in Clinton, S.C., and was the daughter of James Fred and Dorothy Farley Mann. Frank was raised in Greenville and graduated from Greenville Sr. H.S. in 1959.

Frank Looper, 18, joined the U.S. Navy on Nov. 2, 1959, and served on the U.S. Algol (#54) out of Norfolk, VA. He made the rank of RD3 and completed his four-year tour in 1963. He served in the Navy Reserves until his death in 1975.

Upon his return to Greenville in 1963 Frank enrolled at N. Greenville College and transferred to Furman University in 1966. He graduated from Furman on June 7, 1970, with a B.A. in Economics and Business Administration.

Frank Looper, 30, joined the Greenville Sheriff's Office in October of 1971 and was assigned to the narcotics unit. He left the force for 14 months to conduct criminal investigations for Tom Greene, the 13th judicial circuit solicitor. Lt.

Looper returned to the Sheriff's Office in Aug. of 1973 to head the narcotics squad. His six-man squad made 257 narcotics cases in 1974.

Frank Looper was single and lived with his parents in the house adjacent to the Looper garage at 1190 Pendleton St. He and his parents were members of the Pendleton Street Baptist Church.

Lt. Looper was survived by his mother, Vera Mann Looper, 57, and his grandfather, Rufus Franklin Looper, Sr., 83, of Greenville. His mother was not only grief stricken by the murder of her husband and son, but was under treatment for a "heart defect." A memorial fund for the widow/mother was set up by the Greenville News-Piedmont Co. and raised $2,293 by Feb. 15.

The body of Lt. Looper lay in state at the Thomas McAfee Funeral Home on Sunday, Feb. 2. A burial service for both Lt. Looper and his father was held at Graceland Cemetery on Monday, Feb. 3. The service was conducted with "military rites by the members of the Naval Reserve" and included the Furman ROTC color guard and the Navy Reserve honor guard. Hundreds of uniformed police officers from throughout Greenville and surrounding counties attended the service. The procession from the funeral home to Graceland was led by police motorcycles with flashing lights.

In 1996 the grave of Lt. Looper is easily found at Graceland Cemetery in the Looper family plot (marked by a 3 x 6 ft. stone monument inscribed "LOOPER") 50 yards northwest of the graves of Sheriff Hendrix Rector (1919) and Greenville Police Chief J.F Holcombe (1915)—also killed in the line of duty. He is buried beside his father, Rufus F. Looper Jr. (Aug. 27, 1917-Feb. 1, 1975), grandfather, R.R. Looper (Oct. 21, 1892-May 6, 1979), and grandmother, Leora H. Looper (Aug. 11, 1891-Sept. 12, 1971). His grave marker reads:

R. FRANK LOOPER III
RD3 US NAVY
Dec. 30, 1940 - Feb. 1, 1975

Lt. Looper's mother, Vera Mann Looper, , 71, died on Feb. 24, 1989, and was buried beside her son and husband. Her obituary in the *Greenville News* listed only her brother, Elmo Mann of Greenville, as her survivor.

In 1996 Lt. Looper had no direct descendants remaining in Greenville County. Also, in 1996, the Looper family home and garage had been torn down and the site at 1190 Pendleton St. was occupied by a branch post office.

A plaque commemorating the death of Lt. Looper is displayed in the lobby of the Greenville County Law Enforcement Center. The plaque lists the recipients of the annual R. Frank Looper Memorial Award given each year to the Greenville County Sheriff's Office Outstanding Officer of the Year. The first recipient was James K. Hallaway in 1977.

The name of Rufus Frank Looper, III, is inscribed (East Wall, Panel 18, Line 3) on the National Law Enforcement Memorial in Washington, D.C., and a plaque bearing his name is displayed at the S.C. Criminal Justice Hall of Fame in Columbia.

SOURCES: *Greenville News*, Feb. 1,2,15, 1975, Feb. 26, 1989; Greenville Cemetery indexes; Furman University Registrar's file on Frank Looper; Greenville H.S. Yearbook for 1959; Burial records and grave markers at Graceland Cemetery; Greenville County criminal court case #75-GS-2183, 2184 & 2185; and records of S.C. Dept. of Corrections for Charles Wakefield.

#29 MATHEW M. BEACHAM, JR.
Greenville Police Dept.
Died of heart attack during a chase on Sept. 20, 1983.

THE EVENT

Greenville Officer Mathew M. "Monty" Beacham, Jr., 40, a 16-year veteran, died of a heart attack while chasing a youth who had escaped from the lobby of the Greenville County Law Enforcement Center. He became the 10th Greenville officer killed in the line of duty.

Mathew M. Beacham, Jr.

Mark Anthony Austin, 17, and a 16-year-old youth were arrested about 12:30AM on Tuesday, Sept. 20, for the theft of a car from a lot on Laurens Road. A night magistrate set bond at $10,500 for a charge of grand larceny, auto theft for both youths. Anthony was in the process of being taken to the detention center when he "broke free and ran out the front doors" of the Law Enforcement Center about 3:30AM.

Officer Monty Beacham was working the third shift as desk officer when Anthony "made a break for it." Beacham, Gantt District Officer Ed Whitmire and a sheriff's deputy ran after Anthony. Several hundred feet outside the LEC, Beacham complained of chest pains and was taken to Greenville Memorial Hospital by ambulance and admitted to the Coronary Care Unit. Beacham suffered a massive heart attack and died 14 hours later (5:30PM on Tuesday, Sept. 20). His death was ruled as "line of duty" since the heart attack occurred while on duty and during a police action.

THE PERPETRATOR

Mark Anthony Austin, 17, of 12 Keat St., was captured later the same day. However, Austin was not charged in the death of Officer Beacham and thus was not considered the perpetrator in this case. He was prosecuted for grand larceny, auto theft.

THE OFFICER

Mathew Montgomery "Monty" Beacham, Jr., 40, was born on Oct. 26, 1942, in Greenville to Mathew Montgomery Beacham, Sr., and Annie White Beacham. He was the second of two sons. His father drove a trolley in downtown Greenville before he died of a massive heart attack in 1943 when Mathew was a baby.

Monty was raised in Greenville and graduated from Holmes H.S. in 1960. He then attended the Holmes Bible Institute, a theological seminary run by the Pentecostal Holiness Church, from 1960-1964. After graduation from the seminary he was a minister with the Fountain Inn Pentecostal Holiness Church for three years from 1964-1967.

Mathew married Jean Hayes of Liberty, SC, on Aug. 3, 1969. Their first child, Mathew Montgomery Beacham, III, was born on June 22, 1970. A second child, William Charles Beacham, was born on Oct. 12, 1974.

Beacham joined the Greenville Police Dept. on June 13, 1967, and completed the Basic Police Recruit Training on Nov. 18, 1968. He was a detective in the I.D. Division until July 1, 1976 when, with the consolidation of law enforcement services, he was transferred to the Greenville County Police Service Bureau and worked there until Feb. 15, 1982, when he was reinstated to the Greenville Police Dept. Also, while still a Greenville Police Officer, he was sworn in as a state constable on June 27, 1978, giving him jurisdiction outside Greenville County. He was a 16-year law enforcement veteran at the time of his death.

Beacham was an expert in crime scene investigation and completed special training in photography (1971), fingerprint classification (1971), advanced latent fingerprint (1976), instruction in crime investigation and physical evidence collection (1976), death investigation (1978) crime scene processing and forensic laboratory procedure (1978), and advanced latent fingerprint teaching (1983).

Officer Beacham was well-known and well-liked by his colleagues. In 1973 he was elected treasurer of the Greenville chapter of the National Union of Police Officers. Officer W.C. Dees, who was one of his early training officers, became his partner for three years and served as best man at his wedding. One of his supervisors was Capt. Mike Bridges, later the Chief of Police. Chief Harold C. Jennings described Beacham as a "fine police officer and always a Christian gentleman...he exemplified good, clean living."

Officer Beacham was a member of the Geer Memorial Baptist Church in Easley, worked with the youth training program and sang in the church choir. He and his wife often sang duets during services. He was also a 3rd degree Mason in Easley Lodge No. 189 and was a Cub Scout Master. He lived at 301 Sharon Lane in Easley with his wife and two boys.

Funeral services for Monty Beacham were arranged by the Robinson Funeral Home and were held at the Geer Memorial Baptist Church on Friday, Sept. 23, 1983. The 45-minute service was conducted by Rev. Luther M. Price of the Geer Memorial Baptist Church and was attended by hundreds of uniformed police officers as well as family and friends. The flower-laden casket was flanked by a police honor guard. Uniformed officers served as pallbearers.

There was no eulogy other than the reading of a personal statement written by Monty Beacham before his death that gave his religious history and told of his "finding peace with God" on May 14, 1981, during a church revival. The closing words were:

Ever since that night, I give my testimony every chance I get. I want to tell people of what God has done for me and that he can do the same for you.

Burial was at the Flat Rock Baptist Church Cemetery. A procession of 40 police cars with flashing blue lights escorted the funeral procession the four miles from the church to the cemetery. A brief service was held at graveside.

Mathew M. Beacham, Jr., 40, was survived by his wife, Jean Hayes Beacham, 35; his mother, Annie White Beacham, 78; two sons, Mathew Montgomery Beacham, III, 13, and William Charles Beacham, 8; and a brother, A.D. Beacham of Oklahoma City, OK.

In 1996 the gravesite of Mathew Beacham is easily found at the Flat Rock Baptist Church Cemetery on Highway 178, 3 miles from Highway 123, Liberty exit. The marker reads:

Mathew M. Beacham, Jr.
1942-1983

Also on the grave marker is a metal ribbon which reads, "MTY-LTT" (He will be loved More than yesterday but less than tomorrow). The only other grave in the family plot is that of Cecil Bennett Hayes, Mathew Beacham's father-in-law. His father and mother are buried in Woodlawn Cemetery in Greenville.

In 1996, Jean Hayes Beacham had remarried (now Mrs. Roy Lee Moore) and worked in medical records at St. Frances Hospital in Greenville. She lived in Liberty, S.C. as did her sons Mathew M. Beacham, III, 25. and Charles Beacham, 21. Both boys graduated from Liberty H.S. Mathew was married and had two children (the grandchildren of Officer Beacham), Mathew M. Beacham, IV, 4, and Jamie Leigh Beacham, 3, and worked as a security guard at St. Frances Hospital. He would be easy to pick out by any visitor to the hospital as he is 7'2" tall. Charles Beacham was a partner in his step-father's construction company. Officer Beacham's brother, A.D. Beacham, died in 1996 and was a past general secretary and treasurer of the Pentecostal Holiness Church in the United States.

The name of Mathew Montgomery Beacham, Jr., is inscribed (West Wall, Panel 1, Line 6) on the National Law Enforcement Memorial in Washington, D.C., and a plaque bearing his name is displayed at the S.C. Criminal Justice Hall of Fame in Columbia.

SOURCES: *Greenville News*, Sept. 20,21,23, 1983; and interview with Jean Beacham Moore.

#30 VALDON OSBORN KEITH
S.C. State Constable
Shot & killed during car chase of robbers on Nov. 28, 1985.

THE EVENT

S.C. State Constable Valdon Osborn Keith, 46, was killed early Thanksgiving Day, 1985, when he was shot in the head while riding in a patrol car that tried to "box in" a vehicle occupied by two men fleeing an armed robbery. The two armed robbers/killers were convicted and sentenced to long prison terms. The "shooter" escaped from prison in 1994 but was recaptured after being featured on the TV program "Unsolved Mysteries" in 1996.

At 12:35AM on Thanksgiving morning, Nov. 28, 1985, two armed men, Samuel Leroy Wodke, 40, and Wilbur Rutledge "Rusty" Corvette, Jr., 32, entered The Family Mart on East North Street in Loehmann's Plaza in Greenville. Wodke, unmasked and armed with a machine gun, stood at the door while Corvette, armed with an automatic handgun and wearing a dark-colored ski mask, went to "the booth where the safe was kept."

Valdon O. Keith

There were approximately 20 employees and 35 customers in the store at the time of the robbery. The employees and customers were ordered to the back of the store or forced to lie on the floor while Corvette took $8,800 in cash and an additional $1,200 in food stamps and checks. Wodke fired two shots into a soft drink display with the automatic handgun "when he saw someone get too close." No one in the store was injured during the robbery.

After the robbery the two armed men fled in a 1981 Chevrolet Chevette driven by Samuel Wodke. Wodke's son, Richard, 18, was waiting in the car. A witness followed the robbers' car north on Howell and Edwards roads and then returned to the store to give police a description of the getaway car and the direction it was traveling. Police broadcast a description of the getaway car and Greenville Sheriff's Deputy Park Evans spotted it as it turned from Rutherford Road onto S.C. 291. He followed the car to Piney Mountain Road where it turned north to S.C. 253 (State Park Rd.).

The robbers spotted the "tail" and waited at an intersection for Evan's car to approach. Evans, recognizing that he had been "made" and fearing an ambush, stayed back, and the suspects then turned left onto S.C. 253. A second Sheriff's patrol car was traveling south on S.C. 253 toward the suspects' car. The driver, Deputy Dennis Eubanks, was aware from the police broadcast that the suspects had automatic weapons and had fired shots at the supermarket robbery and thus were extremely dangerous. Not wanting to meet the getaway car "head-on," exposing he and his passenger, State Constable Valdon Osborn Keith, to oncoming fire through the front windshield, Eubanks turned his car around so that it was going in the same direction as the suspects' car.

When the getaway car caught up with the patrol car, "Eubanks slowed, trying to box the car between the two patrol cars" (Evan's patrol car was closely following the suspects' car). The robbers "swung to the right of Eubanks' car" into a parking lot. As they passed the patrol car they "sprayed it with gunfire." Five bullets shattered the windshield and two windows. "Eubanks rolled out of the car and fired six shots at the rear of the suspects' car as it sped off." Shots from the fugitives' car continued as Eubanks rolled out of the driver's side of his car onto the ground and returned fire.

Deputy Eubanks found that his partner, Constable Keith, had been shot in the head. He called for an ambulance and did what he could for the fatally wounded officer until it arrived. Deputy Evans did not pursue the suspects, and instead, stopped to check on the condition of Eubanks and Keith. He realized that other backups would arrive quickly. A third patrol car did arrive within a minute "but by then the suspects were gone." Keith was declared dead at the scene by arriving paramedics.

Police notified surrounding jurisdictions of the description of the getaway car (the 1981 Chevrolet Chevette with bullet holes in the back) and the two armed robbers (two white males, one described as "6-foot-1 and 175 pounds" and the other as "shorter and stocky, about 180 pounds with curly dark hair and a moustache"). The car was found 12 hours later in Gaston, a rural section of Lexington County. It was parked at the residence of the person who loaned it to two men.

THE PERPETRATORS

Given the names of the two men who had borrowed the getaway car, police quickly located the first suspect, Samuel Leroy Wodke of Lexington County, and arrested him at 9:50PM on Friday, Nov. 29, in West Columbia as he left a restaurant with a woman. He was unarmed at the time and was overpowered by more than 20 law enforcement officers from Lexington and Greenville counties. Wodke was taken to the Greenville County Detention Center and held without bond. His son, Richard, was arrested a short time later.

Wilbur Rutledge Corvette, Jr., of Chesterfield Square was arrested on Tuesday, Dec. 3, in Lexington County on two armed robbery warrants issued in Charleston County. The three were held in the Greenville County Detention Center until the March, 1986, trial.

Samuel Wodke and Corvette were charged with armed robbery and first degree murder. Richard Wodke was charged with being an accessory before and after the fact of murder and armed robbery. Thirteenth Circuit Solicitor Joe Watson announced that he planned to seek the death penalty against Samuel Wodke and Rusty Corvette.

Samuel Leroy Wodke, 40, of Lexington County, was on intensive supervision parole at the time of the murder of Constable Keith. He was serving a 20-year state sentence for an armed robbery in Berkeley County, S.C., when he was paroled on Jan. 28, 1985 (ten months before the murder). Before parole he had been on work release at the Campbell Pre-Release Center in Columbia.

Wilbur Rutledge Corvette, Jr., 32, of Chesterfield Square, was also on parole at the time of the Keith murder. He was from a middle-class family in Charleston but had been "in trouble" since he was a juvenile. In 1977 he was convicted of grand larceny and sentenced to six years in jail and five years probation but was paroled by S.C. authorities in October, 1980. He testified for the prosecution in the 1983 trial of Newby Franklin Love and four other defendants in connection with the seizure of more than $325 million in cocaine at the Sumter County airport on Dec. 20, 1982. At the time the seizure was the "largest such bust in the state's history and was called by authorities the fourth largest in the nation's history."

On April 21, 1983, Corvette pled guilty to conspiracy to smuggle marijuana and conspiracy to violate anti-racketeering laws. In return for his co-operation as a state witness, Corvette was given a more lenient sentence than his partners—two consecutive five-year terms in federal prison. However, U.S. District Judge Charles Simmons shortened Corvette's 10 year sentence to 40 months after learning that the government violated Corvette's plea agreement by including his criminal history in a pre-sentence report to the sentencing judge. In Jan. of 1985 (10 months before the Keith murder) he was already on parole from that sentence.

A plea bargain was struck with Corvette and the younger Wodke to testify against Samuel Wodke, "the shooter." Wodke's trial was held March 5-8, 1986, before Judge C. Victor Pyle, Jr. Solicitor Joe Watson prosecuted the case for the state while Greenville County Public Defender Pete Partee and Harold Christian, Jr., defended Wodke. Jury selection took 1 & 1/2 days and the jury was sequestered for the entire trial.

Richard Wodke testified that the trio had initially planned to rob a money courier leaving an Ingle's grocery store by running his car off the road and robbing him. However, they lost him and then decided to rob the Family Mart. He also testified that he saw his father shoot the constable with a machine gun.

Sam Wodke stopped the car, then slowly drove around the right side of the police car at about five to 10 miles per hour, his son said.

As Sam Wodke passed, he raised a 9mm machine gun, extended it out the driver's side window and pulled the trigger, Richard Wodke testified. "That's when I put my head down between the seats."

Wodke said his father then drove him and Corvette to a hotel in Spartanburg where Corvette and the elder Wodke counted the money. Sam Wodke gave him $165 and told him to catch a bus, Richard Wodke said. (*Greenville News*, 3/6/1986)

Several witnesses, who had been customers or employees at the Family Mart, testified that Corvette, wearing a ski-mask walked up to a manager's booth in the front of the store and pointed a .45 caliber pistol at the manager's nose and demanded money while Samuel Wodke, who was not wearing a mask, "crouched" by the front door with a machine gun "braced against his shoulder."

On the second day of the trial Samuel Wodke and Corvette "pointed the trigger finger at each other." Wodke claimed that Corvette shot the constable while Corvette, testifying for the state, claimed that Wodke fired the fatal shots. Corvette also read passages from letters from Samuel Wodke which he received while both were in jail awaiting trial in which they planned to blame the shooting on Richard Wodke, Samuel's son. Thus the state presented evidence that Samuel Wodke was willing to frame his own son for the murder. The state also presented physical evidence that suggested that Samuel Wodke was "the shooter."

The jury deliberated only an hour before returning a verdict of guilty on March 7. The sentencing hearing followed the verdict to determine whether Wodke would receive a life sentence or death. The state presented evidence of Wodke's prior record and reminded the jury that Wodke was a "con man" who plotted to blame his own son for the murder. "He conned his own lawyer by telling him Richard did it. If you buy that Rusty Corvette pulled the trigger, then he has conned you too." The state closed with the words:

"On November 28 on State Park Road, you had the epitome of good in Valdon Keith. A businessman, a father, a man who volunteered his time for the good of the community. At the same time, three feet away, you had Sam Wodke. Good and evil three feet apart. Evil won." (*Greenville News*, 3/9/1986)

Samuel Wodke conceded that he committed the armed robbery but told the jurors, "I give you my word as a man that I did not shoot Valdon Keith." Wodke called Corvette a "thug" and a "liar". Defense attorney Partee reminded the jury that Corvette was the real "con man" and that he had gotten away with over "100 years of crimes" in exchange for his testimony in the 1983 drug trial and now was avoiding the death penalty by "selling out" Wodke by blaming him for the killing of Keith. Partee called Corvette a "vulture, a rat gnawing at somebody's bones...He is a snitch, a dope dealer and a killer."

The jury evidently had some doubts as to who actually fired the shots at Constable Keith as it returned a recommendation for a life sentence to the judge. The jury might have believed that the "real killer" was Corvette or simply had some doubt that Wodke was the killer. Judge Pyle sentenced Samuel Wodke to life plus 25 years.

Two months after Samuel Wodke's trial (on July 8, 1986), Corvette pled guilty to robbery with a deadly weapon (the murder charge was dropped in the plea bargain) and was sentenced to 21 years in prison. At the sentencing hearing, Solicitor Joe Watson told Judge William H. "Howard" Ballenger that all state evidence showed the slaying was a "spontaneous" act by Wodke and conceded that be believed Corvette "did not intend for the shooting to occur." Watson also told the judge that trying Corvette for murder would be unfair since he would be subject to the same maximum sentence (25 years plus life) given to the more culpable Wodke who was spared from the death penalty by a jury. Corvette would be eligible for parole after only 7 years of the 21 year sentence.

Richard Wodke was given a 10 year suspended sentence while being placed on intensive probation for 5 years. The probation was to be suspended if the younger Wodke entered a branch of the armed services.

Corvette was paroled from his 21 year sentence on Sept. 8, 1993, after serving seven years and 10 months. No one appeared at his parole hearing to speak in opposition to his parole because police and the Keith family were not notified of the hearing. However, Corvette was arrested and incarcerated in a federal prison because the 1985 armed robbery and murder of Keith constituted a violation of his federal parole granted in 1985. Corvette was incarcerated at the federal prison in Butner, N.C., until his mandatory release on Feb. 9, 1996.

Constable Keith's widow, daughter (Julie Ann), and his son, Gary Allen Keith, traveled to Butner, N.C., in 1995 and successfully opposed an earlier release date.

On Jan. 8, 1994, Samuel Leroy Wodke, 49, and another convicted killer Danny Lail, 47, escaped from the Kirkland Correctional Institution by prying open a steam tunnel manhold cover, sawing through three sets of bars with a hacksaw, breaking the lock of a boiler room located outside the security fence, and driving a state vehicle past the front gate. The two inmates were allowed to work on a horticulture crew near the manhole even though Wodke had been caught trying to escape through the same tunnel in 1987 and though Lail had been seen by a corrections officer in another manhole 10 days earlier.

Investigators described the escape as involving a "comedy of errors" and six prison employees were reprimanded or suspended. Newspaper reports after the escape indicated that "less than 300" of the 2,855 inmates who escaped from S.C. prisons from 1972-1994 escaped from maximum or medium security prisons. S.C. ranked 23rd among the states in 1992 with 3.5 escapes for every 1,000 inmates.

Lail was arrested on Feb. 2, 1995, in Naples FL. However, Wodke was still at large by March of 1996 when his escape was shown on TV's "Unsolved Mysteries." He had earlier been featured on "America's Most Wanted." On March 30, 1996, Wodke was arrested in Morgan City, La, after being a fugitive for almost 27 months. Authorities received a tip on his whereabouts through the TV show, "Unsolved Mysteries" and "stormed" his hotel room with a SWAT team. Wodke had been working under an alias for a year as a welder in Morgan City.

Samuel Wodke was charged with grand larceny of a motor vehicle, kidnapping and escape and was returned to prison in S.C. As of April, 1996, he was still incarcerated in a S.C. prison and had not been arraigned on his recent escape warrant. His next parole hearing date was scheduled for April 13, 1998.

THE OFFICER

Valdon Osborn Keith, 46, was born on March 5, 1939, in Pickens, S.C., to Kenneth O. and Bonnie Keith. The ancestors of the Keith family had lived in the Upstate for almost 250 years as Cornelius Keith, born in Scotland "of royal lineage dating from 1010 A.D.," became in 1743 one of the first white settlers in what later became known as Pickens County. He traded a pony for the Oolenoy Valley which was occupied by the Cherokee Indians. An historical marker at the Oolenoy Baptist Church in Pickens County marks the grave of Cornelius Keith who died in 1808 at the age of 93. More than 125 descendants of Cornelius Keith gathered at the gravesite on April 15, 1956, to dedicate the monument.

Valdon was the oldest of four boys and was raised with his brothers in Berea. He attended the public schools in Berea and went thru the 11th grade at Berea H.S. After H.S. Valdon worked for Covil Insulation and was self-employed as a carpenter (doing remodeling work) until his death.

On Dec. 22, 1982, Keith received his commission as a state constable and began working as a volunteer (unpaid) with local law enforcement officers. He had decided that he wanted to pursue law enforcement as a career and thus began working in that capacity as a volunteer constable until he could gain full-time employment. He had planned to take criminal justice courses at Greenville Tech to pursue his goal of becoming a full-time police officer. He had no formal training for his work as a volunteer constable but was trained to shoot and allowed to carry a gun.

As a duly authorized state constable, Keith had jurisdiction throughout S.C. and thus Greenville County law enforcement officers liked to have him around in case they had to cross over into another county. Keith worked 10-20 hours per week as an unpaid volunteer and usually rode with other officers on weekends and holidays (he was killed on Thanksgiving Day).

Valdon Keith was survived by his second wife, Barbara, 41 (whom he married in 1972), and their son, Gary Allen Keith, 12; by two children from a prior marriage, Julia Ann Yates, 25, and Valdon Scotty Keith, 19; by a granddaughter, Carrie Yates, 4; by his step-son (from Barbara's first marriage) Christoper Lollis, 20; by his three brothers, Earl Keith, 42, Larry Keith, 36, and James Keith, 33; and by his mother, Bonnie Keith, 62, and grandmother, Olive Roper Keith, 90. All lived in Greenville County.

The funeral for Constable Keith was held at the Thomas McAfee Funeral Home Chapel in Greenville on Saturday, Nov. 30, 1985. Hundreds of uniformed police officers filled the chapel joined by friends and family of the slain officer. Rev. J. Frank Sanders of Travelers Rest and Dr. Douglas N. Baker, pastor of the Berea First Baptist Church (Keith's church) spoke at the service. Baker quoted a law enforcement prayer, "May time never erase the sacrifice that was made. May this man stand forever as one who went down brave."

After the 30-minute service, a procession of patrol cars with emergency lights flashing traveled from the chapel to Graceland Cemetery for the burial. "There, under gray skies threatening rain, officers ringed the burial site as the coffin was put in the ground."

In 1996 the grave of Constable Keith is easily found at Graceland Cemetery. A three foot stone marker inscribed "Keith" marks the family plot which includes a place for his widow. His marker reads:

Valdon O. Keith
March 5, 1939
Nov. 28, 1985
Forever in Our Hearts

Three infant children from his first marriage (James W. Keith, Oct. 3, 1958-Jan. 29, 1959; Larry Dean Keith, Jan. 22, 1963-Jan. 31, 1963; and Brenda Jean Keith, Jan. 22, 1963-Jan. 27, 1963) are also buried at Graceland.

In 1996 Barbara Keith, 51, worked at Mayfair Mill in Easley. Gary Allen Keith, 22, worked at the Greenville County Detention Center. Christopher Lollis, 30, lived in Easley with his two children Brittany, 9, and Bryson, 4. Julia Ann Yates, 35, lived in Greenville with her daughter, Carrie, 15, and Valdon Scotty Keith, 29, lived in Greer with his daughter, Tiffany, 5 (Carrie and Tiffany are grandchildren of Constable Keith).

Valdon's mother, Bonnie, 72, remained in Greenville in 1996. His father, Kenneth O. Keith, died in 1979 and was buried in the cemetery adjoining the Berea Baptist Church near Valdon's grandparents, Grover Matthew Keith

(1885-1957) and Olive Roper Keith, (1895-1990). His brothers (Earl, 52; Larry, 46; and James, 43) also lived in Greenville County in 1996.

The name of Valdon Osborn Keith is inscribed (East Wall, Panel 44, Line 15) on the National Law Enforcement Memorial in Washington, D.C., and a plaque bearing his name will be displayed at the S.C. Criminal Justice Hall of Fame in Columbia in 1996. A plaque honoring Valdon Keith is also displayed in the lobby of the Greenville County Detention Center.

SOURCES: *Greenville News,* April 16, 1956, Nov. 29,30, Dec. 1,3,5,6, 1985, March 9, Nov. 27, 1986, Jan. 10, March 16,22, 1984, March 5-9, July 9, 1986, Sept. 9, 1993, April 10, 1994, March 31, 1996; Greenville County criminal court case #86-GS-23-1319 & 86-GS-23-0959,1960; Records of S.C. Dept. of Corrections; and interviews with Barbara Keith and James Keith.

#31 WILLIAM MAHON BANKS
Greenville County Deputy Sheriff
Killed in traffic accident on June 9, 1989

THE EVENT

Greenville County Deputy Sheriff William Mahon Banks, 28, was killed on June 9, 1989, when his patrol vehicle was hit broadside by a pickup truck that ran a stop sign. The 17-year old driver of the pickup was convicted of reckless homicide.

At 11:45PM on Friday, June 9, 1989, Deputy William ("Bill") Banks, 28, was on patrol when his patrol car was hit on the driver's side by a pickup truck driven by Leon Christopher Garrett, 17, of Pelzer, at the intersection of Old Pelzer Road and Estes Road, near Piedmont. "The impact pushed the patrol car completely out of the roadway." Deputy Banks died "instantly" of multiple body trauma and was pronounced dead at the scene.

THE PERPETRATOR

Leon Christopher Garrett, 18, of Pelzer, was charged with reckless homicide. He was treated and released from Greenville Memorial Hospital after the accident.

William Mahon Banks, 28, a Greenville County, South Carolina Deputy Sheriff, was killed on June 9, 1989, when a pickup truck ran a stop light and hit his vehicle. Banks graduated from Ware Shoals High School in 1979 and served four years in the U.S. Army. His name is inscribed on the National Law Enforcement Memorial in Washington, DC.

Records in Greenville County criminal court indicate that Garrett was found guilty at trial of reckless homicide on Oct. 17, 1990. The three-day trial before Circuit Judge Don Rushing included testimony by a friend of Garrett's that he often sped down Estes Road on his way to work and turned off his headlights and ran the stop sign at Old Pelzer Road.

A state Highway Patrol trooper said Garrett probably was traveling 63 mph before the collision, and a forensic chemist said tests showed that the headlights on Garrett's truck weren't on before the accident. (*Greenville News*, 10/18/1990)

Solicitor Warren Mowry, who prosecuted the case for the state, told the jury that Garrett never exercised any regard for the safety of others when he was driving and that he ran the stop sign on purpose, causing the wreck that killed Banks. He noted that "this was not a mere accident where the stop sign slipped up on an unsuspecting motorist" but was a "deliberate act."

The jury deliberated for only 30 minutes before returning a verdict of guilty of reckless homicide. Judge Rushing sentenced Garrett to up to five years in prison under the Youthful Offender Act. The newspaper reported that Judge Rushing also "chastised" Garrett at the sentencing and said:

"This is not what I call a typical reckless homicide case....your prior acts are just absolutely appalling. There's a close question of whether you should have been indicted for murder in this case. (*Greenville News,* 10/18/1990)

The victim's father, Billy Banks, said after the trial that he was satisfied with the sentence "so far" indicating that he hoped Garrett would serve the full sentence.

Leon Christopher Garrett, 19, was given a conditional parole and released on Oct. 31, 1991, after serving only 13 months of his 5 year sentence.

THE OFFICER

William Mahon "Bill" Banks, 28, was born on April 13, 1961, in Laurens, SC, to William "Billy" and Dorris "Dot" Mahon Banks. He was the oldest of two sons.

Young Bill grew up in Ware Shoals in Greenwood County. He attended Ware Shoals Jr. H.S. and Ware Shoals H.S., graduating in 1979. He attended Clemson University in 1979-1980 (majoring in engineering) and Piedmont Tech in Greenwood in 1980-1981 & 1985-1986.

Bill served in the U.S. Army from 1981-1984, serving in the military police. He went through basic training at Ft. McClellan, AL, and was later stationed at Ft. Stewart in Savannah, GA, and in Hohenfels, Germany.

Upon discharge from the Army, Banks returned home and joined the Greenwood County Sheriff's office in July of 1984. He graduated from the Police Academy in Columbia in 1984 and served as a Greenwood deputy until Jan. 5, 1987, when he joined the Greenville County Sheriff's Office in Greenville. He was a 2 & 1/2 year veteran of the Greenville Sheriff's Office (and 5 year law enforcement veteran) at the time of his death. Bill Banks was single and lived at the Barrington Parks Apts in Greenville. He was a member of the Calvary Baptist Church.

The funeral for Deputy Banks was held on Monday, June 12, at the First Baptist Church of Ware Shoals, S.C. The visitation was held the day before at the Parker-White Funeral Home. The Rev. Ronnie Powell and Sheriff Johnny Mack Brown delivered eulogies. Sheriff Brown called Banks a "soldier-the epitome of a true professional who did his job and did it well."

The Honor Guard of the Greenville County Sheriff's Dept. served as pallbearers. Hundreds of uniformed police officers from the Upstate area attended the funeral and burial services. The funeral procession from the church to the cemetery included over 75 law enforcement vehicles.

The burial service, held at the Oakbrook Memorial Park in Greenwood, was conducted with full police and military honors (e.g., the folding of the flag by the honor guard, a gun salute).

In 1996 the grave marker of William Banks at Oakbrook Memorial Park in Ware Shoals reads:

DEPUTY WILLIAM M. BANKS
APRIL 13, 1961
JUNE 9, 1989

William Banks was survived by his parents William "Billy" Banks, 55, and

Dorris "Dot" Mahon Banks, 54, and a brother, John Lee Banks, 21, all of Ware Shoals.

The 7th annual "Cultured Cowboy Championship Rodeo," held June 23-29, 1989, was dedicated to the memory of Deputy Bill Banks who "helped behind the scenes" of the prior six rodeos. Also, Sheriff Brown presented a "gold-plated, wood-mounted" plaque to the Banks family in 1989 at a ceremony at the Greenville County Law Enforcement Center. The plaque featured Bank's deputy sheriff's badge.

The name of William Mahon Banks is inscribed (West Wall, Panel 9, Line 3) on the National Law Enforcement Memorial and a plaque bearing his name is displayed at the S.C. Criminal Justice Hall of Fame in Columbia. In May of 1990 William and Doris Banks attended a memorial service in Washington, D.C. at the National Law Enforcement Memorial which included the reading of the name of William Banks and the other officers killed the prior year.

Also, in May of 1990, Bank's parents attended a seminar in Columbia sponsored by the newly formed S.C. chapter of Concerns for Police Survivors (C.O.P.S.) The organization offers emotional and psychological support to relatives, friends and co-workers of law enforcement officers who have been killed in the line of duty. The SC chapter was formed by Dillon resident Paula Radford whose husband, George Radford, a S.C. Highway Patrol officer, was murdered while transporting a suspect in his patrol car.

SOURCES: *Greenville News,* June 11, 1989, *Greenwood Index Journal*, June 11,12, 1989; *Piedmont People,* June, 1990; Greenville County criminal court record of Leon Christoper Garrett, #90-GS-23-0932; records of S.C. Dept. of Corrections; and interview with William Banks.

#32 JAMES RUSSELL SORROW
Greenville Police Dept.
Shot & killed during foot chase on Sept. 19, 1996.

THE EVENT

Greenville Officer James Russell Sorrow, 26, was shot and killed on Sept. 19, 1996, at the end of a foot chase of a man wanted on an outstanding warrant. The killer escaped the scene but was captured in Greenville six days later after an intensive manhunt. Sorrow was the first City of Greenville officer killed in the line of duty in 25 years (since Officer Frank Chasteen in 1971).

Around 4:45PM on Thursday, Sept. 19, 1996, Greenville Officer Russ Sorrow, a 4-year veteran, was on patrol near the corner of Endel and Gower on the "Westside" when he spotted Joseph R. Sheppard, 20, a man wanted on an outstanding warrant. When Sheppard saw the uniformed officer he began running. Officer Sorrow gave chase which led to a house at 74 Endel St. Inside the house Sorrow was able to grab Sheppard but another man in the house, Draco Olandis Sullivan, 19, intervened and knocked Sorrow to the floor allowing Sheppard to escape.

James Russell Sorrow

Sorrow used his police radio to call the dispatcher to request an ambulance as he had been hit in the head and "received a gash over his eye." Sorrow then ran outside to continue the chase, not knowing that Sheppard was waiting outside. He "ran into a hail of gunfire from a man waiting in ambush." Sheppard had hidden around a corner and shot Sorrow two times with a .22-caliber semi-automatic handgun "at close range" as he ran toward him. The officer fell to the ground with his gun still in its holster. Sheppard then approached the prone and wounded officer and fired five more times, striking him four times in the back of the head and once in the buttocks.

Several people nearby heard the gunshots, saw a man running away, and found Sorrow lying on the ground. Two witnesses saw the gunman "standing over the fallen officer pointing a weapon at him" and then flee. One witness ran to the scene and "picked up Sorrow's radio and called for help." The wounded officer was taken to Greenville Memorial Hospital with what Dr. Alfred Nelson described an "unsurvivable wounds." Sorrow's wife, Joy, who worked at American Federal Bank in Greenville, was taken by officers to the hospital "where her husband lay mortally wounded." Russ Sorrow died at 8:05PM, three hours after being shot.

THE PERPETRATOR

A large team of law enforcement officers from the City of Greenville, the Greenville Sheriff's Office, the Highway Patrol, S.C.L.E.D., A.T.F., and

D.E.A., headed by Greenville Major W.L. Johnson began a massive manhunt for Joseph R. Sheppard, 20. The searchers "wore bulletproof vests, SWAT gear and grim looks." They concentrated on the Westside neighborhood where the shooting occurred and where Sheppard lived (at 11 Fulton St.).

Bloodhounds and a helicopter were brought in to aid in the search. However, Sheppard was not captured until Wednesday, Sept. 25, six days after the murder, partly because many persons aided and abetted his escape from capture after the murder. However, several citizens did help including Sheppard's mother who made a public plea for her son to give himself up. In fact, a community rally was held on Sunday, Sept. 22, to encourage cooperation with the police and Sheppard's mother again made a public plea for her son to surrender.

Police eventually charged ten persons with accessory after the fact of murder: Clarence Darrell Thornton, 35; Angel D. Johnson, 19; Anthony B. Sheppard; Nancy M. Workman, 40; Charles William Poole, 21; George H. Smith, Sr., 20; Lewis Anthony Fuller, 20; Reggie Lavon Cole, 26; Leroysha Janiell Johnson, 25; and Drako Olandis Sullivan, 19. Sullivan, the man who assaulted Sorrow inside the house at 74 Endel St., allowing Sheppard to escape the house and wait in ambush outside, was also charged with aiding and abetting a fugitive. Sheppard was moved to the Pickens County Detention Center so that "he wouldn't have contact with the others arrested as accessories."

The police received 269 tips over the six days before Sheppard's capture on Sept. 25. Sheppard "topped" CrimeStoppers Most Wanted List with a $1,000 reward offered for information leading to his arrest. In addition, the City of Greenville offered a $10,000 reward for information leading to Sheppard's arrest and conviction.

The arrest of Sheppard on Sept. 25 came about as a result of a tip that he was hiding in a room at the Cricket Inn on S. Pleasantburg Dr. A heavily armed SWAT team evacuated the hotel and nearby Dixie Restaurant before calling for Sheppard to surrender. The fugitive, realizing that he could not escape, opened the door and surrendered.

Sheppard had a lengthy criminal record. His father, James Mackey, told reporters that his son had "been trouble since he was 14 years old." He "had been convicted of assault and battery of a high and aggravated nature, larceny and receiving stolen goods" and was on probation at the time of the murder. He was also wanted on two bench warrants, one for Family Court (for outstanding child support) and one for failing to appear in court in July on drug, burglary and resisting arrest charges.

Police charged Sheppard with murder and prosecutor Joe Watson said that he would seek the death penalty. Police found the murder weapon though it was "in parts" after an effort had been made to destroy it. Lab tests indicated that the .22 caliber pistol found was the gun that killed Officer Sorrow.

The disposition of his case was not included in this book since the murder occurred just as the book was about to be mailed to the publisher.

THE OFFICER

James Russell Sorrow was born on March 22, 1970, in Greenwood, SC. to Rev. J.C. and Claudine Reynolds Sorrow. He was the fourth of four children.

The Sorrow family, which had a long history of ministers in the family, moved periodically as James' father "pastored" different churches in the Upstate. Russ grew up in Batesburg, Tryon NC, and Ware Shoals. He attended Tryon Elementary and Tryon Middle School for grades two through seven (1977-1983). "Rusty" was a star little league baseball player and was selected as a Polk County All-Star. He also played football at Tryon Middle School. He later attended Batesburg/Leesville Jr. High School and Ware Shoals H.S., graduating in 1988. In H.S. James played on the football and baseball teams and also was a member of the band.

Sorrow attended Clemson University from 1988 to 1990 and played trumpet in the Tiger Band. He also worked for a time with United Parcel, Westinghouse Corp. and Defiance Metal before working briefly as a detention officer at the Greenville Detention Center.

Russ Sorrow joined the Greenville Police Dept. in 1992 fulfilling a lifelong ambition to be a police officer. Several members of his family had been in law enforcement. An uncle, Norman Sorrow, retired as a captain from the Greenville County Sheriff's Office while another uncle, William R. Berry, retired as a captain from the Greenville Police Dept.

Russ joined the Greenville Police Dept. on June 1, 1992, and graduated from the South Carolina Police Academy later that year. He was a member of the Fraternal Order of Police, the South Carolina Law Enforcement Officers Association and the Greenville Police Officers Pistol Club. He was a 4-year veteran of the Greenville Police Dept. at the time of his death and served as a patrol officer during his entire tenure.

Two years earlier Russ Sorrow shot and killed a homeless man "who was brandishing what Sorrow believed was a .45 caliber semi-automatic. It was a plastic gun." He was exonerated for the shooting but received counseling for the distress it caused him.

Russ was a "religious man" who came from a religious family. His father was a Pentecostal minister. He met his future wife Joy Barden at a church youth camp in southern Greenville County. They married in 1993. Russ was often described as a "family man" who cared deeply for his wife and child and extended family. Russ and his wife attended the Belton Pentecostal Holiness Church.

James Russell Sorrow was survived by his wife Joy Barden Sorrow, 25, of Williamston; by his 5-month old son, Matthew Christian Sorrow; by his parents, Rev. J.C. and Claudine Reynolds Sorrow of Greenwood; by two sisters, Donna Sorrow Milford of Abbeville and Micki Sorrow of Greenville; by a brother, Keith Sorrow of Spartanburg; by his wife's parents, Rev. and Mrs. Dennis Barden of Belton; by his sister-in-law, Paige Barden Jay of Ninety-Six; and by his stepgrandfather, William Payne of Piedmont.

Two memorial funds (one at the American Federal Bank in Greenville where the widow worked and the other by the state F.O.P. at the National Bank of South Carolina) were established for the Sorrow family. In addition the family received death benefits from the City of Greenville and the U.S. Justice Dept.

A candlelight vigil in memory of Officer Sorrow was held by fellow officers outside the Greenville County Law Enforcement Center on Friday night, Sept. 20. A large candle at the base of the flagpole "first ignited a single candle and then multiplied through the crowd." Police Chaplain Dr. John C. Vaughn spoke briefly at the service.

The visitation was on Saturday, Sept. 21, at the Cox Funeral Home in

Belton, SC. The funeral service was held at 3:00PM on Sunday, Sept. 22, at the Belton Pentecostal Holiness Church (where the officer was a member). A newspaper reported that

They came by the hundreds, in convoys from across the state, law officers in blue forming solemn lines outside a country church Sunday to pay their respects to a fallen comrade.

Amid a show of solidarity that included state Attorney General Charlie Condon and lawmen and men of all stripes, family and friends said farewell to James Russell Sorrow... *(Greenville News,* 9/23/1996)

The church was "packed with as many lawmen as could squeeze into the tan-brick building for the funeral" and "hundreds more, who were unable to get into the church, kept a quiet vigil in the warm sunshine." One of those in attendance was Fountain Inn Sgt. Carlton Pope who would himself be killed in the line of duty two weeks later.

Three ministers eulogized the fallen officer "who lay beneath a flag-draped coffin." Dr. Phillip Morris told mourners that Sorrow was a "Christian law enforcement officer" and "as such was for our society salt and light for the world." Morris told the family that Sorrow would always be a hero and that they would always have his love. He also praised the widow for her support.

"Joy, thank you for letting your husband be what God called him to be. You have much to be proud of. So many people miss their vision of life because somebody tells them to look for something easy. Somebody tells them to look for something that pays a lot of money. But this man knew what God wanted him to do, and he did it. Thank God for that today."

Dr. Morris also thanked Russ' parents for "letting your son be what he wanted to be" and told them that Russ was as much "called" to be a police officer as his father was to be a minister of the gospel. Two other ministers, Dr. Ronald Carpenter and the Rev. Ansel Boggs, a longtime friend of Sorrow's (and the uncle of J.C. Sorrow), also delivered eulogies.

After the funeral service the procession of police vehicles and family cars proceeded to Forest Lawn Memorial Gardens in Abbeville "where Sorrow was laid to rest." The slain officer's father-in-law, Rev. Dennis Barden, "pinned a black ribbon to his coat lapel" and urged other Upstate residents to do the same. Barden said that the family wanted people to wear black ribbons through at least the end of the month as "an outward sign that we as a community will not tolerate this type of senselessness."

The name of James Russell Sorrow will be inscribed on the National Law Enforcement Memorial in Washington, D.C., in 1997 and his name will be read for the first time at the national memorial on May 15, 1997. A plaque bearing his name will also be placed at the S.C. Criminal Justice Hall of Fame in Columbia.

In a strange coincidence, the last two law enforcement officers killed in Greenville County, Deputy Sheriff William Mahon Banks in 1989 and James Russell Sorrow in 1996, were both graduates of Ware Shoals H.S.

SOURCES: *Greenville News,* Sept. 20,21,22,23,24,25,26,27,29, Oct. 4, 1996; The *Tryon Daily Bulletin*, Sept. 25, 1996; and interviews with Dennis Barden and J.C. Sorrow.

#33 CARLTON POPE
Sgt. in Fountain Inn Police Dept.
Killed in traffic accident on Oct. 9, 1996.

THE EVENT

Fountain Inn Sgt. Carlton "Rick" Pope, 29, was killed in a traffic accident on Oct. 9, 1996, just after he broke off a "chase" of another vehicle. He became the first officer killed in the history of the Fountain Inn Police Dept. (founded in 1886).

Around 4:00AM on Wednesday, Oct. 9, 1996, Sgt. Pope was on patrol in his 1995 Ford Crown Victoria police cruiser when he saw a dark-colored Mustang speeding at 100 mph and running without headlights at the intersection of Main and Knight streets in Fountain Inn. Pope "gave chase" and the Mustang sped down S. Main St. with its emergency flashers on (but no headlights) and then onto Interstate 385. The Mustang continued at a high rate of speed on I-385 traveling with emergency flashers on and blinking its headlights.

Carlton Pope

The Fountain Inn police dispatcher notified the S.C. Highway Patrol and other neighboring law enforcement agencies of the chase. Four Laurens County Sheriff's deputies answered the call as the chase proceeded from Fountain Inn into Laurens County. Sgt. Pope, following departmental procedures, was trying to get close enough to get a tag number so that he could break off the chase allowing apprehension of the speeder later. When he could not catch the speeding Mustang, he broke off the chase and radioed in that he was terminating the pursuit and was turning around.

However, as Pope approached the Gray Court exit ramp off I-385, he lost control of his patrol car and hit a patch of trees. Pope was thrown from the vehicle which "burst into flames." He was found by another Fountain Inn officer and a passer-by "lying on his back near his burning car."

Pope was taken by ambulance to Laurens County Hospital where doctors attempted to stabilize him. He was then moved to Greenville Memorial Hospital in an ambulance led by a police escort. He died shortly after 9:00 AM, five hours after the accident.

THE PERPETRATOR

The mustang disappeared and thus the identity of the driver of the vehicle which initiated the chase that resulted in the officer's death was not known. Under S.C. law, conviction on a charge of failure to stop when signaled by a law enforcement vehicle carries a maximum sentence of 25 years in prison if a death results from the chase.

Police were still pursuing leads on the Mustang described as a late 1980s dark blue or black Ford Mustang GT or LX. The Highway Patrol was urging anyone in the area at the time of the chase who saw the vehicle to call.

THE OFFICER

Carlton "Rick" Pope was born on July 1, 1967, in Conway, SC, to Malcolm Patrick and Wanda Dale Alford Pope. He was the second of three children.

Rick's father was in the military and thus the family moved frequently. He attended elementary school in Honolulu, Hawaii, and J.L. Mann H.S. in Greenville, SC. He played H.S. football and graduated in 1985.

After H.S. Rick joined the U.S. Navy serving from 1985-1990. He served on the USS Turner and worked in communications and electronics repairs and installation. Upon discharge from the service Rick joined the N. Charleston Police Dept., graduating from the S.C. Police Academy in Columbia in 1991. He served as a patrol officer in N. Charleston from 1991-1993.

In 1993 Rick joined the Fountain Inn Police Department and was a three-year veteran of the Dept. (and a six-year law enforcement veteran) at his death. He was promoted to Sgt. on Dec. 28, 1994.

Sgt. Pope was well known to the residents of Fountain Inn, a community of only 5,000 residents, and served as the city's bicycle patrolman on holidays and special occasions. Many residents of the community expressed shock when they heard of Sgt. Pope's death and several had "Rick stories" about times he had helped them, made them laugh, etc.

The 17-man Fountain Inn Police Dept. was hit hard by Pope's death as the small department was a close knit "family." All of the officers knew Pope's 5-year-old son, Austin, as his father often brought him to the police station on his days off.

Rick married Angela "Angie" Wilson of Greenville. Their son, Austin Lee was born on Oct. 2, 1991.

Carlton Pope, 29, was survived by his wife, Angela Wilson Pope, 27, and his son, Austin Lee Pope, 5; by his mother, Wanda Dale Alford Pope, of Anchorage, Alaska; by his father and stepmother, Malcolm Patrick Pope, and Catherine Shaw Pope of Pass Christian, Miss.; by a brother, Lonnie Michael Pope, of Columbia; and by a sister, Julia Pope Tolbert, of Saucier, Miss. Julia was a law enforcement officer in Gulfport, Mississippi, and served as a pallbearer at her brother's funeral.

Funeral arrangements were handled by Mackey Mortuary where the visitation was held on Friday evening, Oct. 11. The funeral was held at Mackey Mortuary on Century Drive on Saturday, Oct. 12. Rev. Van B. Thomas, Jr., pastor of the Trinity United Methodist Church in Fountain Inn, conducted the service. Eulogies were delivered by Rev. Thomas and by Fountain Inn Chief A. Keith Morton.

The funeral and burial services were "scripted" by Rick Pope as he had attended the funeral service of Greenville Officer Russell Sorrow two weeks earlier and, knowing that he might meet a similar fate, "went over verbatim what he would like at his funeral" with Chief Morton.

More than 200 people, including scores of uniformed law enforcement officers from around the state, attended the funeral and burial services. The funeral procession traveled from the Mortuary to Cannon Memorial Park in Fountain Inn. The burial service included "a riderless horse. A 21-gun salute. The solemn notes of 'Amazing Grace' played on bagpipes." Pope's widow, Angie, received the American flag that covered her husband's coffin and handed it to their 5-year-old son, Austin, "who clutched it in his small hands."

The name of Carlton Pope will be added to the National Law Enforcement Memorial in Washington, D.C., in May of 1997. His name will also be displayed on a plaque at the S.C. Criminal Justice Hall of Fame in Columbia. A plaque honoring Pope will also be displayed at the Fountain Inn Police Dept.

SOURCES: *Greenville News,* Oct. 10,11,13, 1996; The (Fountain Inn) *Tribune Times,* Oct. 16, 1996; and interviews with Chief A. Keith Morton and Rev. Van B. Thomas, Jr.

The above photos are of the National Law Enforcement Officers Memorial which is located in a park above the Judiciary Square Metro (subway) station in Washington, D.C. The memorial dedicated in 1991, includes more than 14,000 names of law enforcement officers killed in the line of duty since 1794. A visitors' center, located two blocks away (at 605 E. St.), displays numerous photographs and sells souvenirs of the memorial.